IMAGES
of America

The Town of Tonawanda

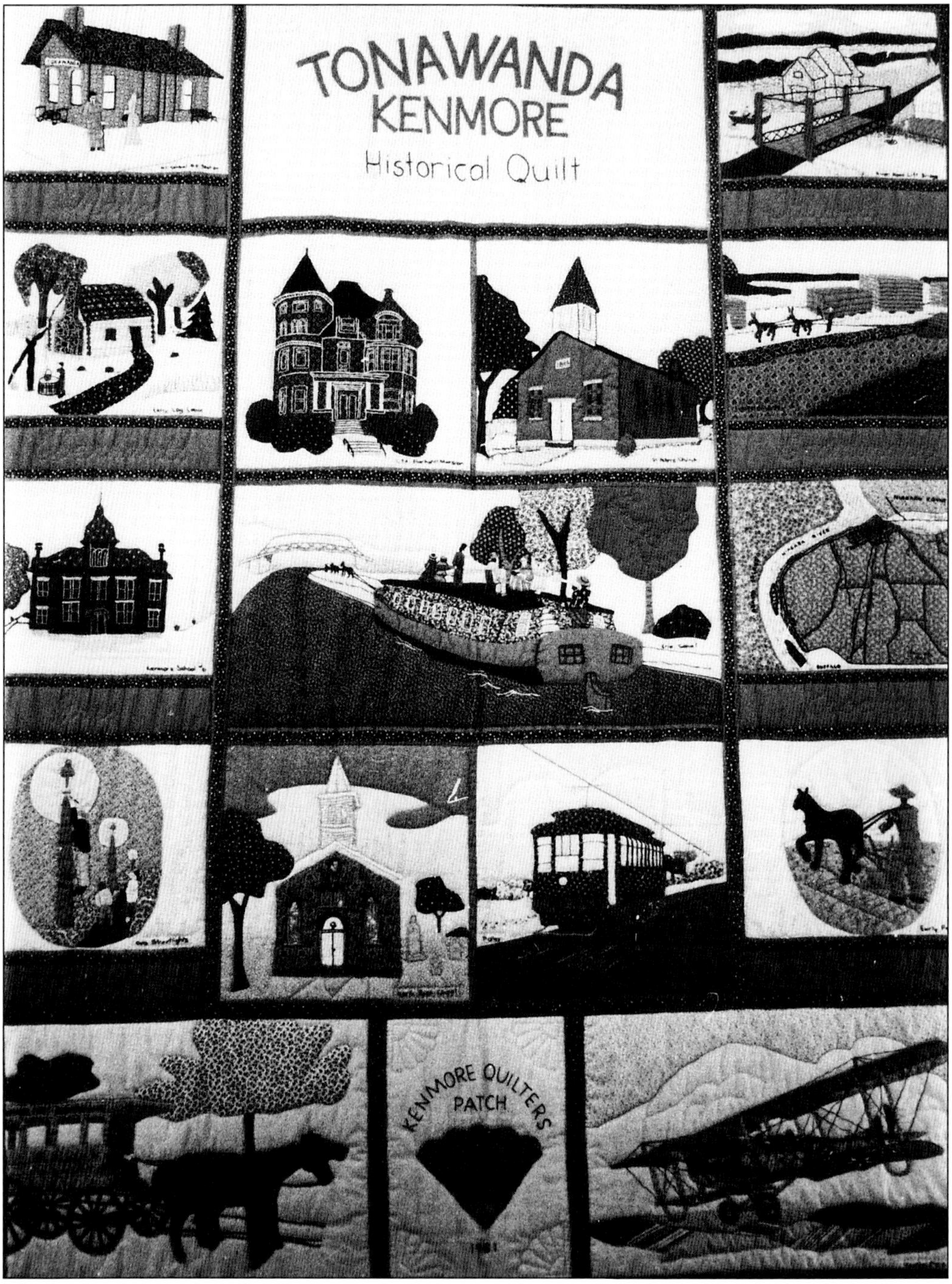

The quilt presented to the Tonawanda-Kenmore Historical Society in 1981 by the Kenmore Quilters Patch. It depicts a variety of historical places and events from 1805 to 1926 in the town.

IMAGES
of America

THE TOWN OF TONAWANDA

John W. Percy

ARCADIA
PUBLISHING

ISBN 978-0-7385-8717-2

Published by Arcadia Publishing
Charleston, South Carolina

Printed in the United States of America

Library of Congress Catalog Card Number: Applied for

For all general information contact Arcadia Publishing at:
Telephone 843-853-2070
Fax 843-853-0044
E-mail sales@arcadiapublishing.com
For customer service and orders:
Toll-Free 1-888-313-2665

Visit us on the Internet at www.arcadiapublishing.com

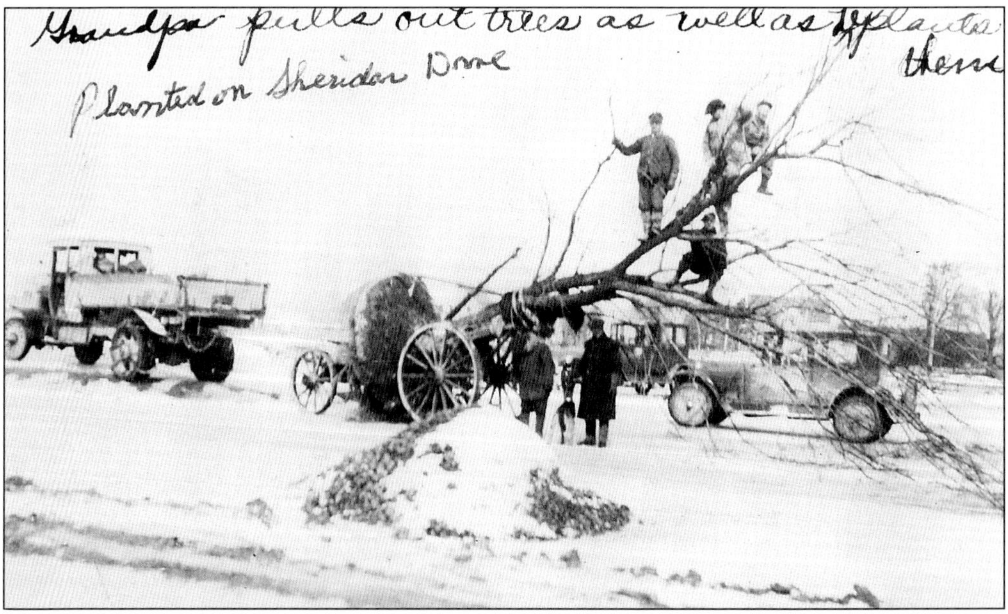

Sheridan Drive in 1925. Large trees were transplanted under the direction of LPA Eberhardt to give the wide new highway a more finished appearance. Cut through farmland, the expensive highway looked desolate before the trees were planted.

Contents

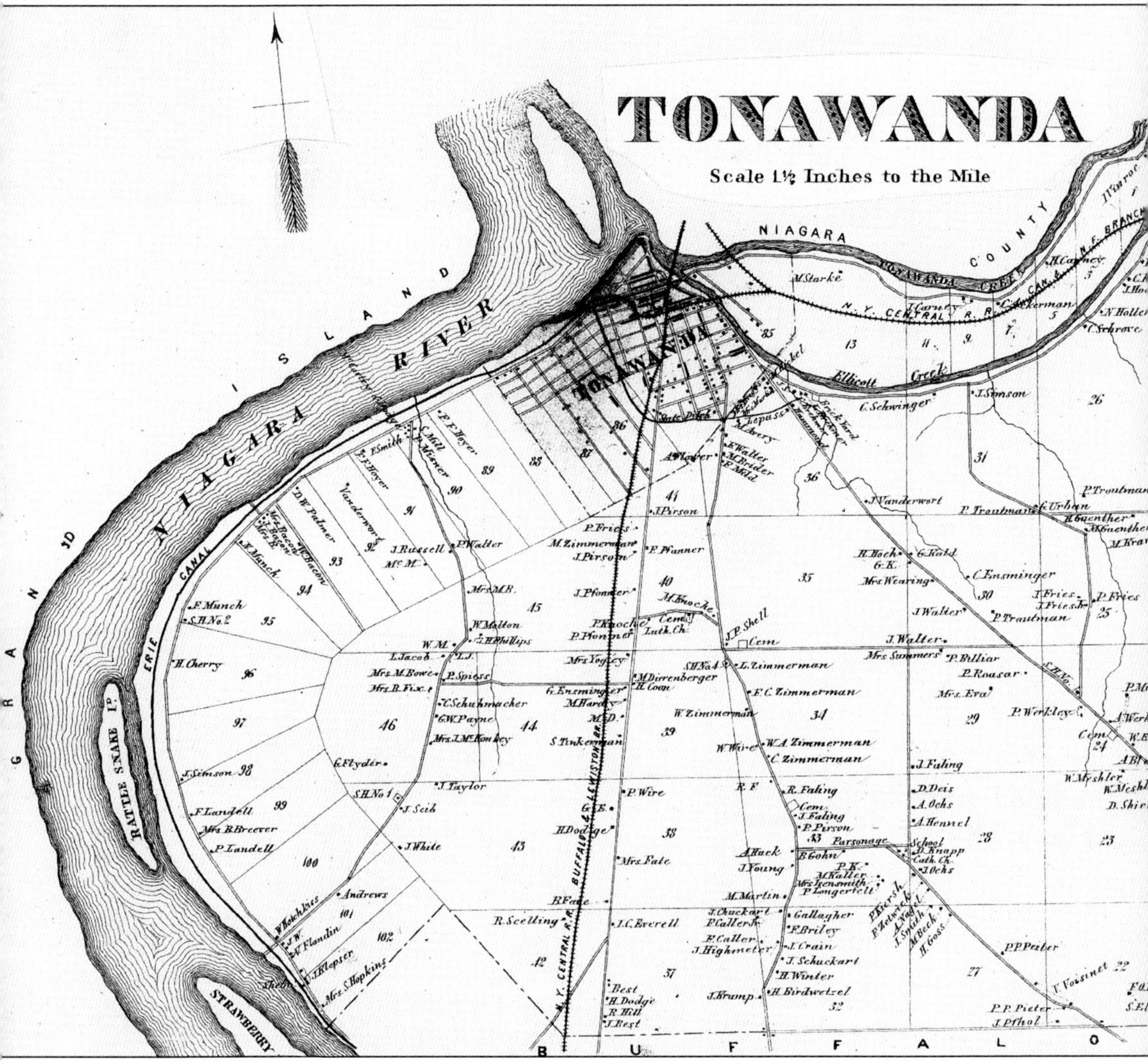

The Town of Tonawanda, from a topographical map of Erie County (Stone and Stewart, 1866.)

Introduction

It was once tagged the "Keystone of the Niagara Frontier." Certainly, it remains one of the leading towns in western New York. The Town of Tonawanda can boast of spawning the Niagara Frontier's pioneer suburban village, becoming the first to develop an extensive and varied industrial base, and being the first town to exceed a population of 100,000 people. This volume in the Images of America series illustrates the changing scene as the Town of Tonawanda passed through successive stages of agriculture, industry, and suburbanization over the past century.

The earliest settlement of the area that would be incorporated in April 1836 as the Town of Tonawanda took place along Tonawanda Creek. In 1805 a handful of pioneers to western New York began to clear a "slash" in the dark forest that covered this region, thereby commencing the agricultural development of the area, which was complete by the time of the Civil War. Other farming communities were established during the early years along the Indian trail that became Delaware Road, at "Mohawk" on the famous Military Road built through the town in 1802–1809, and at "North Bush" on a trail that eventually became Englewood Avenue. Most of the farmers who established their homes in our town were conservative, deeply religious people of German descent, largely Protestant, although the North Bush settlement was Roman Catholic.

Good transportation benefited the area's economy early in our history. The Niagara River, the 1825 Erie Canal, and the 1836 Buffalo & Niagara Falls Railroad, one of the nation's earliest, gave the town a distinct advantage for industrial development over its neighbors. The Erie Canal enabled the East Boston Timber Company to ship the fine white oak they logged on the Grand Island portion of the town to markets on the eastern seaboard. Grand Island became a separate town in 1852. Tonawanda's population center was concentrated at the junction of the three transportation arteries, and in 1854 the Village of Tonawanda was incorporated within the town. By the 1870s a substantial lumber trade had developed here as millions of board feet of lumber from the upper Great Lakes were transferred from lake barges to canal boats. Industrial and commercial growth in the northern part of the town resulted in its incorporation as the separate City of Tonawanda in March 1903. This left the largely rural town with a population of less than 2,000, fewer than lived within its 1850 boundaries.

An altogether new type of development was begun in the southern portion of the town during the 1890s. The changing environment of industrial Buffalo combined with the introduction of the electric streetcar to encourage a few farsighted individuals to develop a new "sub-urban" village within commuting distance of jobs in Buffalo. Kenmore was incorporated as a village within the rural Town of Tonawanda in September 1899.

The southeastern portion of the town, known as the Kenilworth section, was the site of a large racetrack (developed by Buffalo interests) from 1902 until 1908, when changing state laws regarding horse racing caused its closing. The conservative, temperance-oriented residents of Kenmore were not unhappy about its demise. "Palace Park," an amusement resort at Delaware and Knoche Roads, had already met a similar fate in 1901.

Attracted by extensive water frontage, many industries began to locate along the Niagara River around the turn of the century. This Riverside section of the town attracted a considerable number of workers from Serbia, Croatia, and Hungary who provided the work force for the new riverfront industries. The employment opportunities, industrial tax base, and restriction of heavy industry to the western portion of the town encouraged additional suburban growth in Kenmore. By the 1920s the town was a home for electric power generation, and steel, rubber, chemical, and aircraft plants. Other industries, such as oil refining and auto manufacturing, would follow a decade later.

The decade from 1920 to 1930 was a period of tremendous growth in the Kenmore portion of the town. The village population increased from 3,160 to 16,482 in ten years, and most of the available land in the village was built up. Further growth would have to be outside the village limits. The people who made Kenmore their home were mostly working-class people, both blue collar and white collar, with a substantial number of younger professional and business men who saw career opportunities in the village. Family-oriented, the new residents continued the traditions of thrift, temperance, and political conservatism which had guided the founders of the village.

The Great Depression of the 1930s slowed the pace of industrial and residential development in the town. Sheridan Drive, the much-heralded cross-town highway designed to open up the town to further development, appeared to be an expensive mistake as the area's economy floundered. Though certainly scarred by the decade, village and town residents weathered the ordeal better than most communities. There were no local bank failures, and by 1938 industrial growth was once again on the rise.

A rapid immigration of new people to the town who were employed by the burgeoning war industries necessitated construction of low-cost housing in a community which was very "middle class." Much opposition was raised to the construction of the Sheridan Parkside housing project, with fears expressed that such housing would encourage permanent settlement of people who were "not characteristic" of the majority of town residents.

Two changes of note occurred in the population after the war. An increasing number of people from different ethnic backgrounds began to move into the village, especially from Buffalo's west side. The formerly "WASP" Kenmore took on a more cosmopolitan character as Italians, Poles, and by 1964, African-Americans made their homes in the village. At the same time, especially in the 1950s, there was extensive development of new middle-class housing throughout the town. Within that decade most of the idle farmlands were developed by builders, and hamlets such as Brighton, Ellwood, and Kenilworth became hard to identify as separate communities. The town's population nearly doubled from 55,270 in 1950 to 105,032 in 1960. In order to ensure the quality of life residents of the town had come to expect, a new water treatment plant, modern sewage and garbage disposal, and a vast storm sewer system were constructed.

One of the greatest challenges to the community was to provide quality education for a rapidly increasing school-age population. Prior to World War I, small country schools had provided the predominately rural population with basic education through the eighth grade. Gradually, Kenmore's School District No. 1 absorbed the country school districts until Union Free School District No.1, which covers 80 percent of the town, grew to become the seventh largest school district in the state, with over 22,000 pupils enrolled by the mid-1960s. During the 1970s the district's enrollment declined by over 50 percent as the "Baby Boomers" grew up at the same time the nation's birth rate nosedived. During the 1990s modest growth has taken place in the school population. The northeast portion of the town is served by the Sweet Home School District, which has seen even more spectacular growth as new housing continues to be built in the Amherst portion of the district. Through farsighted educational leadership, both school districts have maintained a reputation for excellent scholarship and fine athletic teams.

The development of recreational facilities paralleled that of education. Perceptive town government provided land for parks, such as Lincoln and Sheridan Parks, as early as the 1920s. The first of four public swimming pools was opened in 1954. The world-class athletic center on Pool Plaza was a cooperative project with the World University Games of 1993. Today the town recreation department oversees the operation of the four pools, two ice-skating rinks, two golf courses, a driving range, and other recreational facilities throughout the town and village.

Government in the town has traditionally been characterized as forward-thinking, yet fiscally responsible. Town government has been almost exclusively Republican, though Democrats captured control of the village government for a time during the early 1970s. Democrats representing the town and village have also won most of the seats in the county legislature, the state assembly, and the U.S. House of Representatives in recent years.

Nearly all of the residential land in the town has been built up; the last few years have seen extensive apartment development in the northern sections of the community, and of senior housing in Kenmore. Business activity remains generally healthy in spite of increased competition from the newer shopping malls outside the town. As older industries close their doors, town government has been successful in attracting new firms to locate here, especially in the developing Fire Tower Road industrial park.

Today the Town of Tonawanda is virtually a city in itself. It offers every municipal service and a broad range of housing, business, and employment opportunities. Its people come from every walk of life, from the low-income through the well-to-do, though they are predominately middle class. All major faiths are represented in the numerous churches and temples throughout the community. Varied ethnic backgrounds provide the town with a cosmopolitan population, though less than 1 percent of the residents are non-white. Probably the greatest challenge facing the town is ensuring the continuation of the high quality of life here in the face of an aging infrastructure and changing social trends and economic pressures.

The Tonawanda-Kenmore Historical Society provided most of the photographs for this book. Other contributors included the Historical Society of the Tonawandas, Inc. (HSTI), the Western New York Heritage Institute (WNYHI), and the Buffalo & Erie County Historical Society (B&ECHS). There are also photographs from the author's personal collection. The author would like to thank the many local people who helped identify these images and the staff of Arcadia Publishing, especially editor Sarah Maineri, for their invaluable help with this project.

John W. Percy
Town Historian
October 1996

One

Pioneers

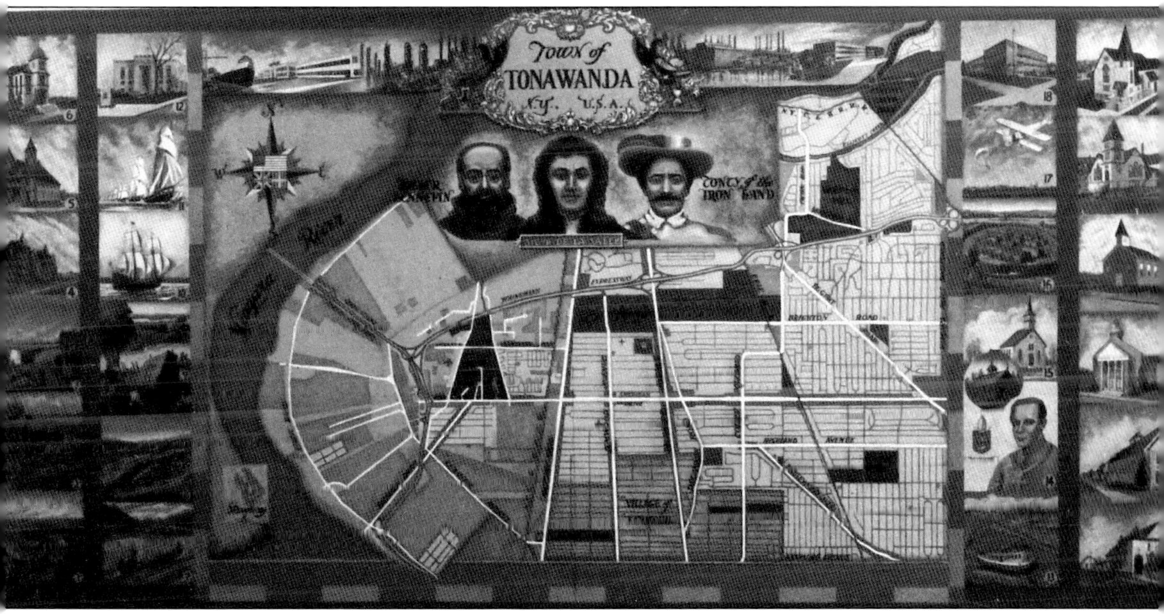

Carlo A. Nisita's historic mural. This large mural, depicting important events in the town from the arrival of early French explorers to twentieth-century technology, hangs above the stairway to the second floor in the Municipal Building. It was painted as part of the town's sesquicentennial celebration in 1986.

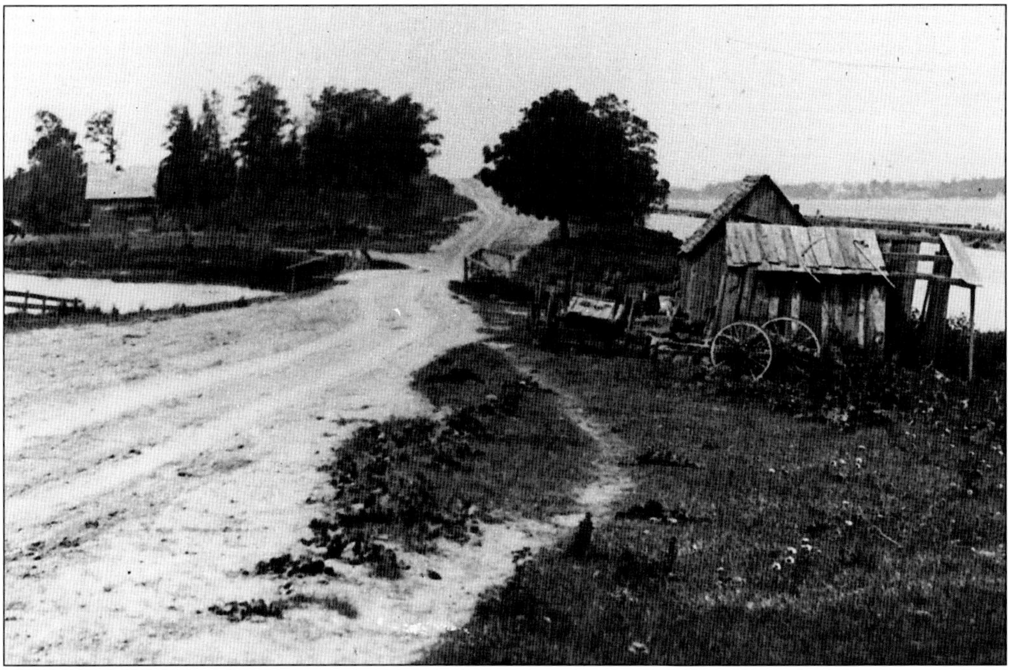

River Road (Niagara Street) at the Two Mile Creek Bridge, *c.* 1895. This bridge replaced an earlier hand-operated lift-bridge which once allowed Erie Canal traffic access to creekside businesses. Outbuildings from the Fix farm back up to the Erie Canal. The tow-path is on the narrow berm between the canal and the Niagara River. Modern Isle View Park and Niawanda Park are located on the filled-in canal bed.

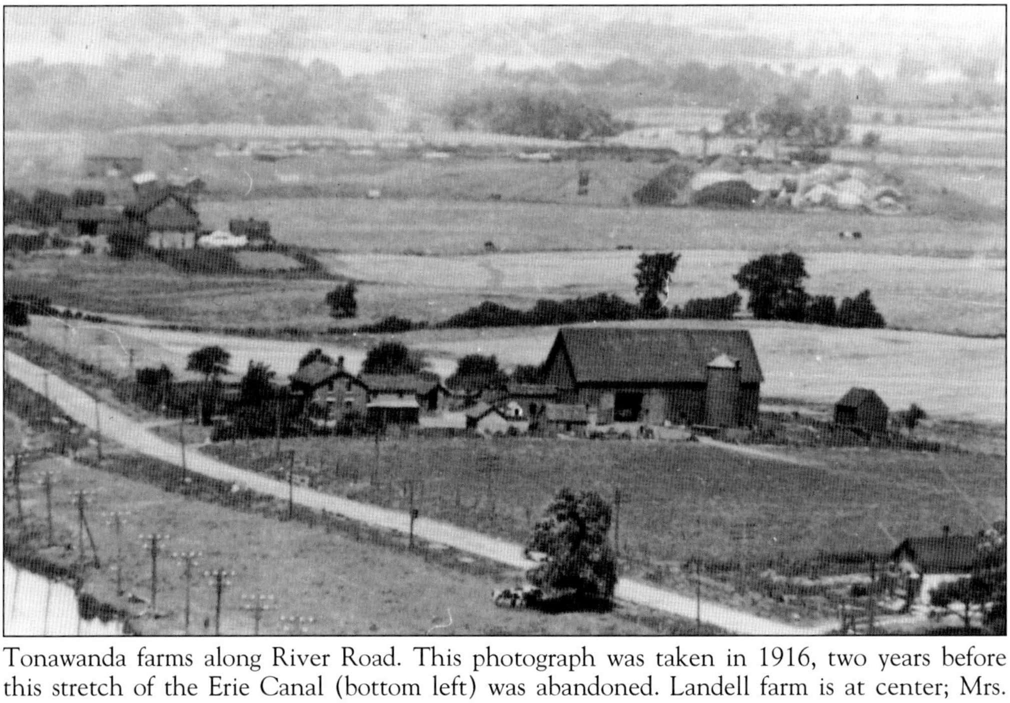

Tonawanda farms along River Road. This photograph was taken in 1916, two years before this stretch of the Erie Canal (bottom left) was abandoned. Landell farm is at center; Mrs. DeGlopper's house is at bottom right.

Hamilton Cherry. Hamilton settled on 300 acres along the Erie Canal four years before the Town of Tonawanda was established. His son Moses, and his grandsons Robert and Carlisle, carried on the family farm which once included Strawberry Island and Rattlesnake Island. In 1907 the Wickwire Steel Company bought much of the property and began erection of a wire mill.

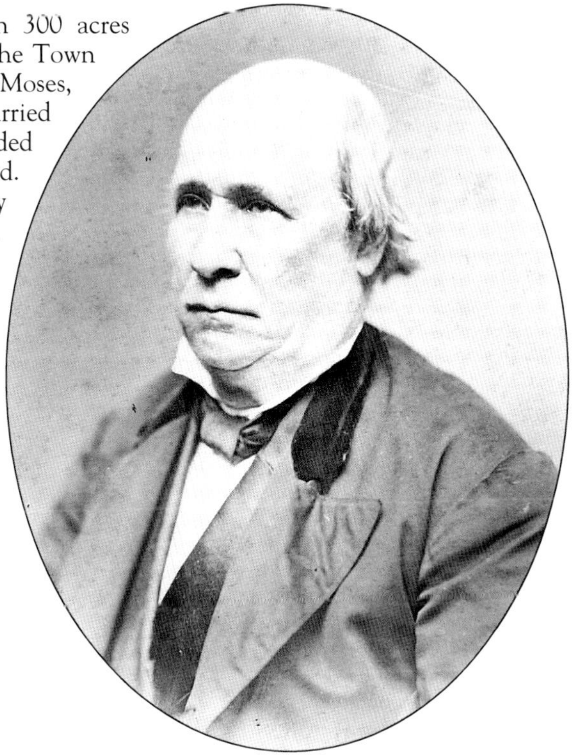

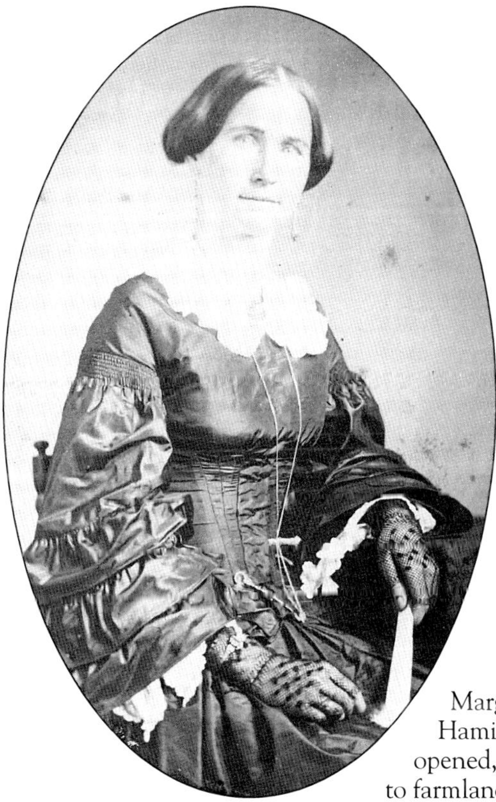

Margaret Cherry Mills (1826–1918), sister of pioneer Hamilton Cherry. Born a year after the Erie Canal opened, she saw the Cherry farm change from wilderness to farmland to steel mill.

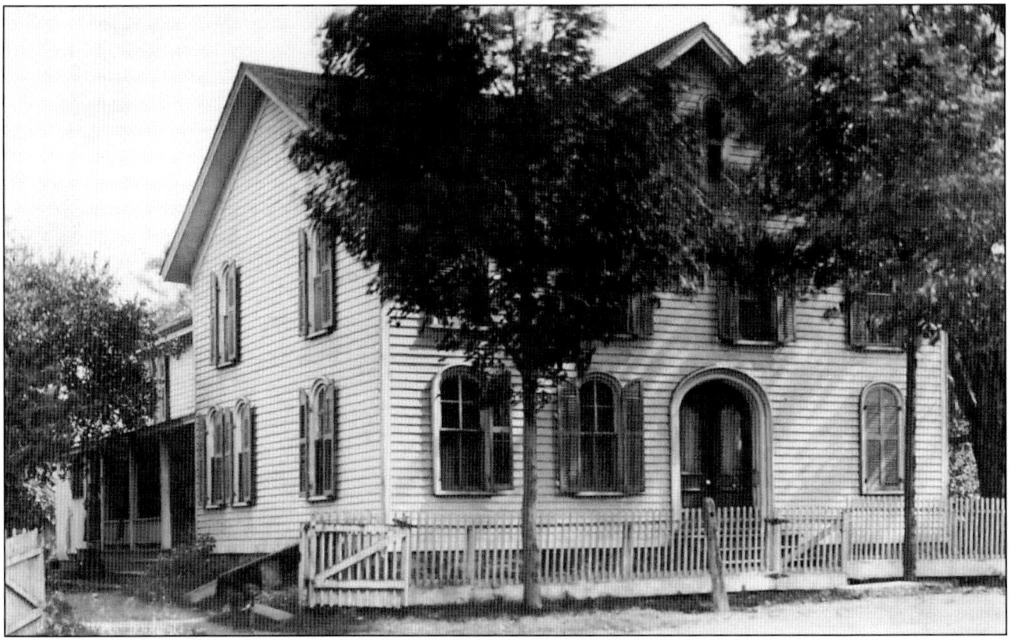

The Cherry home, which faced River Road, the Erie Canal, and the Niagara River for over a century. Meetings of the Tonawanda-Kenmore Historical Society were held here during the 1930s when the structure was nearly a century old.

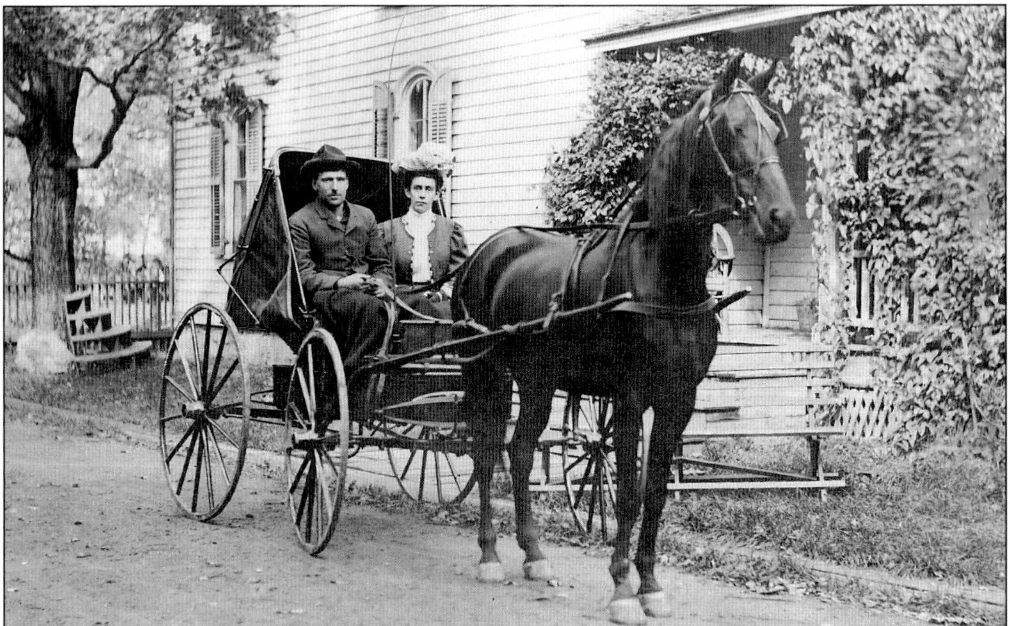

Mr. and Mrs. Robert Cherry at their home on River Road, *c.* 1900. Robert Cherry was a grandson of pioneer settler Hamilton Cherry. The family was active in founding the Tonawanda-Kenmore Historical Society in 1929 and has donated many artifacts that were a part of early farm life.

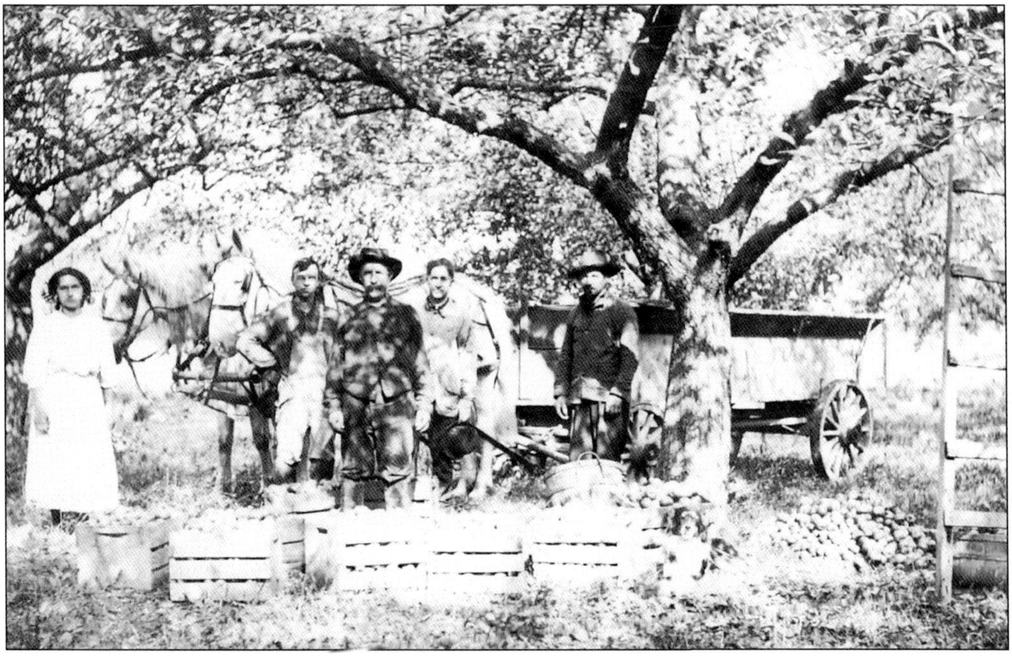

Harvest season in the family orchard on River Road, c. 1900. Moses Cherry (center) and children were photographed with draft-horses, a dog, and crates of fresh-picked pears. There were many nineteenth-century orchards in the town.

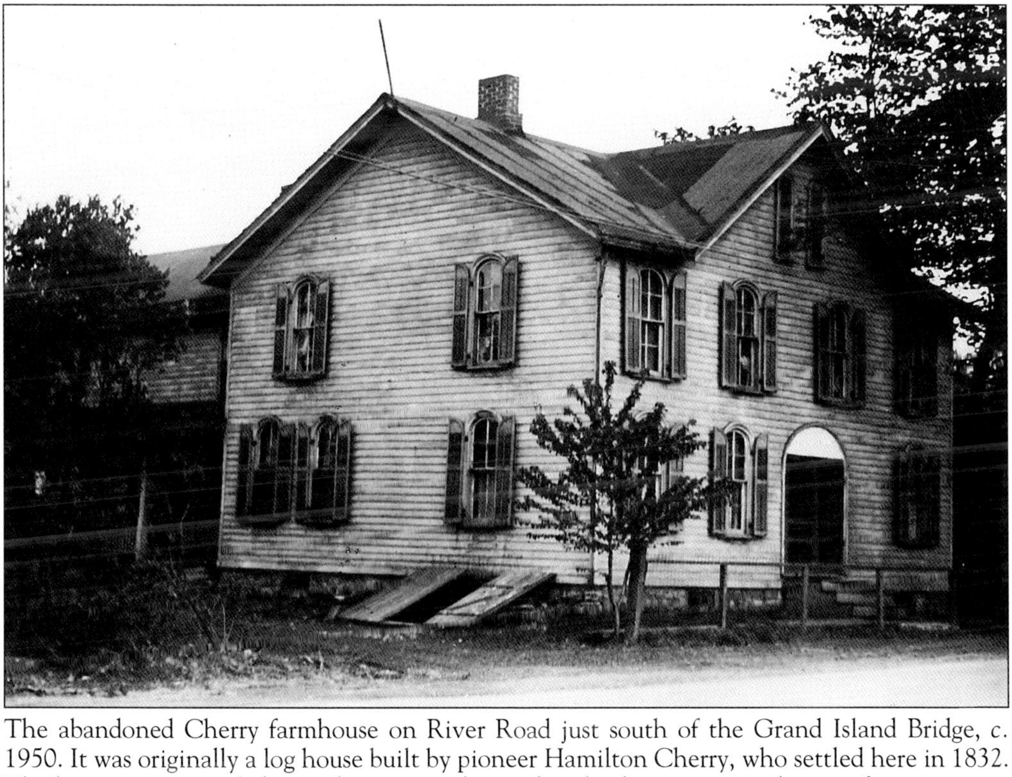

The abandoned Cherry farmhouse on River Road just south of the Grand Island Bridge, c. 1950. It was originally a log house built by pioneer Hamilton Cherry, who settled here in 1832. The home was expanded over the years and served as the first tavern in the area for a time.

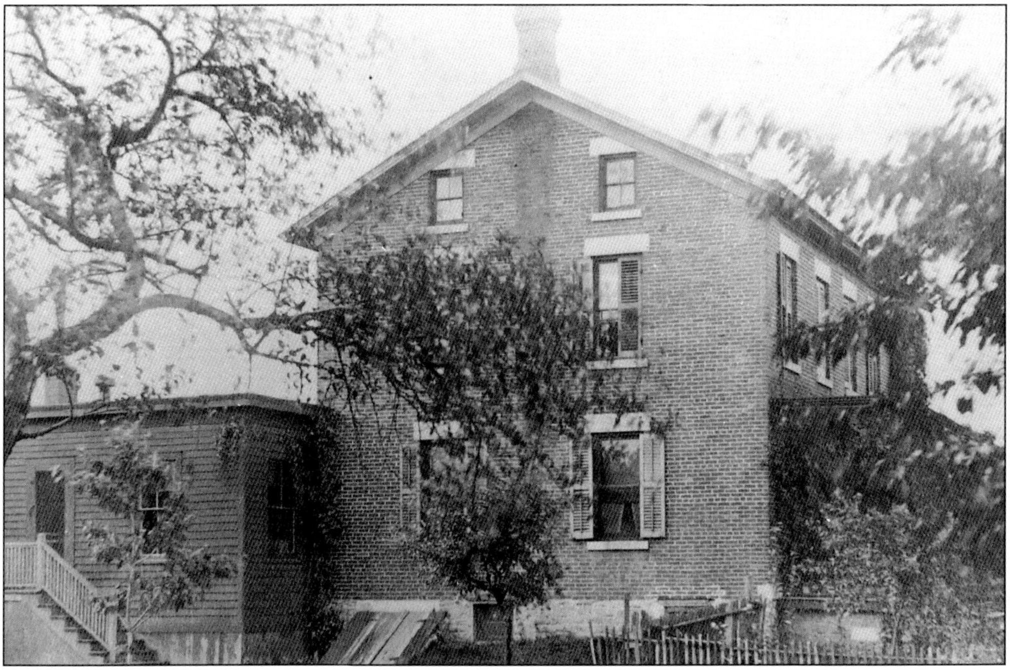

The Nicholas Munch home along River Road, just north of the Grand Island Bridge. Nicholas bought the land after spotting it from a canal boat, then had the home built by an itinerant German brickmaker in 1845. It stood for over 120 years before being torn down c. 1968 to make room for expansion at the Ashland Oil refinery.

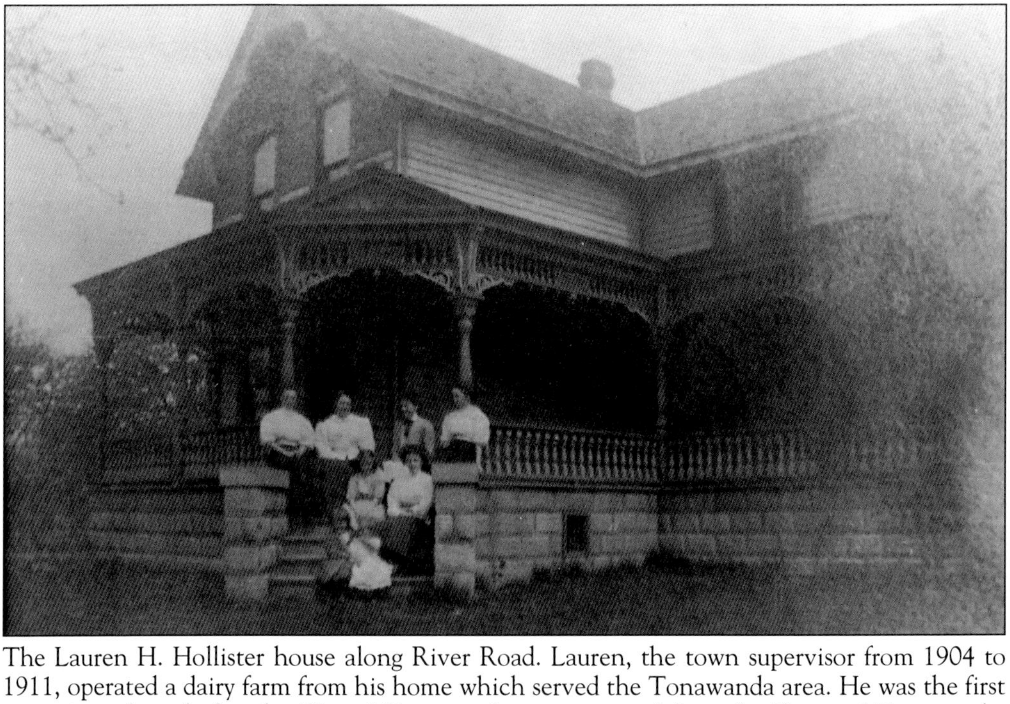

The Lauren H. Hollister house along River Road. Lauren, the town supervisor from 1904 to 1911, operated a dairy farm from his home which served the Tonawanda area. He was the first supervisor elected after the City of Tonawanda was separated from the Town of Tonawanda, and he served four terms.

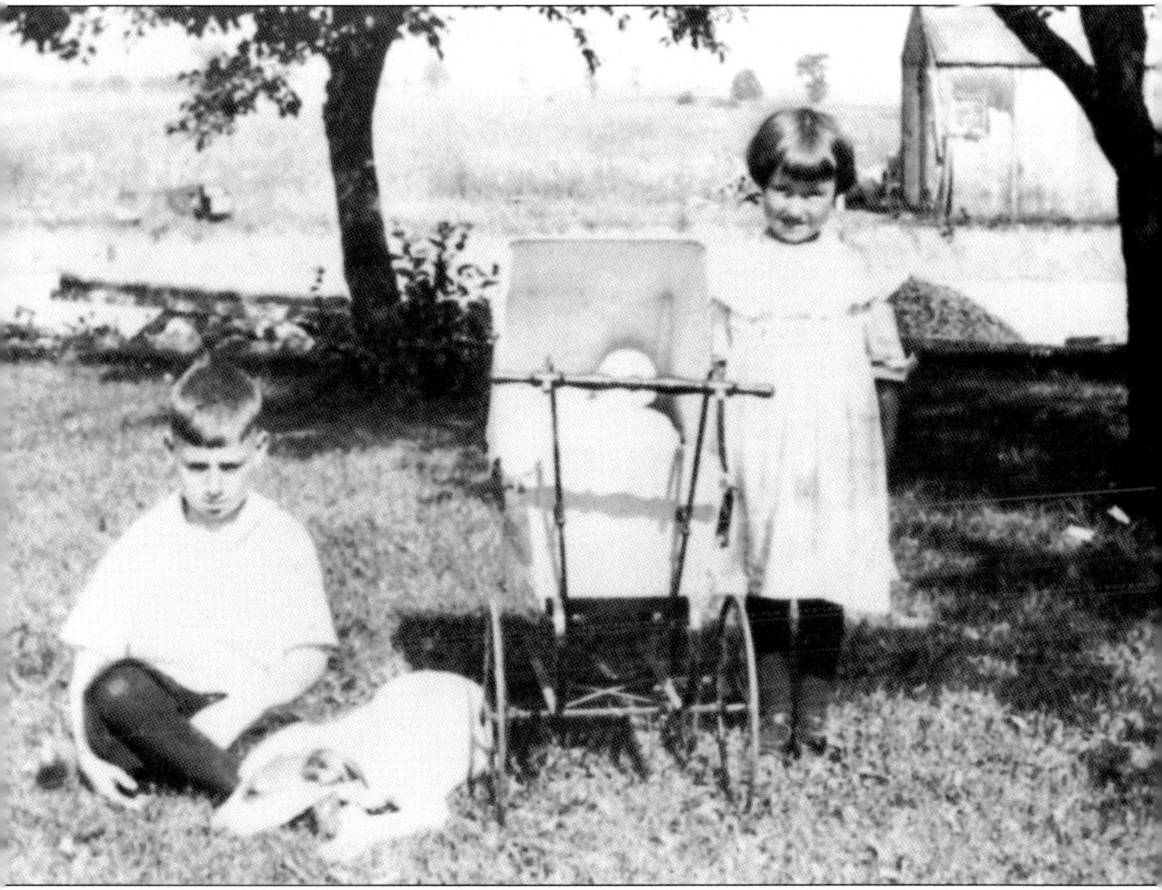

Marian Walter (Supparits) with her doll buggy and brother George with "Spot" on the old Walter farm near the Village of Tonawanda, *c.* 1890. Once children were of school age, they spent much of their time helping with chores on the farms, and had little idle time for play.

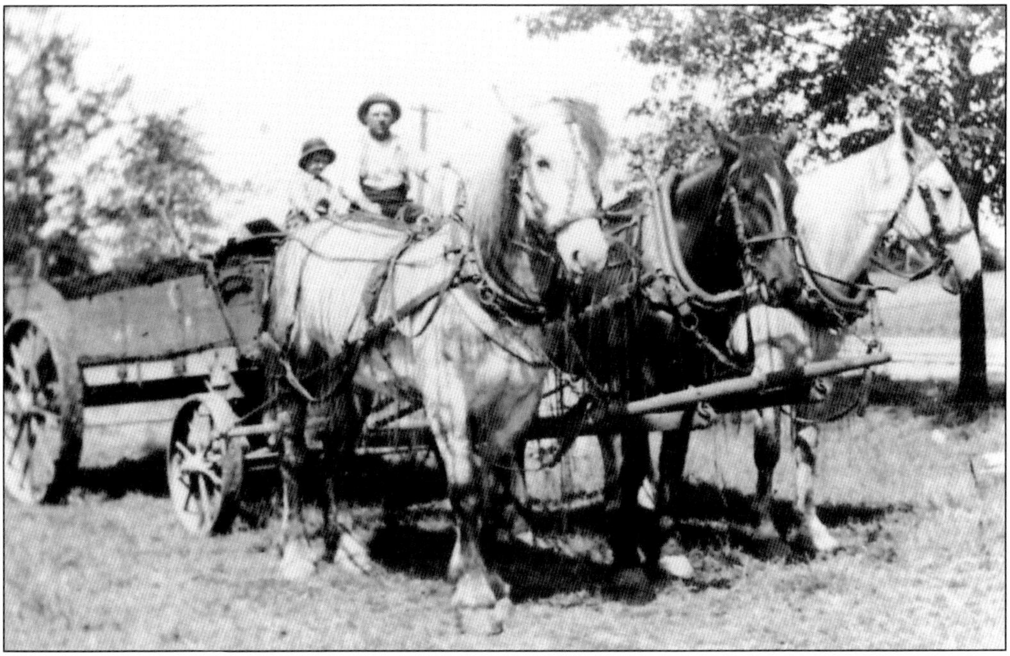

George P. Walter and his son, George K., with three span of horses, *c.* 1890. Father and son are shown here on the old Walter farm along Military Road, where 84 Lumber now stands. Horses pulled most of the farm equipment because the town's farms were generally too small to afford steam traction engines.

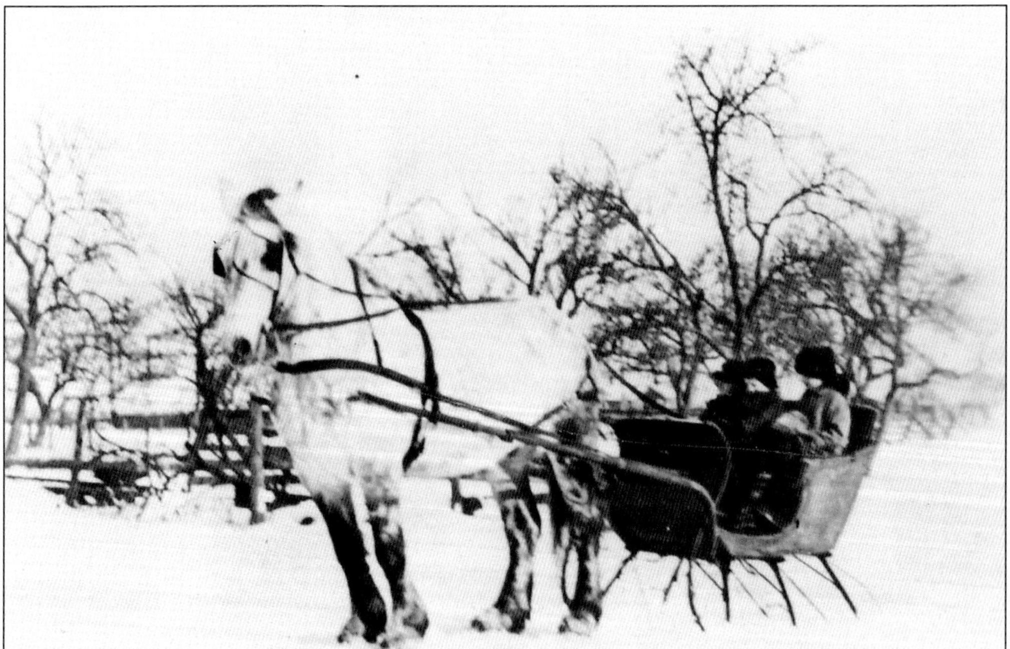

Helen, Laura, and George Walter as youngsters, ready for a sleigh ride. The draft horse was one of several used on the Military Road family farm, located a half-mile north of today's Youngmann Memorial Highway.

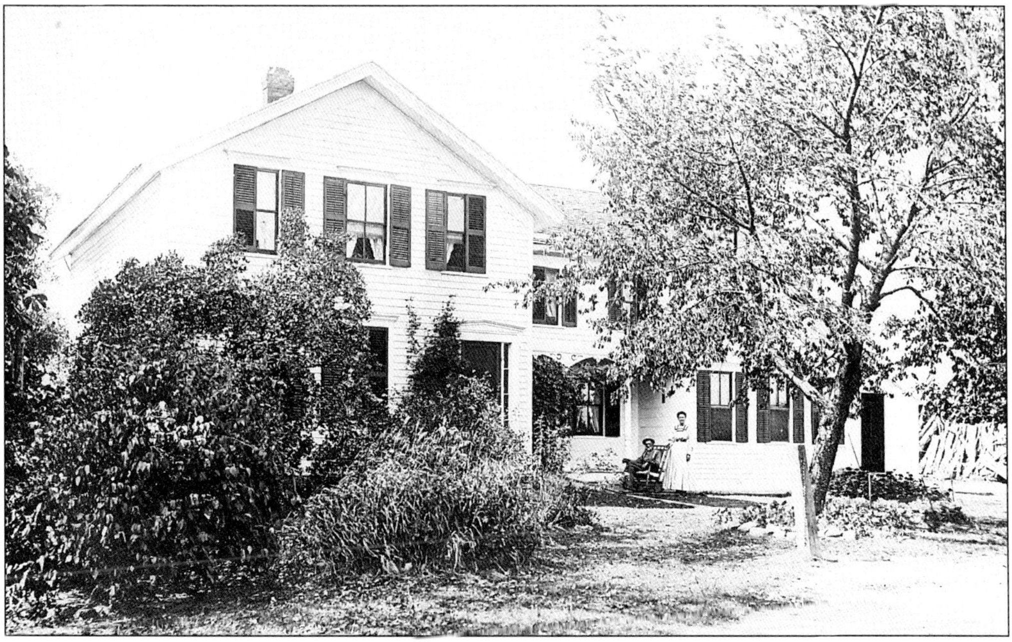

Florence Flyder with her father George at the family farm on the west side of Two Mile Creek Road (near modern Cooper Avenue), *c.* 1900. Their 100-acre farm was one of several in the town which remained active well into the twentieth century.

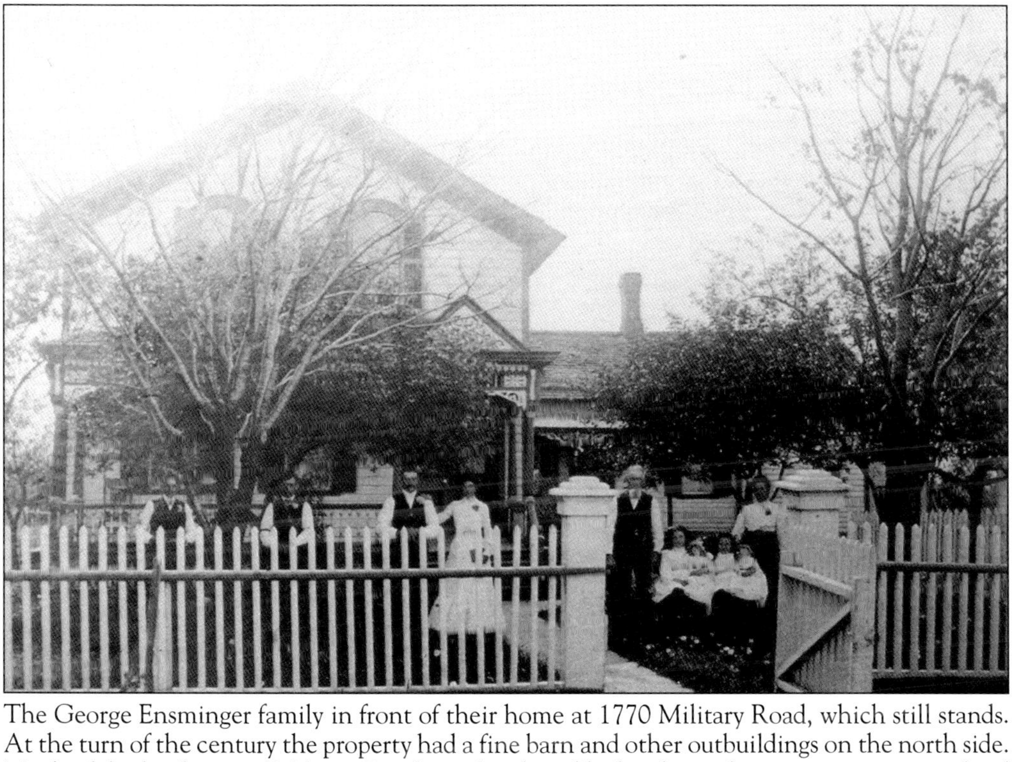

The George Ensminger family in front of their home at 1770 Military Road, which still stands. At the turn of the century the property had a fine barn and other outbuildings on the north side. Much of the land west of Military Road was developed by brothers whose name is memorialized by Ensminger Road.

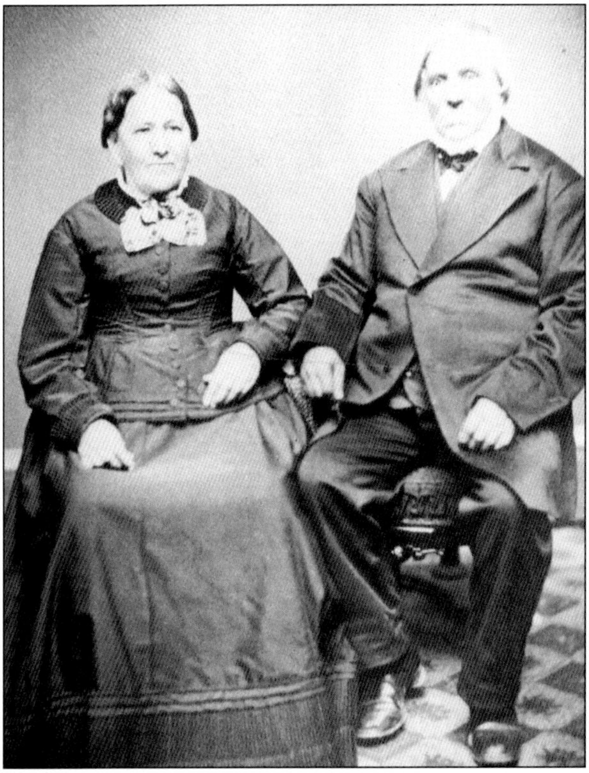

John and Eva Pirson. This couple's pioneer farm was located along the Military Road in the town's "Mohawk" community. The Pirson's original log home was replaced in 1848 by the brick home which still stands at 2250 Military Road. Their old log home was then used as a school for religious instruction by the 1849 St. Peter's German Evangelical Church on Knoche Road, which Mr. Pirson helped finance.

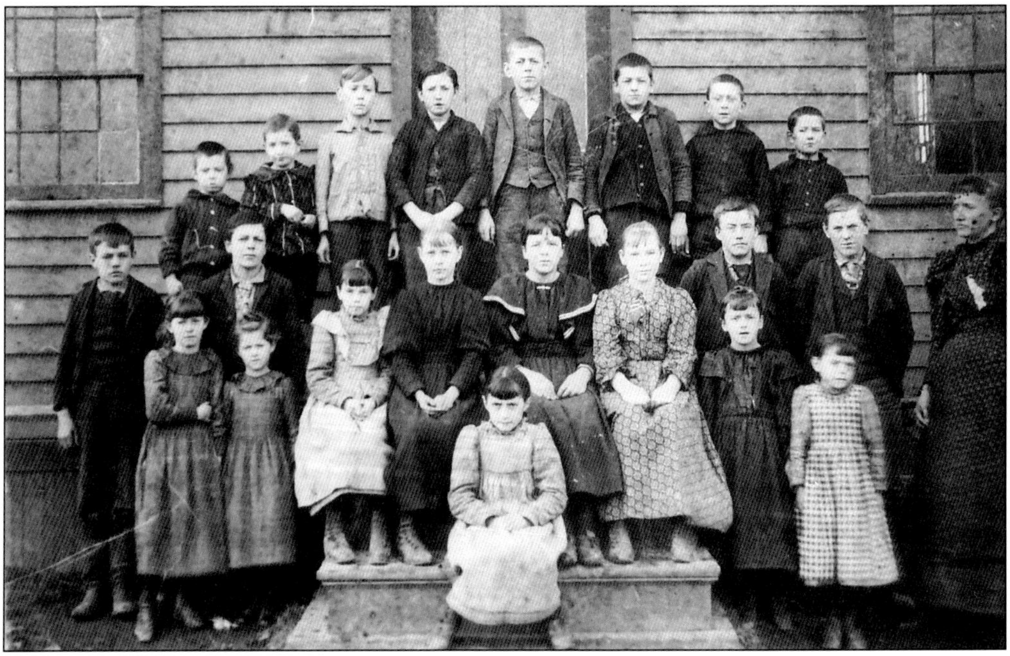

Ida Zimmerman and class, *c.* 1888, at the old one-room School #4, located at Delaware Road and Schell Road (Brighton Road) from 1844 to 1907. The property was sold in 1907 when a larger school was built on School Road; the old school was then moved to the northeast corner of Traverse and Delaware Roads, where it remains part of the home on that corner.

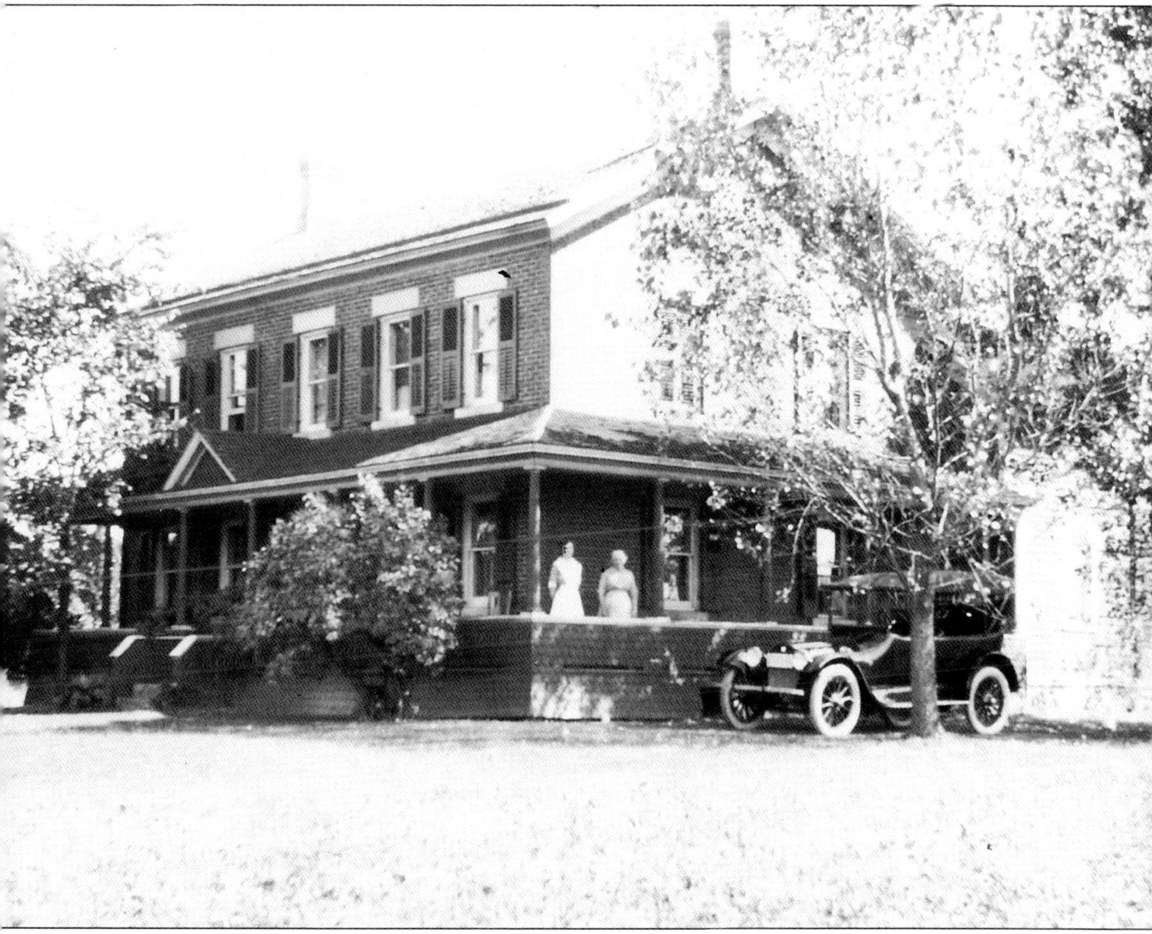

The Philip Knoche home at 204 Knoche Road, *c.* 1918. The home was built in 1849 when a cholera epidemic in Buffalo encouraged men to seek work in the "healthy countryside." The veranda was added later, and then removed after 1920. The 50-acre farm fronted the farm lane which took the family name. This photograph was found on a roll of film that had lain undeveloped for over sixty years.

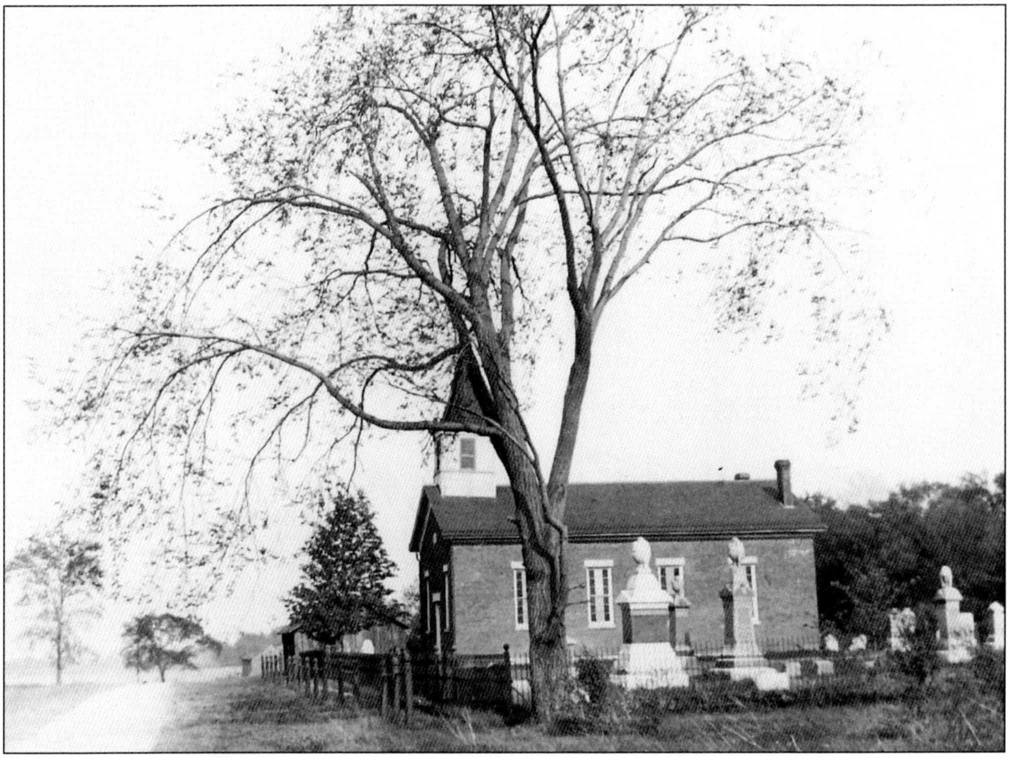

St. Peter's German Evangelical Church in 1918, when Knoche Road was still a dirt lane. Hitching posts stand in front of the cemetery fence. East of the church is the horse shed which provided shelter for the animals during inclement weather. The shed burned about 1922. Burials in the cemetery began in 1847.

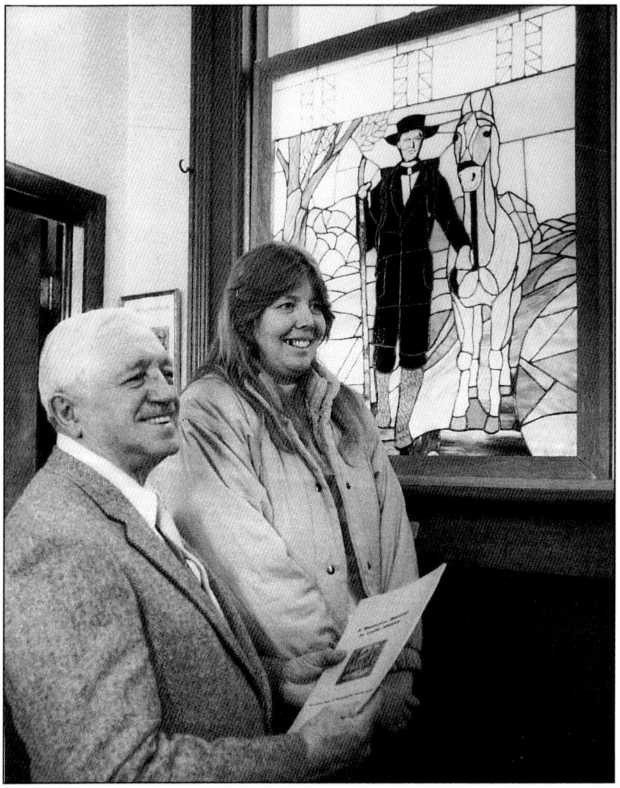

The colored glass St. John Neumann commemorative window at 100 Knoche Road, crafted by Joseph Celano (left). Lora Jane Schultz Ford (right) attended the dedication. The window is a memorial to her mother, Eleanor Schultz, who was instrumental in developing the old St. Peter's church as a historical museum.

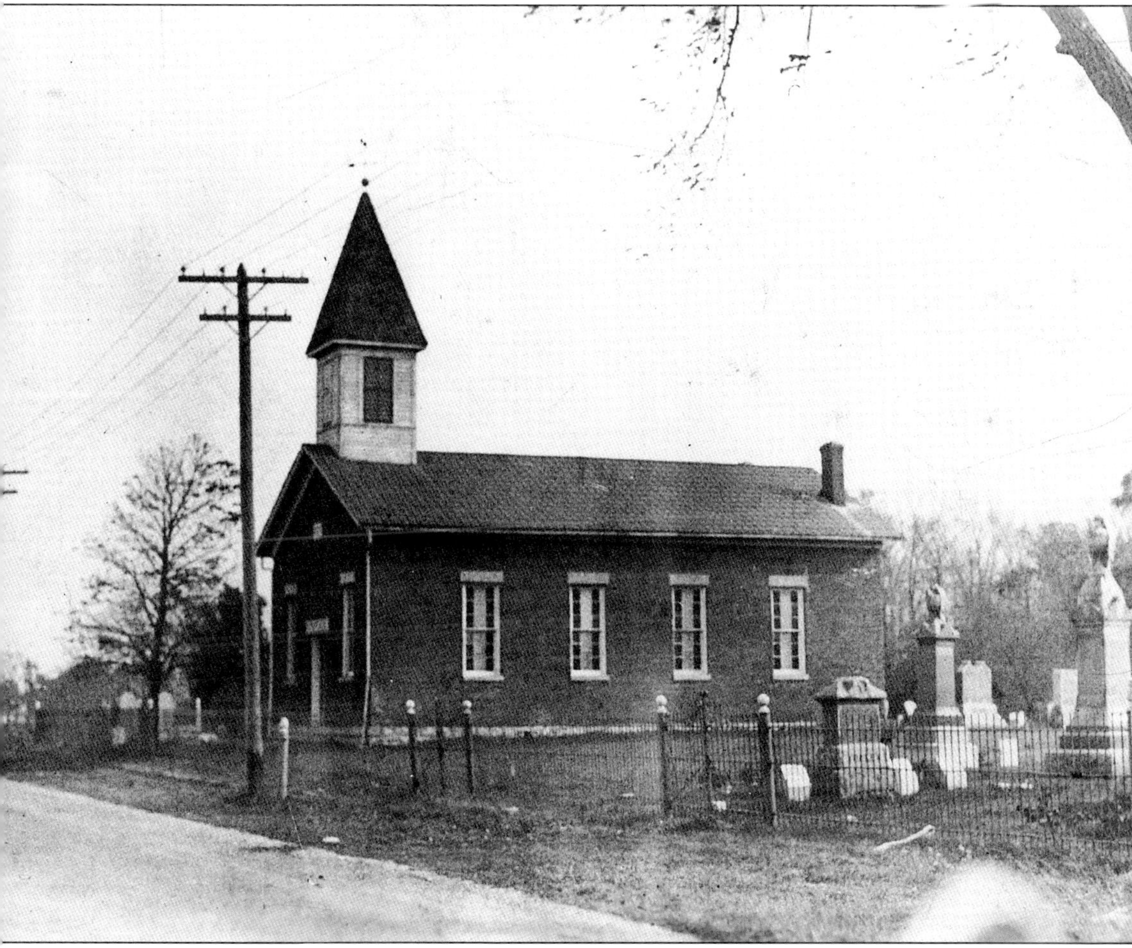

St. Peter's German Evangelical Church on Knoche Road in 1928. The congregation was organized in 1830 and built this church in 1849. Since 1976 the building has housed the Tonawanda-Kenmore Historical Society. The steeple roof has been changed and the road widened since the 1918 photograph on p. 22 was taken.

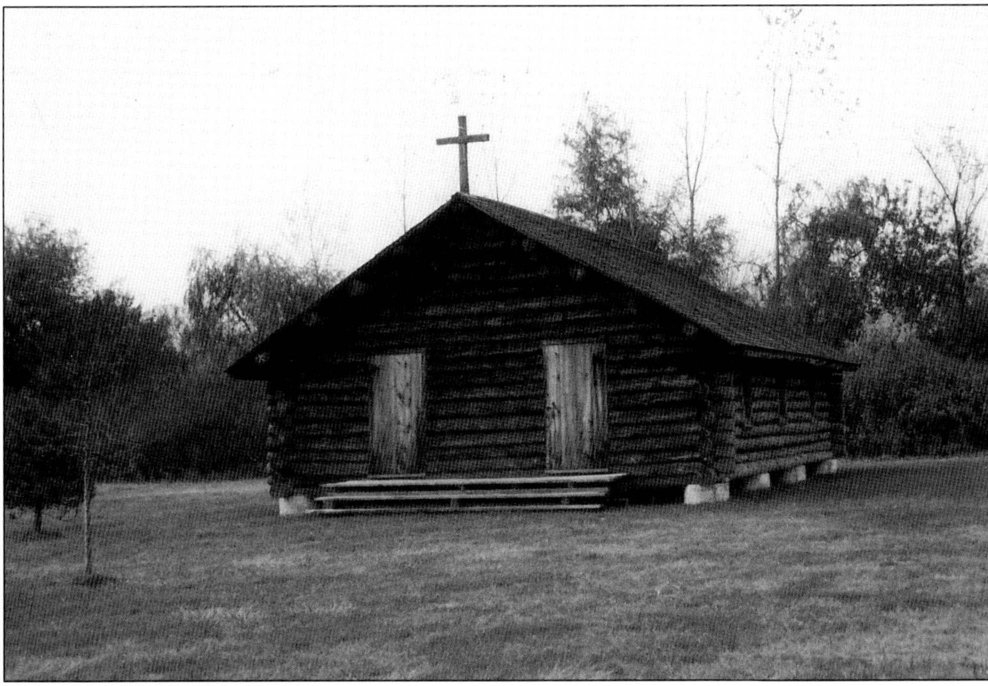

A replica at the Amherst Museum of the North Bush log church. This early Roman Catholic church, erected on Englewood at Belmont about 1833, was served by St. John N. Neumann from 1836 to 1840. Fr. Neumann was canonized in 1977, the first American male to attain sainthood.

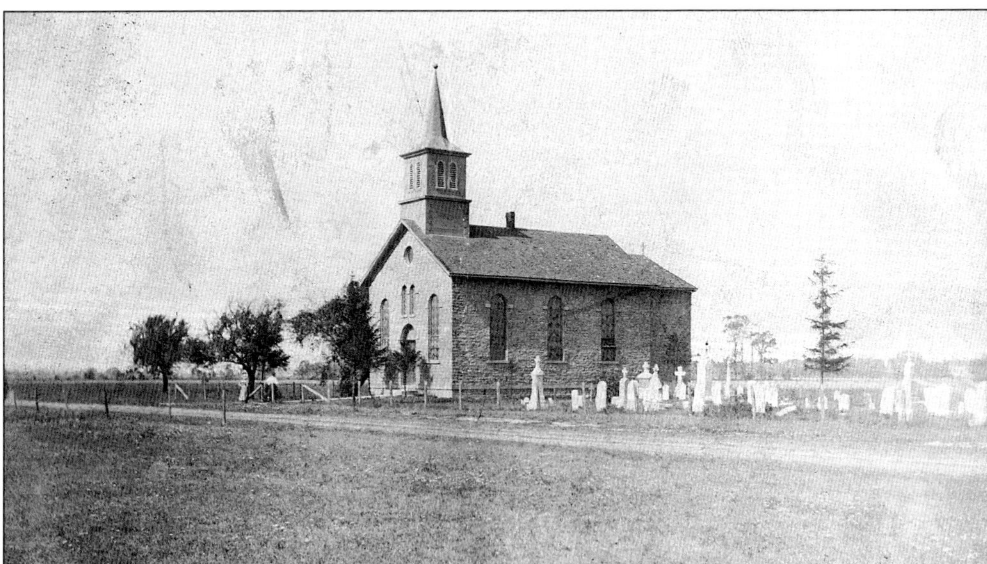

The North Bush Chapel on Englewood Avenue as it looked about 1880. The stone church was erected by German Catholics in 1849–1851 and has been restored by the St. John the Baptist parish. Many early settlers are buried in the North Bush Cemetery.

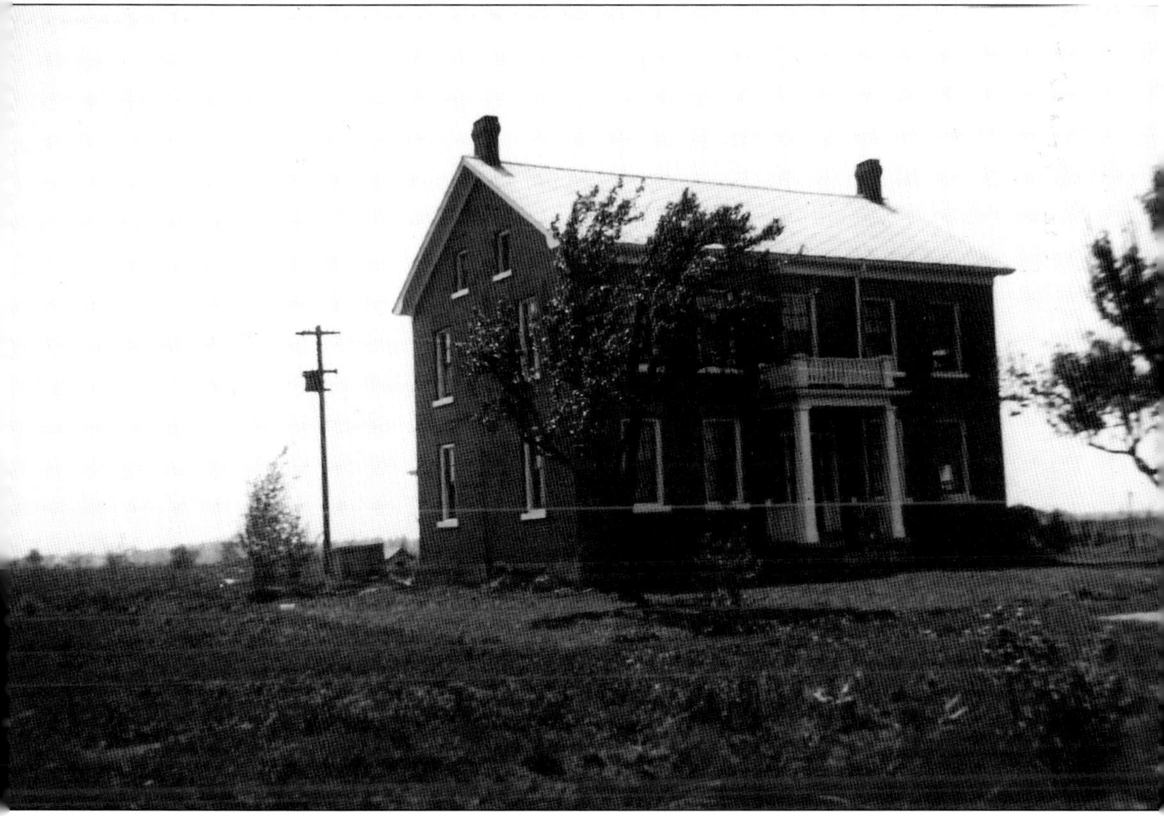

The 1846 Phillip Roeser home faced the "Guideboard Road." This 1938 view from Eggert Road shows the property before the old farm was developed for housing in the early 1950s. The home now fronts Malvern Curve. A popular legend has this home built of bricks imported from England by the English sea captain who first settled here. Recent research shows that Phillip Roeser and his wife Elizabeth were from Alsace in Europe. They farmed their 125 acres until his death in 1881. His son, Phillip Jr., continued to farm here until about 1898, when he sold the property and moved to a better farm in Williamsville because the poor clay soil of Tonawanda was worn out.

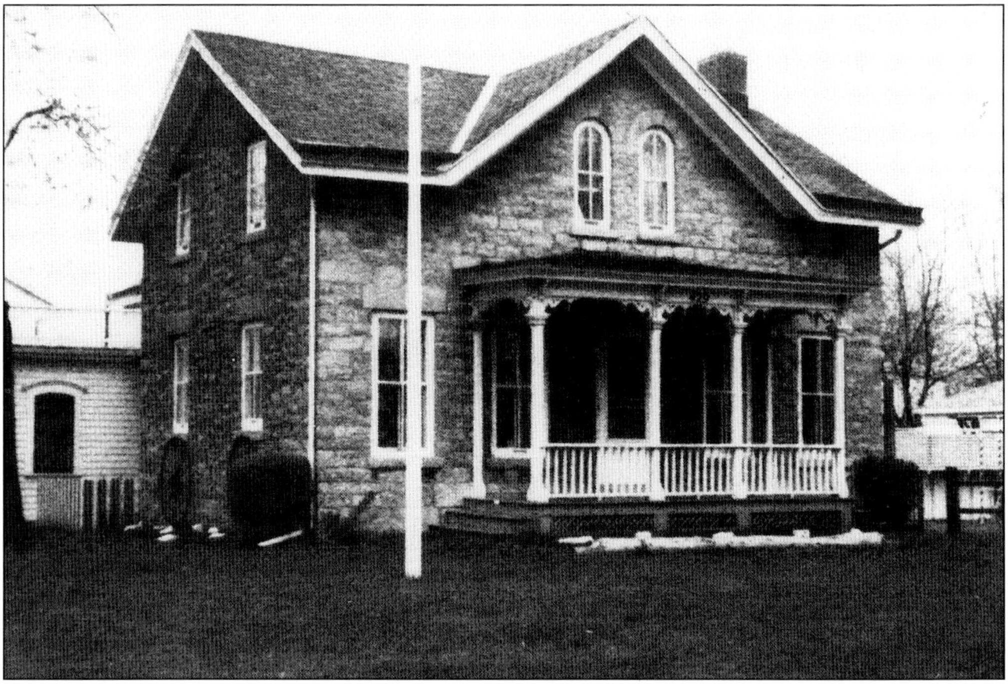

The distinctive pre-Civil War home at 429 Englewood Avenue. This house was built by Louis Voisinet on 102 acres he purchased in 1828. The interior of the home was reconstructed in the mid-1950s; the stone exterior remains little changed. The farmland has become suburban housing and Englewood Avenue businesses.

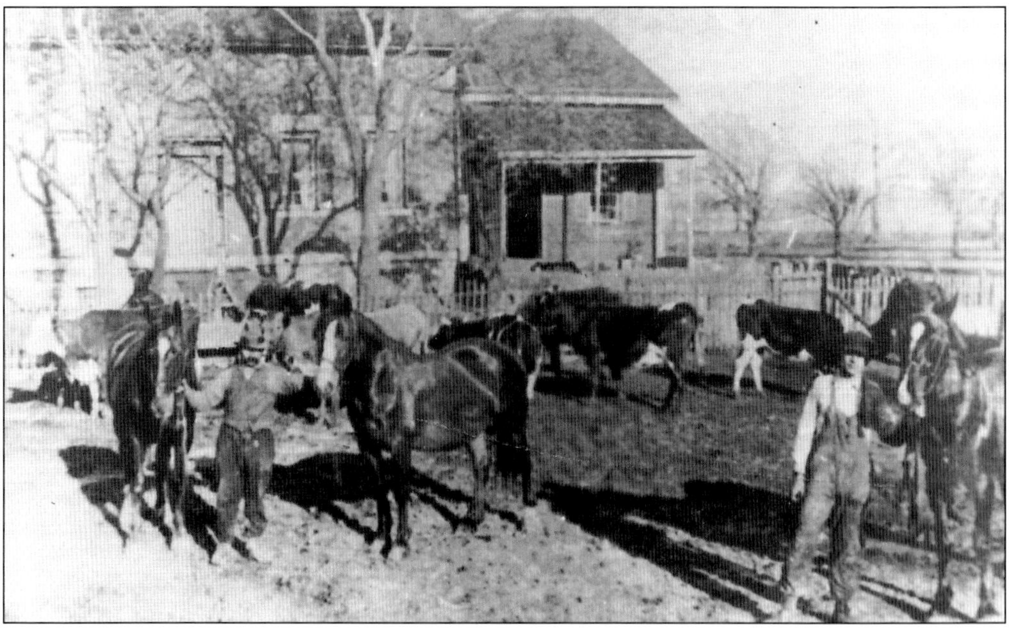

The 1840s Jacob Fries home. Originally fronting Fries Road (as shown in this early twentieth-century view), the rear of the building now "fronts" at 132 Greenleaf Avenue. Fries Road was the farm lane which followed modern Fries, Brompton, and Heritage Roads to reach the extensive family acreage in the northeastern part of the town.

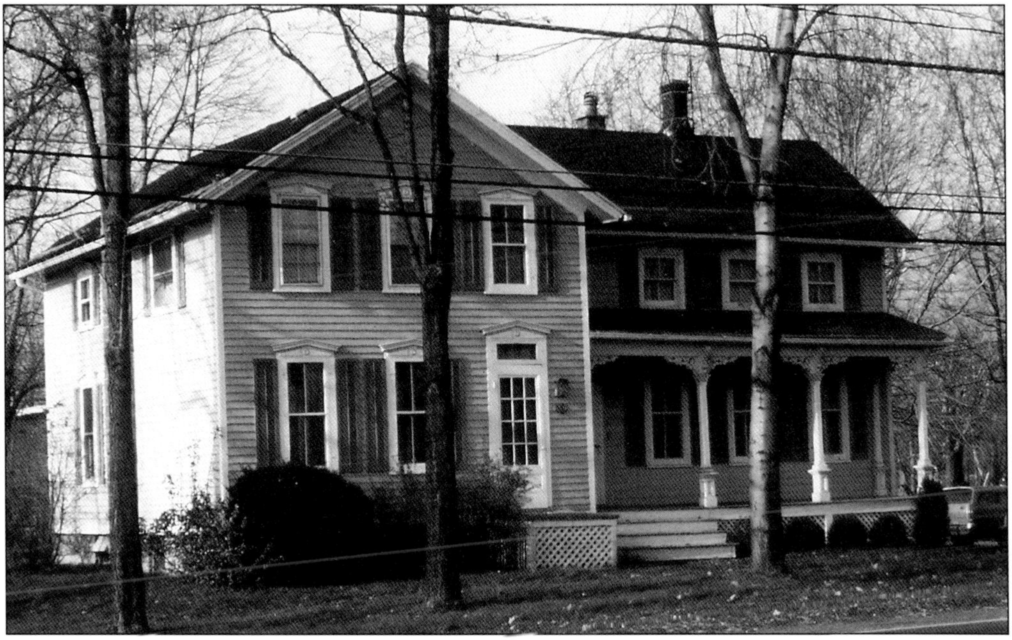

The beautiful pre-Civil War home once located at 2520 Niagara Falls Boulevard. After standing here for over 125 years, this historic residence was lost to the wrecking ball. Alois Rinebold was the owner from 1864 to 1914, having purchased the land from Michael Hickel, who bought it from Christian Schwinger in 1851. His barn stood across Town Line Road (Niagara Falls Boulevard) in Amherst. There is now a car wash on the site of the home.

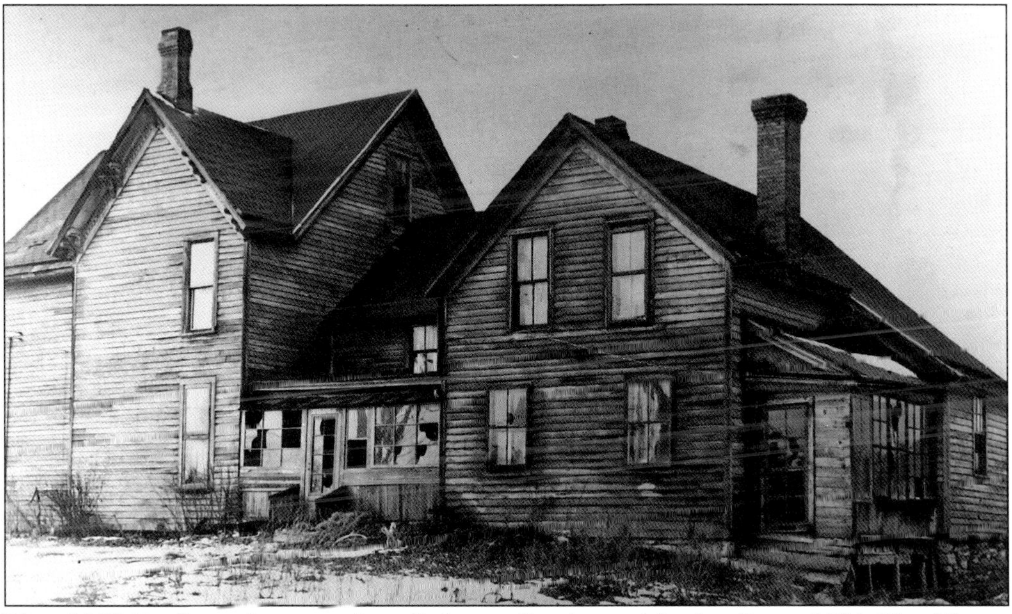

The old Philip Pirson homestead on Delaware Road near Meadow Lane, 1956. The 75-acre farm ran eastward to Belmont and included land where Kenmore West High School is located. The oldest part of the home dates to about 1830. The Pirson family farmed here from 1861 to 1922. The Niagara Mohawk Power Company bought the site to build the automatic transformer station located there now. (WNYHI)

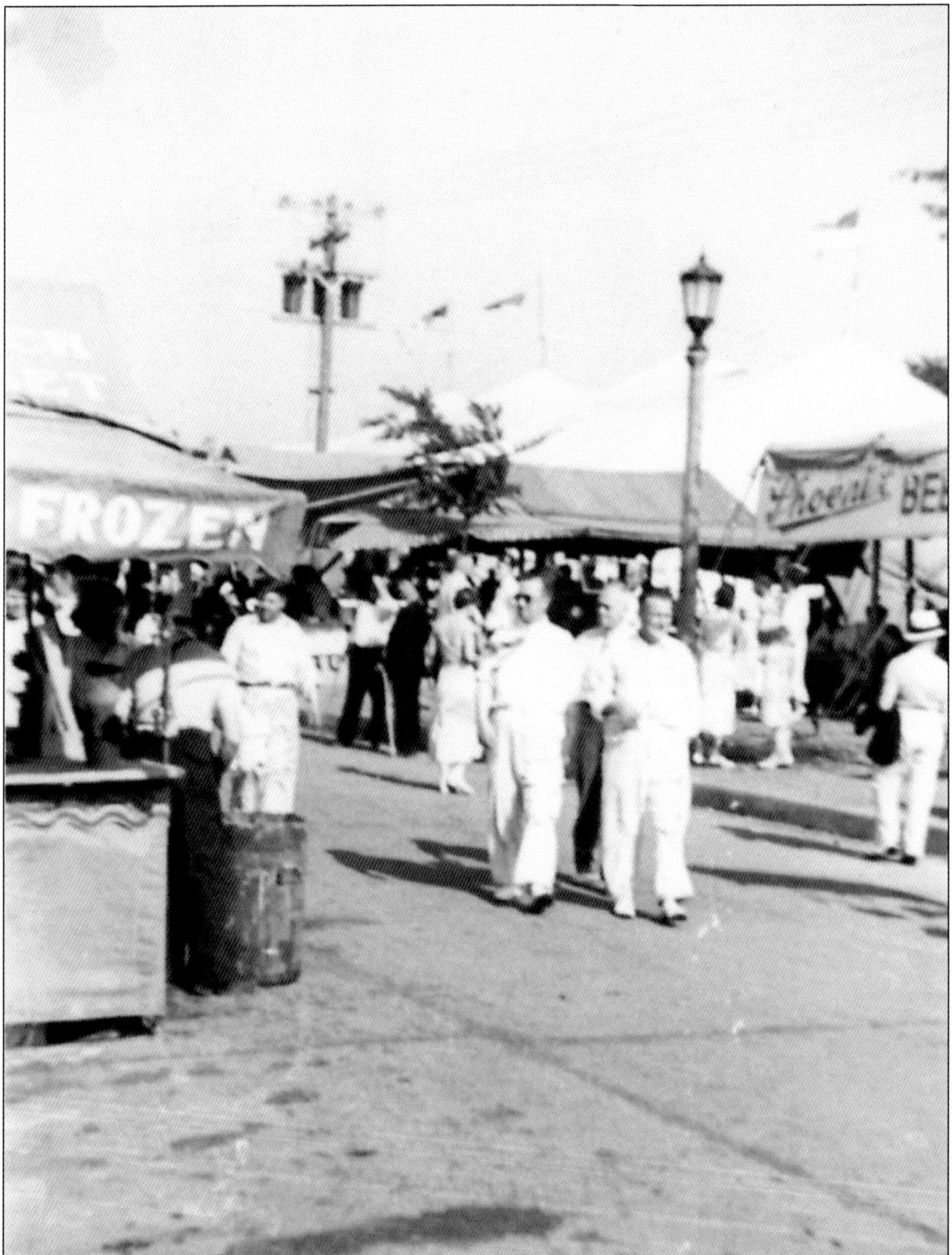

The midway at Centennial Park, July 1936. The Town of Tonawanda celebrated the 100th anniversary of its establishment by the state with a week-long fair on land between Delaware Avenue and Delaware Road (where Sheridan Delaware Plaza is now located).

Two

The Erie Canal

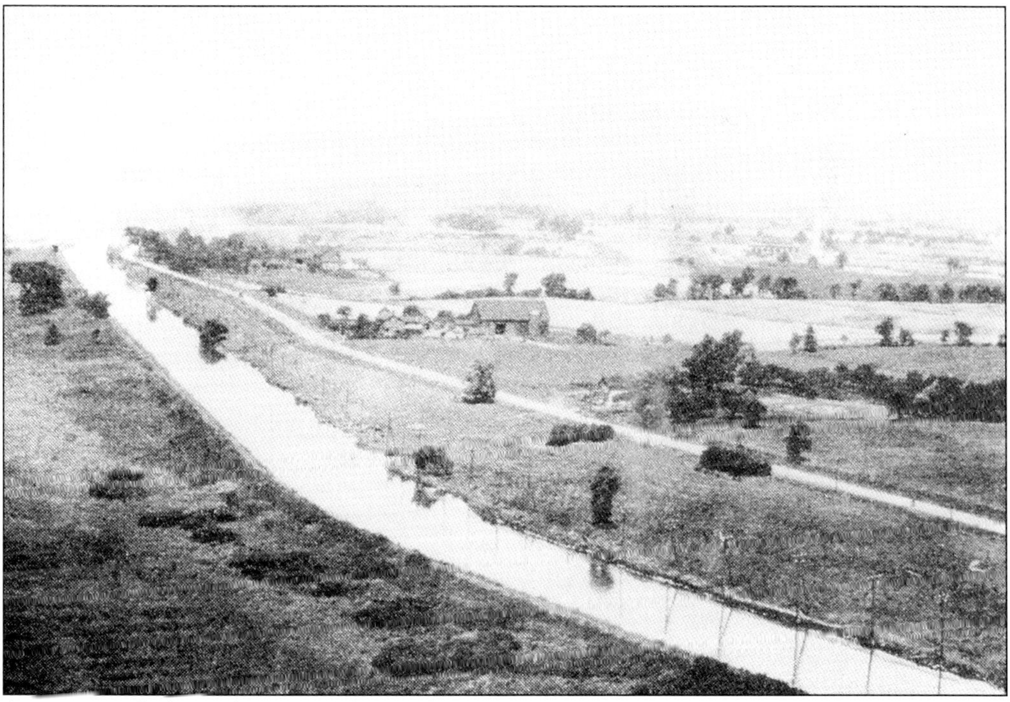

A view north from the top of the smokestack of BG&E's new River Station electric power plant along the Erie Canal in the Town of Tonawanda. The canal paralleled the river through marshy land that teemed with insects and rattlesnakes. In 1918 this portion of the canal bed was abandoned because steam tugs on the new Barge Canal could navigate the Niagara's current. The farms along River Road are located on the historic "Mile Strip" of land.

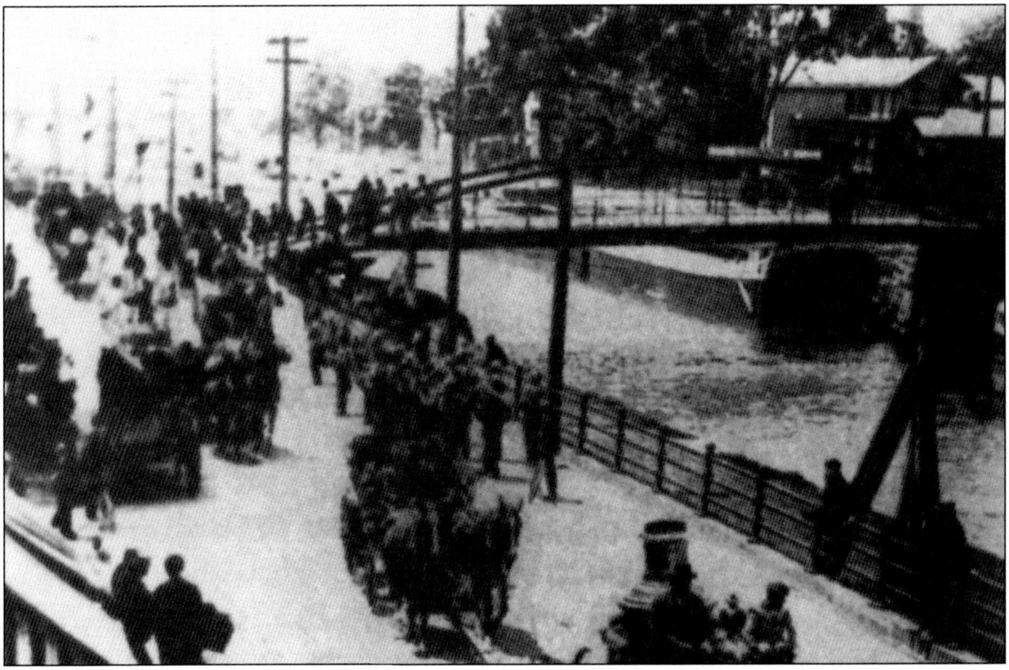

A parade along South Niagara Street at the Main Street bridge over the Erie Canal, *c.* 1860. The young Village of Tonawanda was this area's center for commerce, lumber business, canal-boat building, railroad traffic, and local government during the nineteenth century.

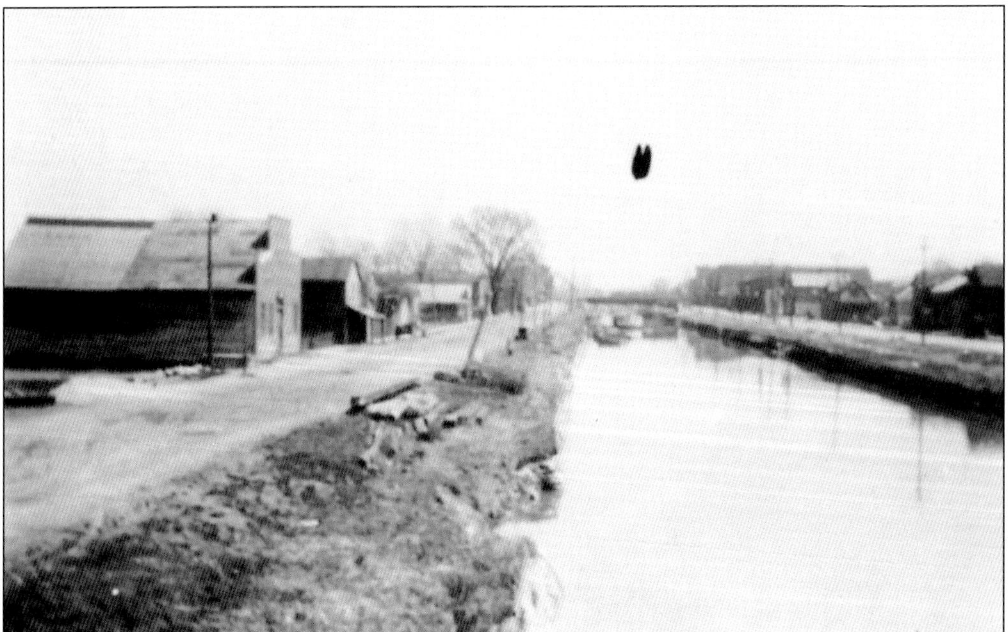

Looking east on the Erie Canal toward the Seymour Street bridge, *c.* 1900. The well-worn tow path is on the right alongside South Niagara Street in the Village of Tonawanda.

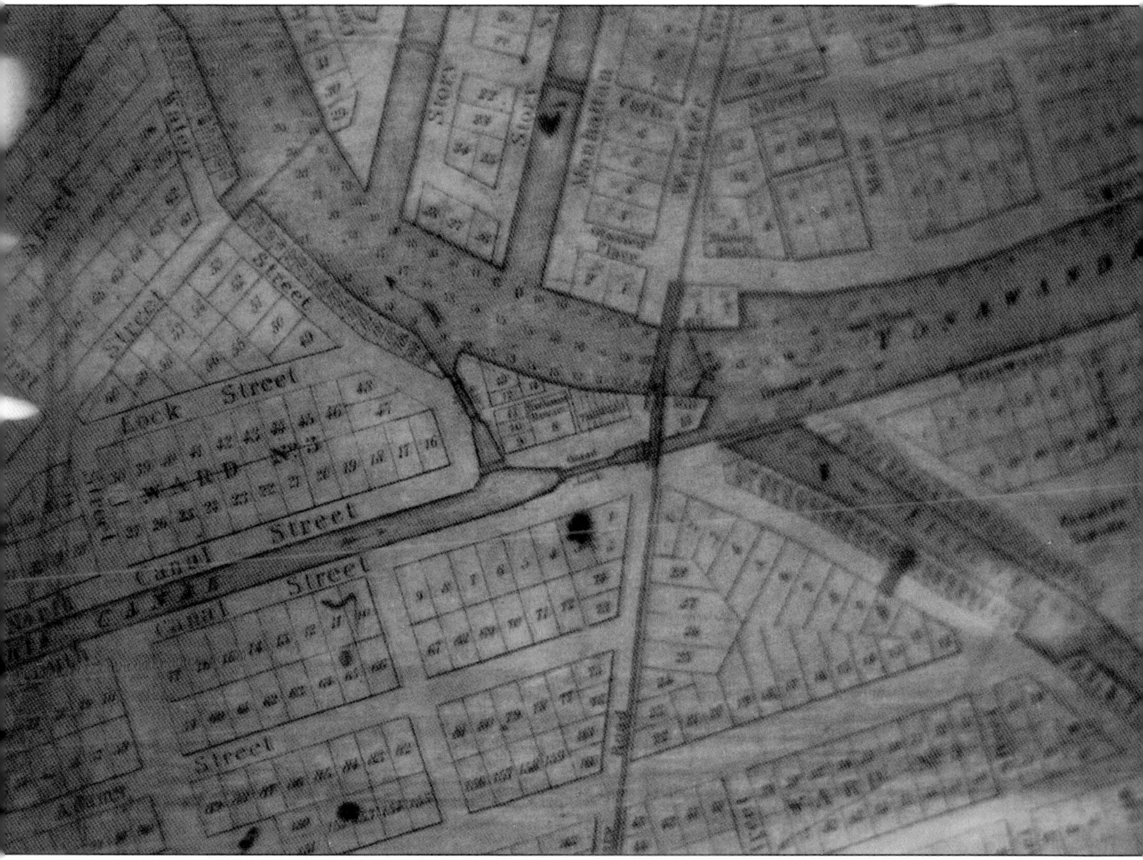

The central portion of an 1837 map of the Tonawandas which shows the route of the Erie Canal through the village. The dam raised the creek 4 feet to accommodate canal boats. The sidecut lock allowed access to Tonawanda's harbor; the guard lock prevented spring flood waters from damaging the sidecut lock. Also note the newly completed Buffalo and Niagara Falls Railroad, one of the nation's earliest. This 1836 railroad was acquired by the New York Central Railroad in 1855. Relocated in 1922, the railroad now serves Conrail and Amtrak.

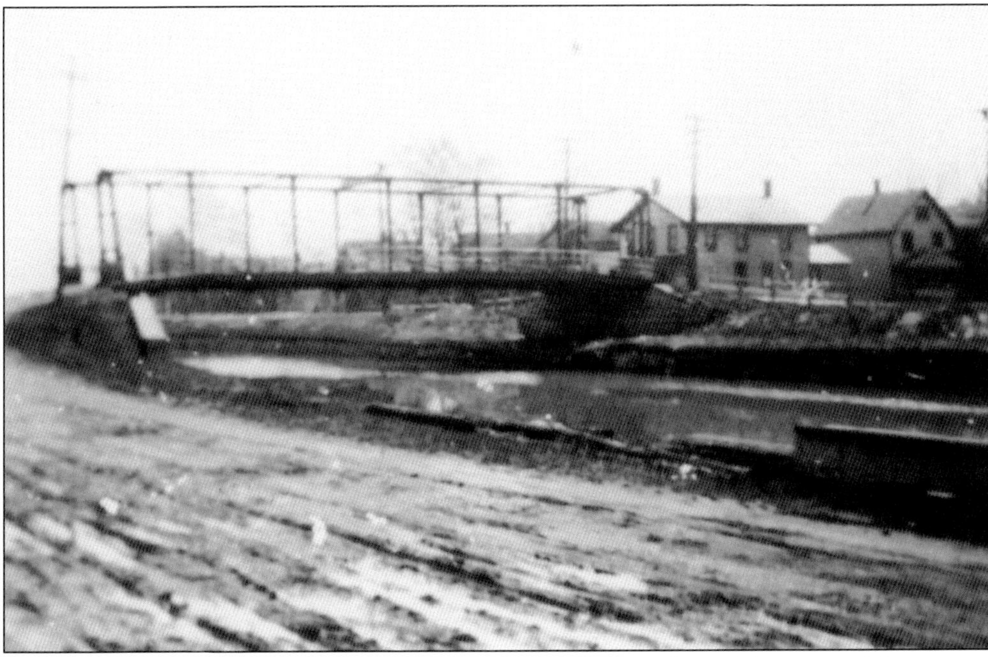

One of the many low bridges ("everybody down") over the Erie Canal. This turn-of-the-century photograph shows the Bouck Street bridge over the canal in the Village of Tonawanda.

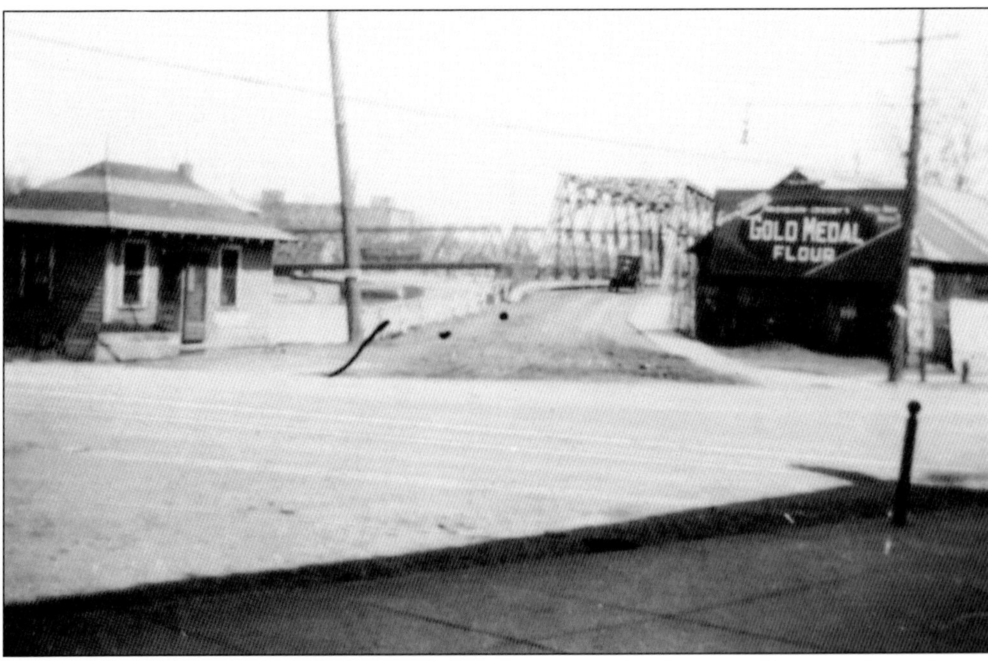

East Niagara Street in an early twentieth-century view. This bridge still carries East Niagara Street across the mouth of Ellicott Creek. The old Village of Tonawanda separated from the Town of Tonawanda in March 1903, when it was chartered by the state as a city. The old Delaware Street bridge across the canal can be seen in the distance.

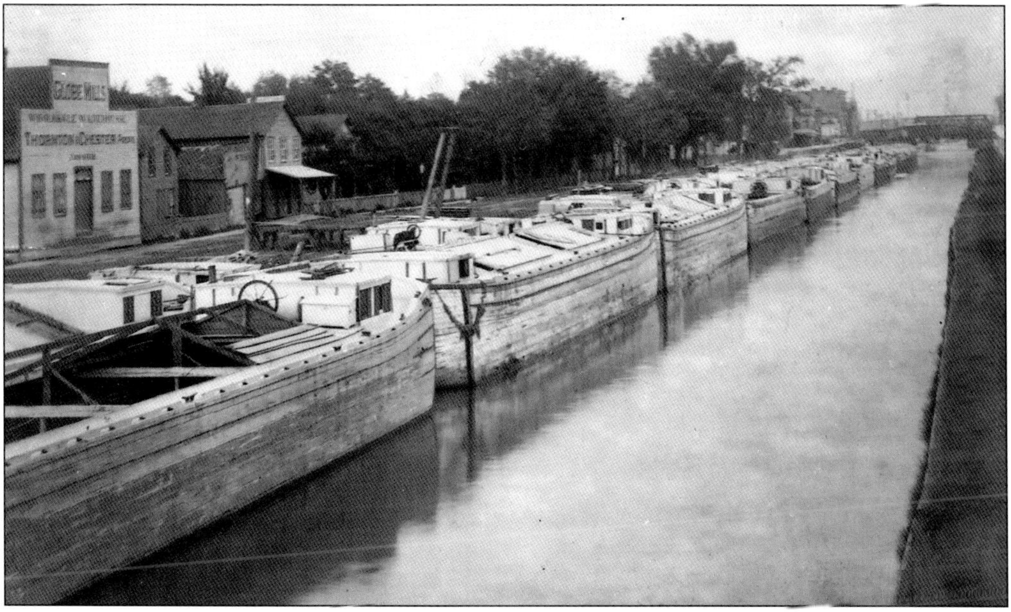

Idle Erie Canal barges along South Niagara Street, *c.* 1895. Globe Mills was a wholesale warehouse in the Village of Tonawanda owned by Thornton & Chester, Proprietors. (HSTI)

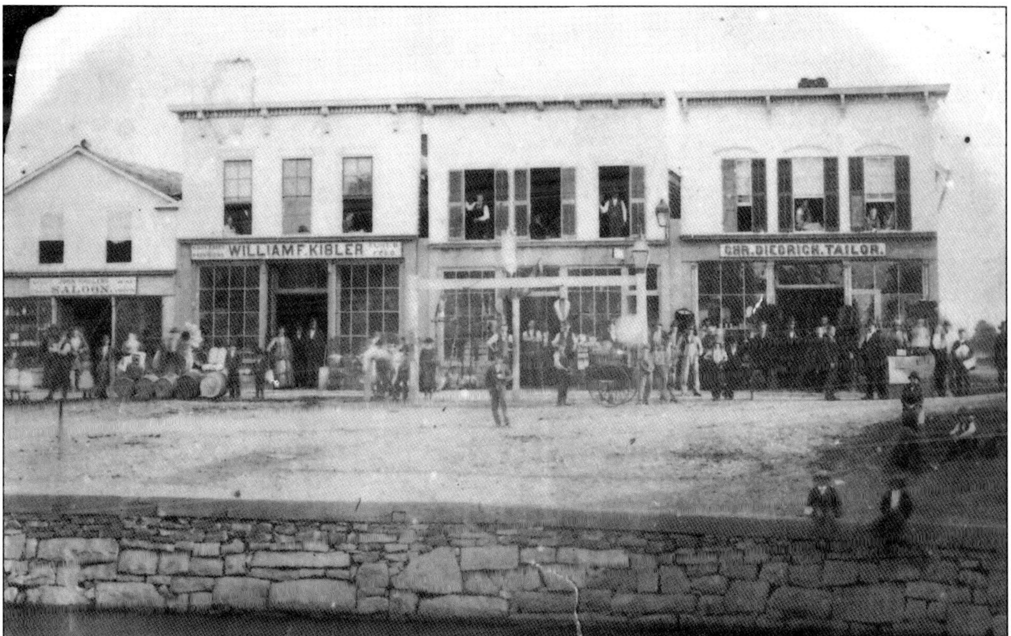

Stores alongside the Erie Canal and Niagara Street, *c.* 1890. Charles Hallers ran the saloon, William F. Kibler sold groceries, provisions, flour, and feed, and Charles Diedrich did tailoring for the "canawlers." (HSTI)

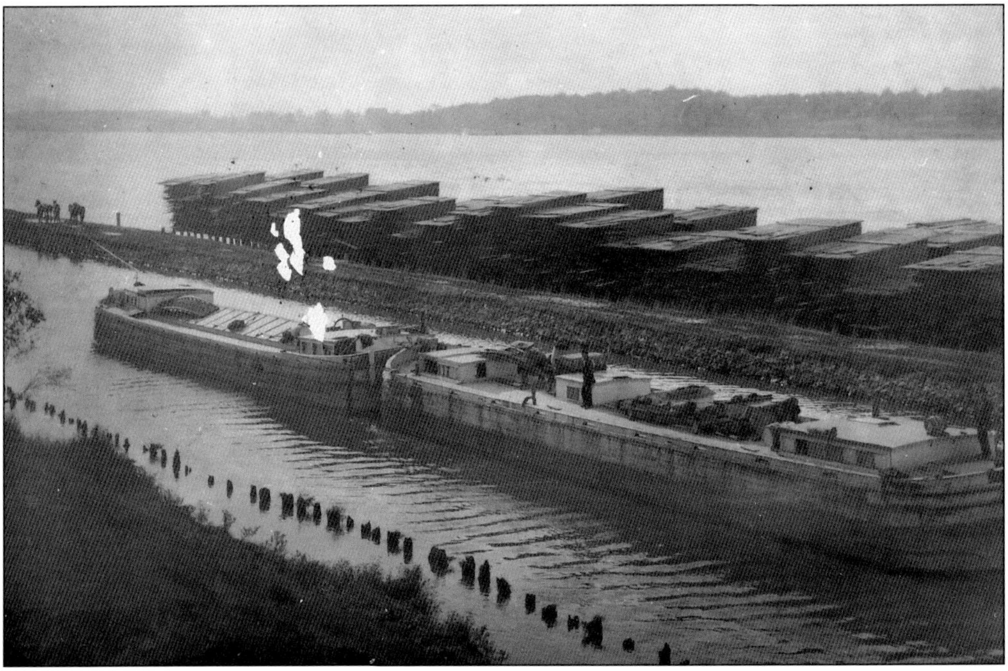

Erie Canal barges in the summer of 1894. This "horse boat and consort" are being pulled toward Buffalo in the area which is now Niawanda Park. The Tonawandas were one of the leading lumber processing centers of the world. Lumber was stacked from this area as far down the river as Gratwick in North Tonawanda. (HSTI)

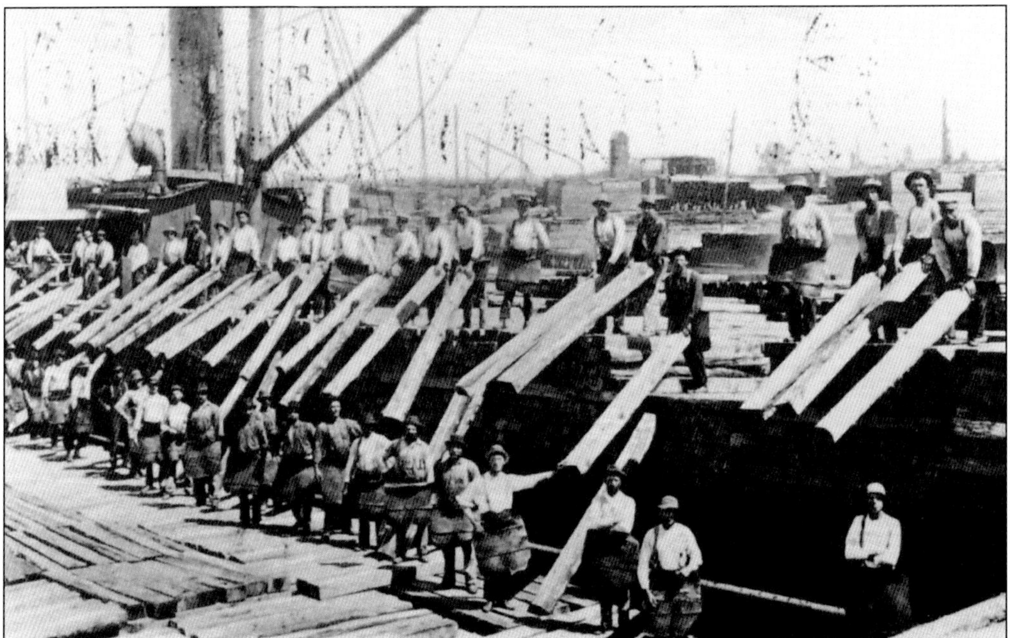

"Lumber shovers," railroad ties, and a lake steamer at Tonawanda. This classic 1890s photograph illustrates the protective clothing each man needed for the job. Heavy gloves and a leather apron enabled each "dockwalloper" to slide lumber across his knees. (WNYHI)

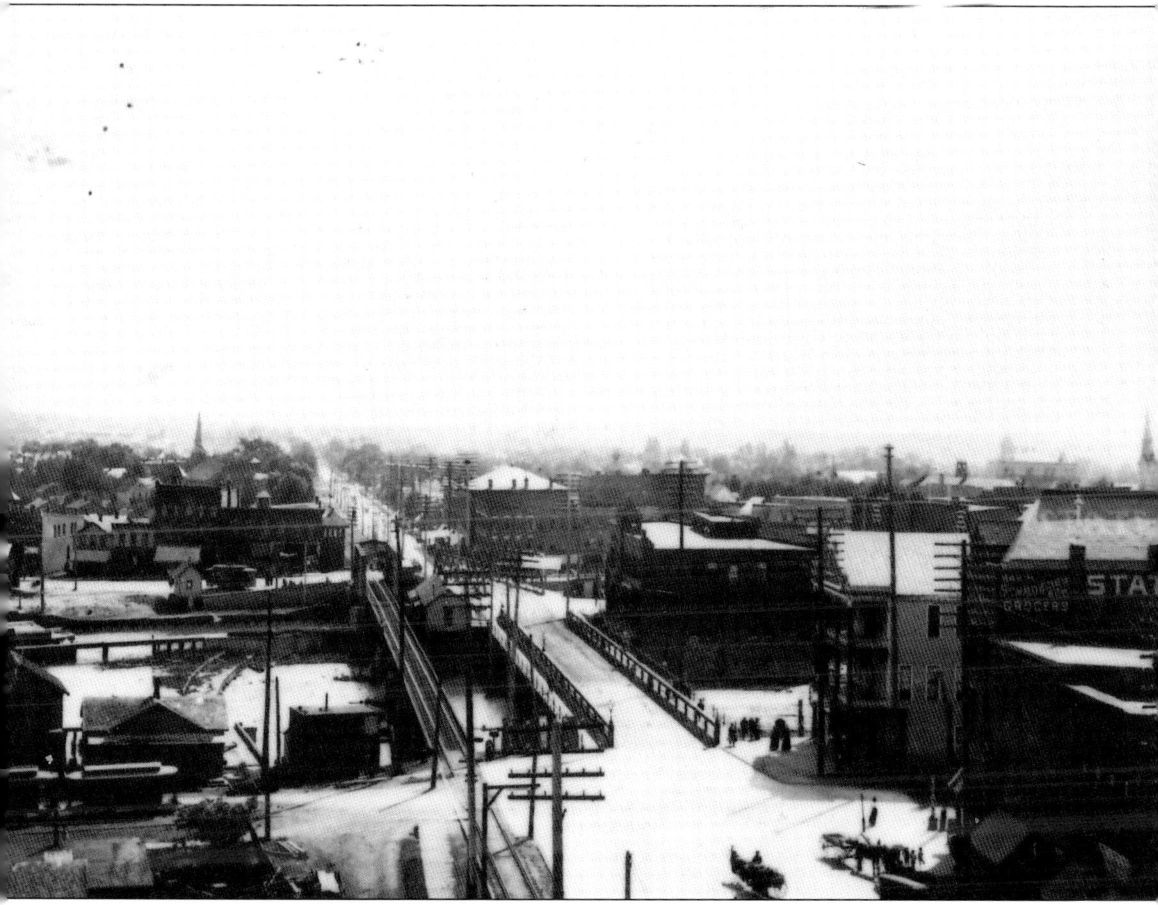

A view of the Long Bridge over the Erie Canal connecting the villages of Tonawanda (across the canal) and North Tonawanda, *c.* 1895. The New York Central Railroad bridge is to the left of the Long Bridge. The Tonawanda station was located just across the bridge until the 1870 station was built at Grove Street. The NYCRR, built in 1836, connected Buffalo with Niagara Falls. (HSTI)

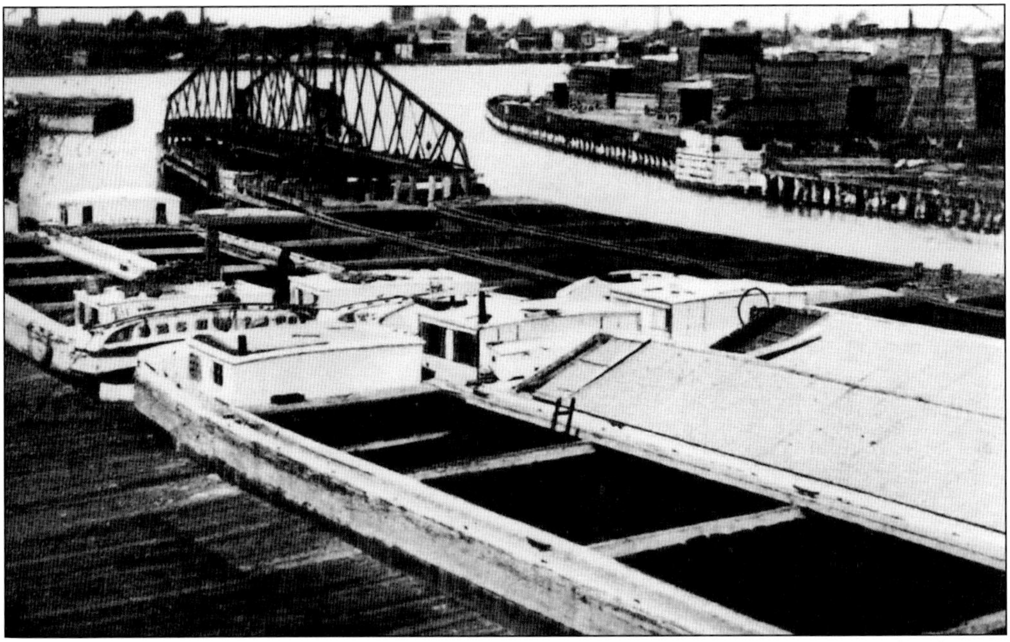

The railroad swing bridge, with Tonawanda Island in the background. The bridge enabled trains to cross the mouth of Tonawanda Creek to service the lumber yards along the Little Niagara River. Barges are tied up five deep along the south side of Tonawanda Creek. Townhouses face this site now, an area once known as "Goose Island," surrounded by the canal, the creek, and the Niagara River. (WNYHI)

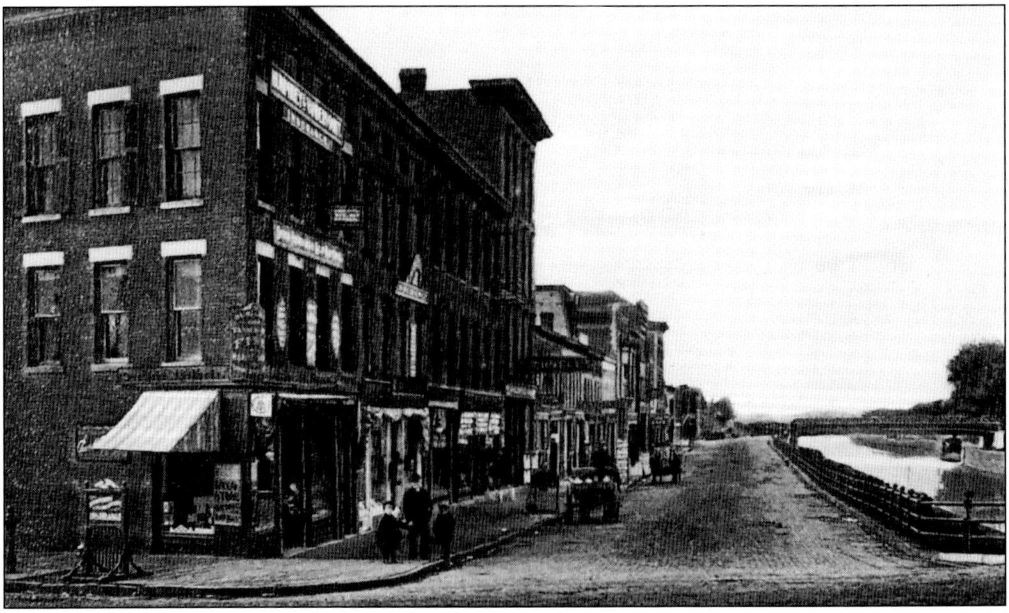

"Downtown" Tonawanda when it was still a village, a century ago. This view from an old postcard looks southwest along South Niagara Street. Humphrey & Vandervoort insurance agency signs dominate their home office at the corner of Main Street, and in the distance the old Seymour Street bridge crosses the Erie Canal. The agency is still active in the area. (WNYHI)

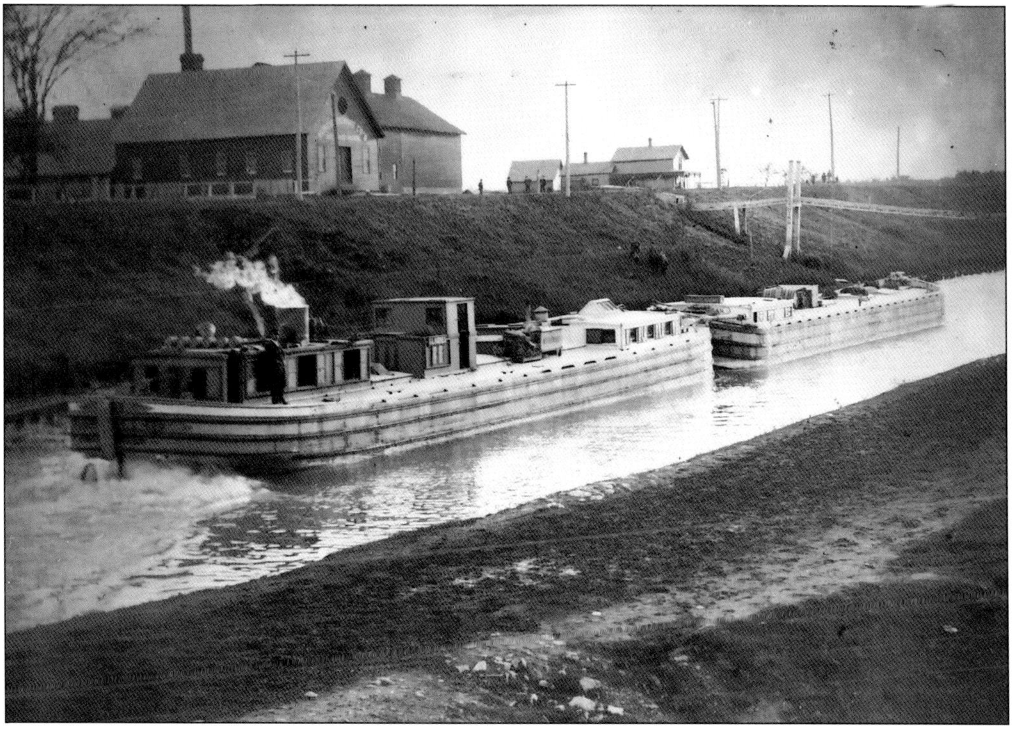

A steam-powered Buffalo-bound barge along the Erie Canal during the 1890s. The brick building stood at Niagara Street and Hinds Street in the Village of Tonawanda where a Wilson Farms mini-plaza is today. (HSTI)

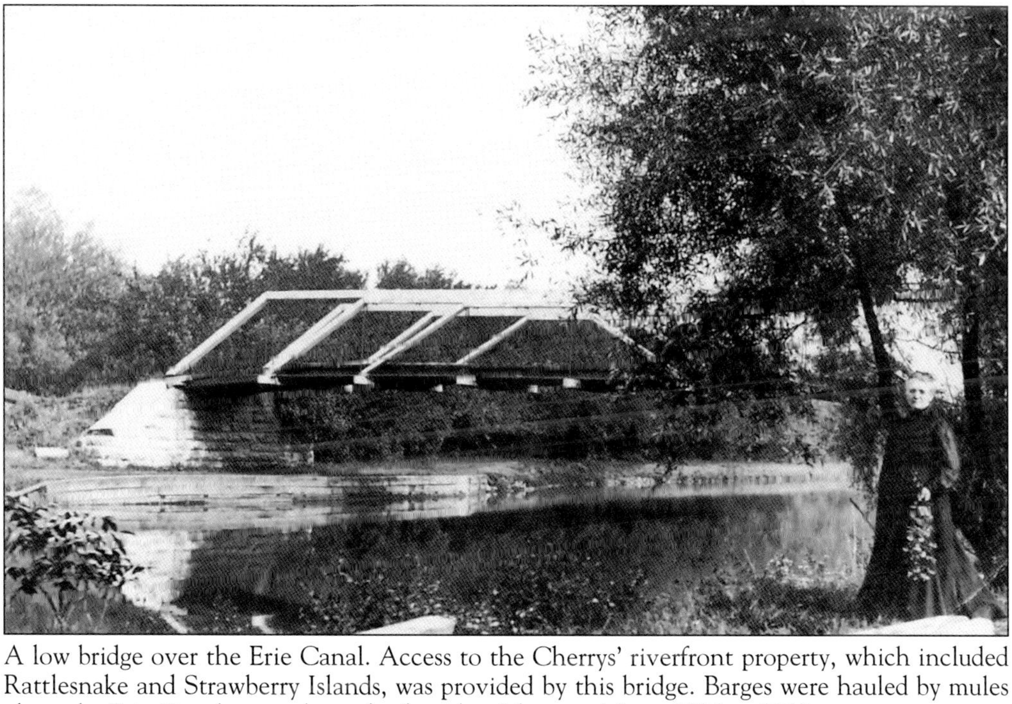

A low bridge over the Erie Canal. Access to the Cherrys' riverfront property, which included Rattlesnake and Strawberry Islands, was provided by this bridge. Barges were hauled by mules along the Erie Canal towpath on the far side of the canal from 1825 to 1918.

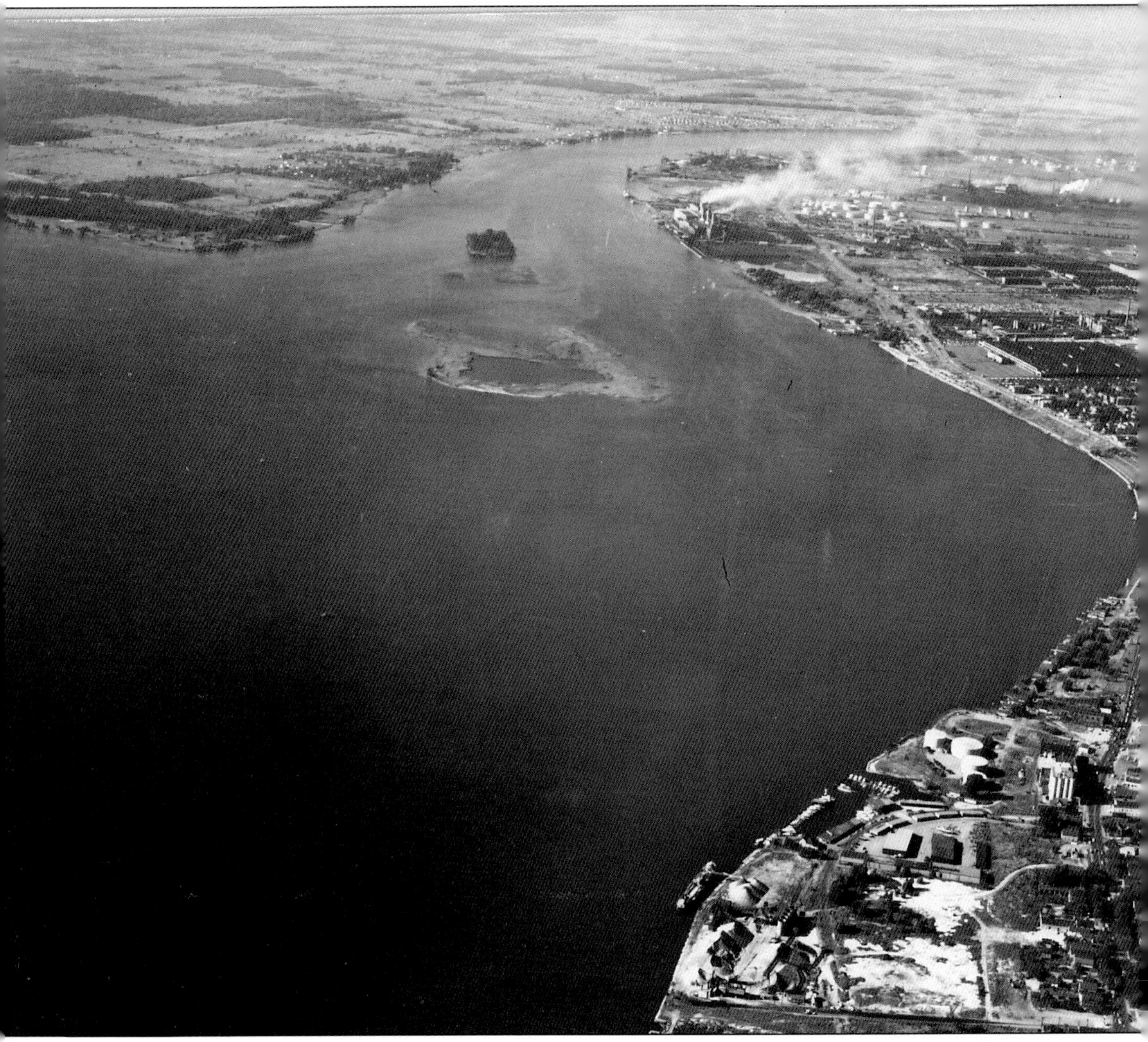

The western part of the town as seen from the air over Buffalo's Riverside area, October 5, 1954. Grand Island is at top. Strawberry Island and Motor Island mark the entrance to the Niagara River's east channel. The Chevrolet engine plant is opposite Strawberry Island and the smoky Huntley Steam Station is farther downriver. The Niagara Thruway along the river follows the old Erie Canal bed. (WNYHI)

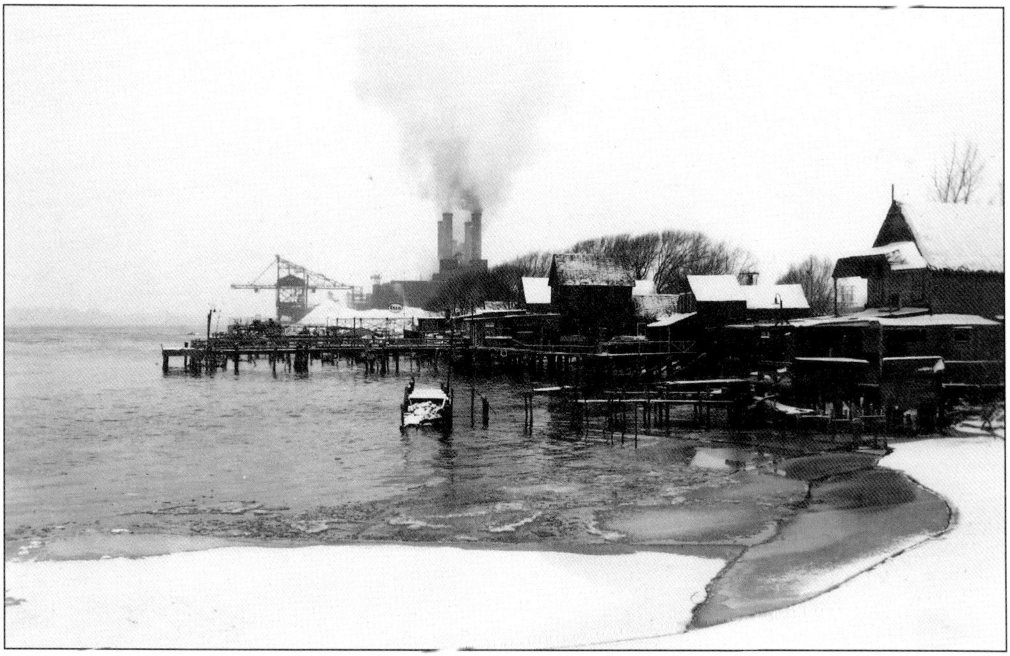

"The Marsh" along the Erie Canal towpath north of Vulcan Street during the nineteenth century. The community had a reputation as a center for "rumrunners" during Prohibition. The Huntley electric power plant appears in the distance in this c. 1950 photograph. The community was razed in 1957 for construction of the Niagara Thruway.

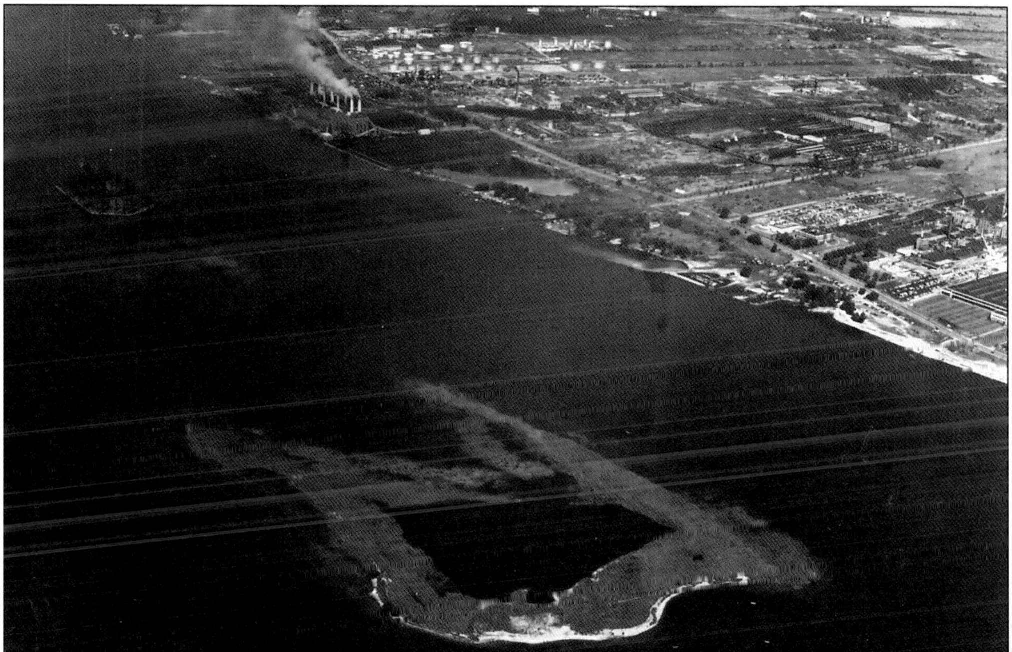

Strawberry Island from the air, October 5, 1954. Much of the gravel from this once-200-acre island has been dredged out for construction material. Motor Island is at left across from the smoking Huntley Steam Station. (WNYHI)

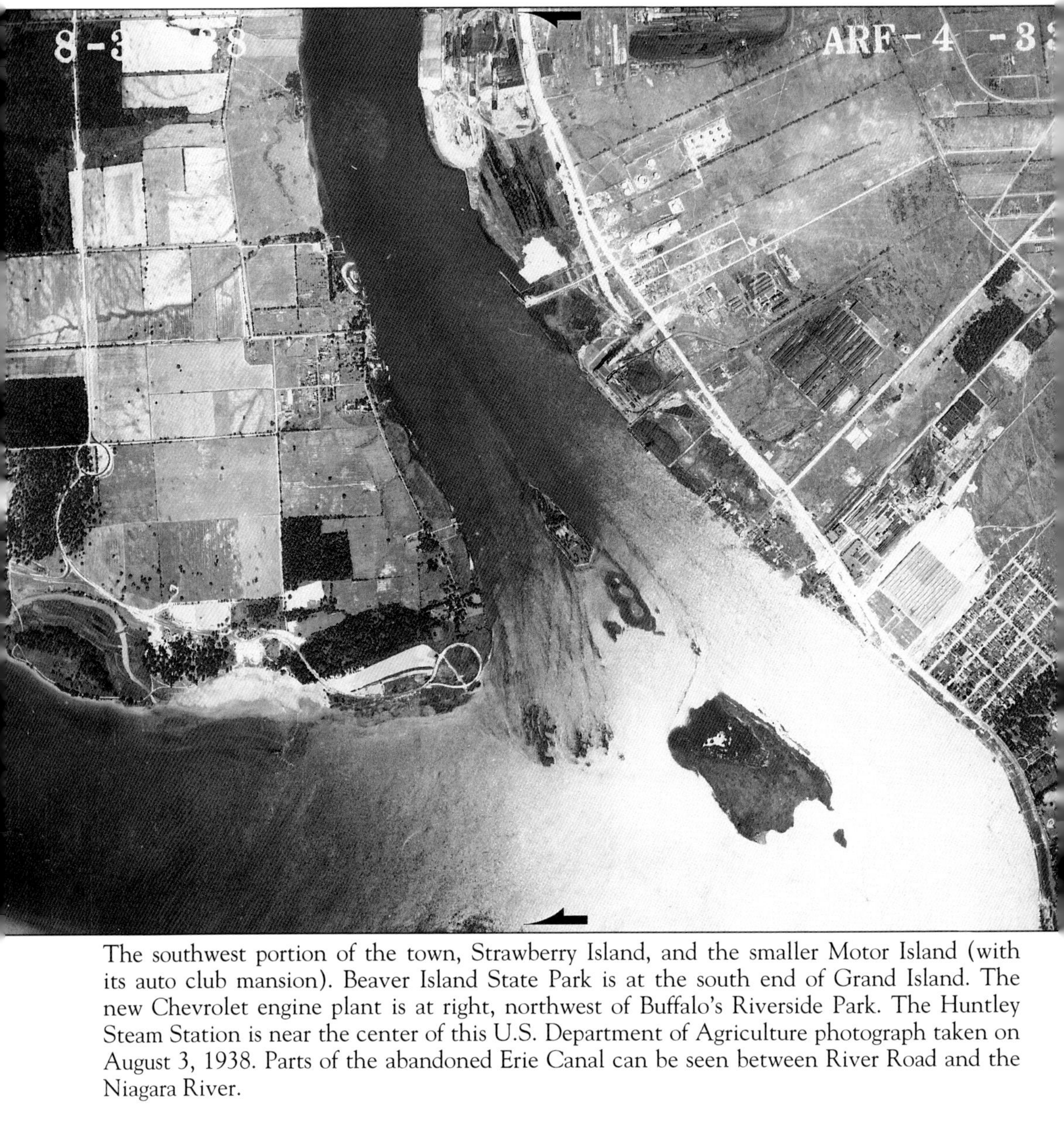

The southwest portion of the town, Strawberry Island, and the smaller Motor Island (with its auto club mansion). Beaver Island State Park is at the south end of Grand Island. The new Chevrolet engine plant is at right, northwest of Buffalo's Riverside Park. The Huntley Steam Station is near the center of this U.S. Department of Agriculture photograph taken on August 3, 1938. Parts of the abandoned Erie Canal can be seen between River Road and the Niagara River.

Three

THE RISE OF INDUSTRY

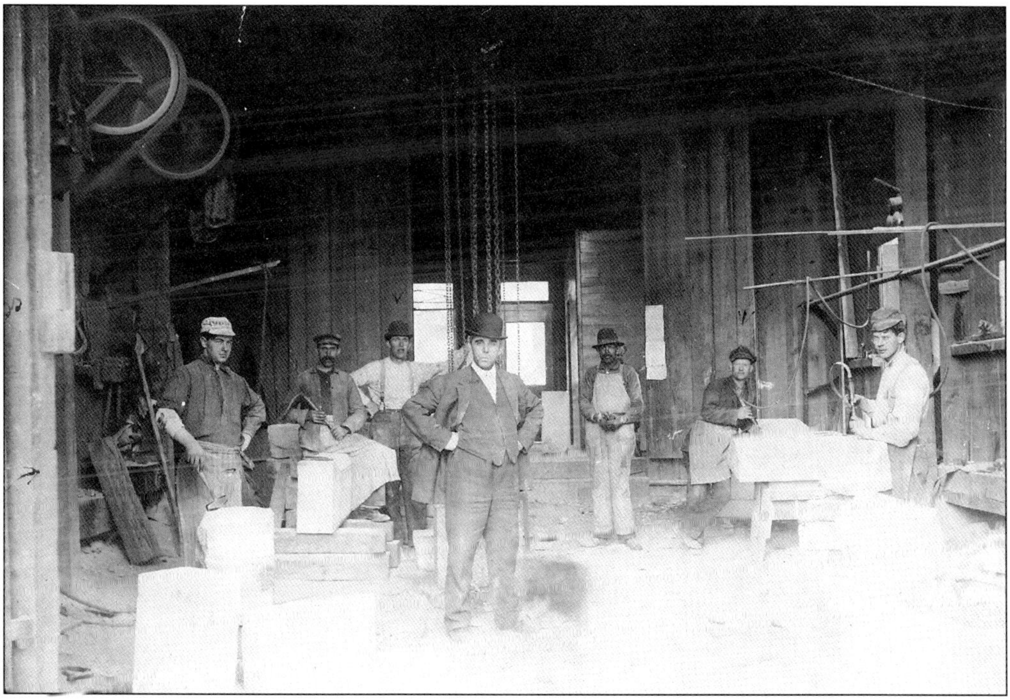

Ball Brothers, a tombstone company. Located on Delaware Avenue opposite the end of Shell (Brighton) Road, the company provided monuments, as shown in this c. 1900 photograph, for a large share of the grave sites. It was convenient to the Elmlawn, Mt. Olivet, and St. Peter's cemeteries. The building was demolished in the 1980s.

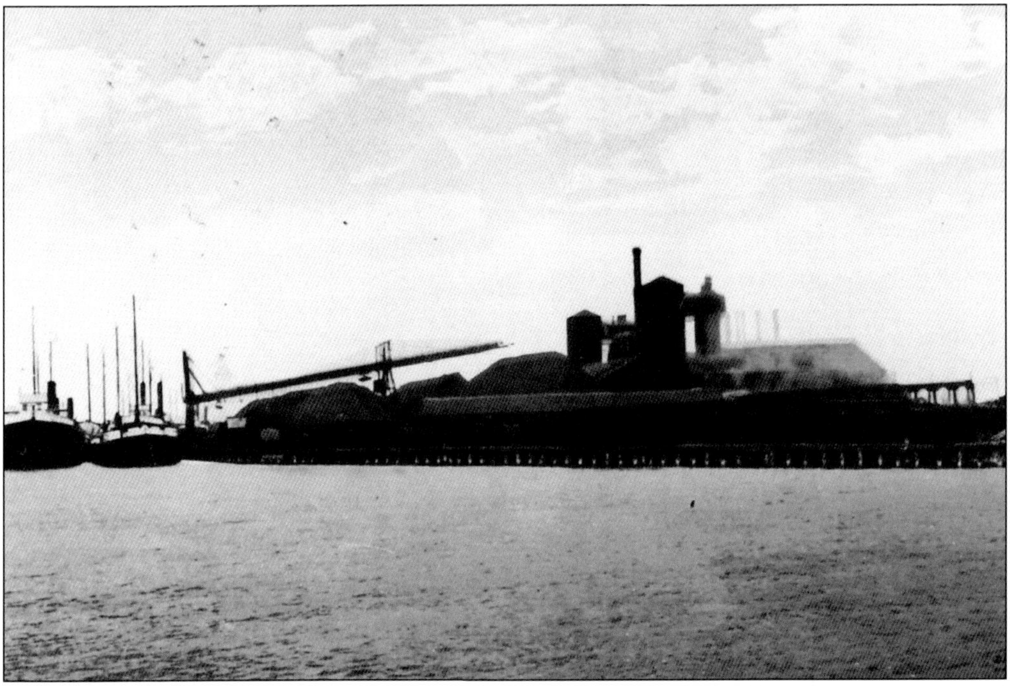

The Wickwire-Spencer Steel Corporation on River Road. Iron ore and limestone were shipped here via lake boat; coal arrived by both boat and train. The company, which opened in 1908 and closed in 1964, made rod and wire products which were shipped by rail and water to the world market. (WNYHI)

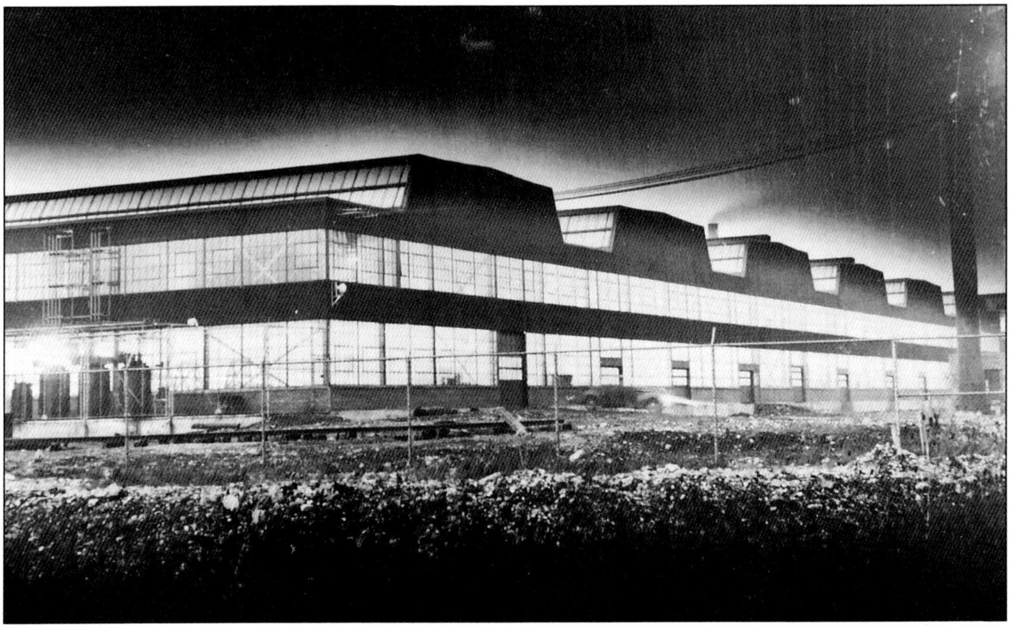

The former Wickwire-Spencer steel mill on River Road during World War II. As shown in this nighttime 1943 photograph, the mill operated around the clock. Thousands of out-of-state people came here to work in the war plants; many stayed on as permanent town residents after the war. (WNYHI)

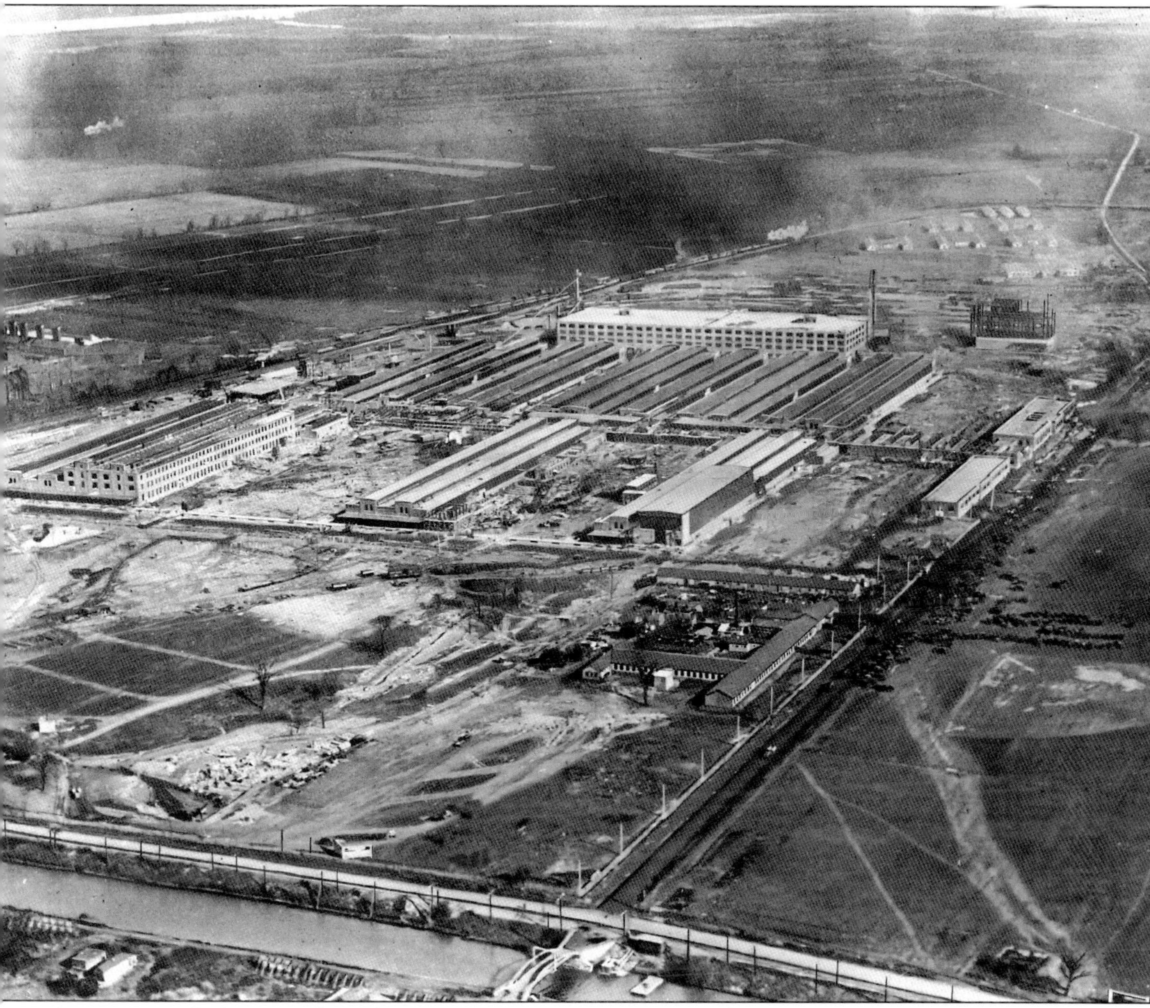

A 1921 aerial photograph of the new Dunlop Tire and Rubber Company plant on Two Mile Creek Road (later Sheridan Drive). River Road and the abandoned Erie Canal are in the foreground. The bridge over the canal led to "The Marsh" and the upper Grand Island ferry landing. Sawyer, Kaufmann, and James Avenues can been seen at upper left. The open area at right was later developed as the Dunlop Golf Course. The Niagara Thruway passes through that area now.

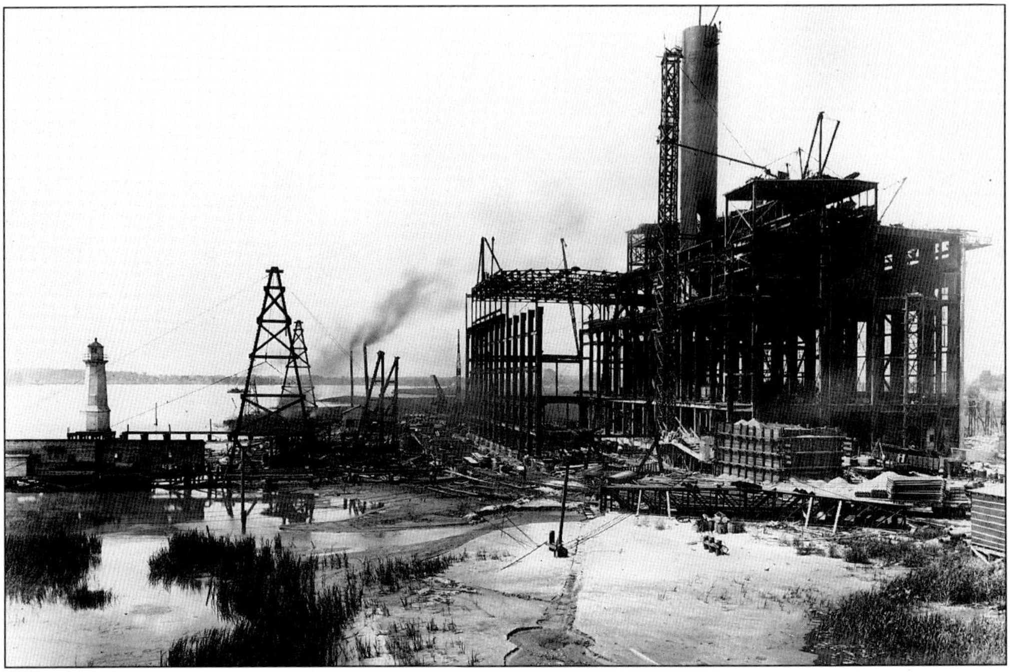

Buffalo General Electric's steam generating station under construction, August 10, 1916. This facility later became part of the Niagara Hudson System and today continues as a supplier of electricity to the Niagara Mohawk Power Corporation.

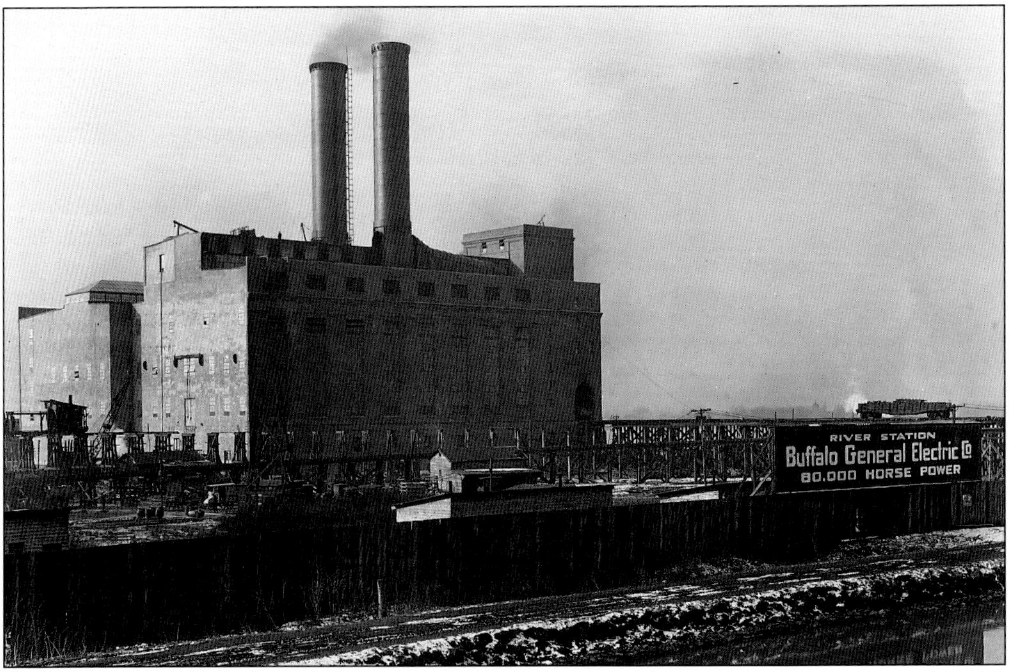

The Buffalo General Electric steam generating station on the Niagara River, December 11, 1916, the year the facility was put into operation. The station was later named for Charles R. Huntley, BGE's president. The coal-fired plant was built to supplement the Niagara Falls hydroelectric plants during a time of rapidly increasing demand for electric power.

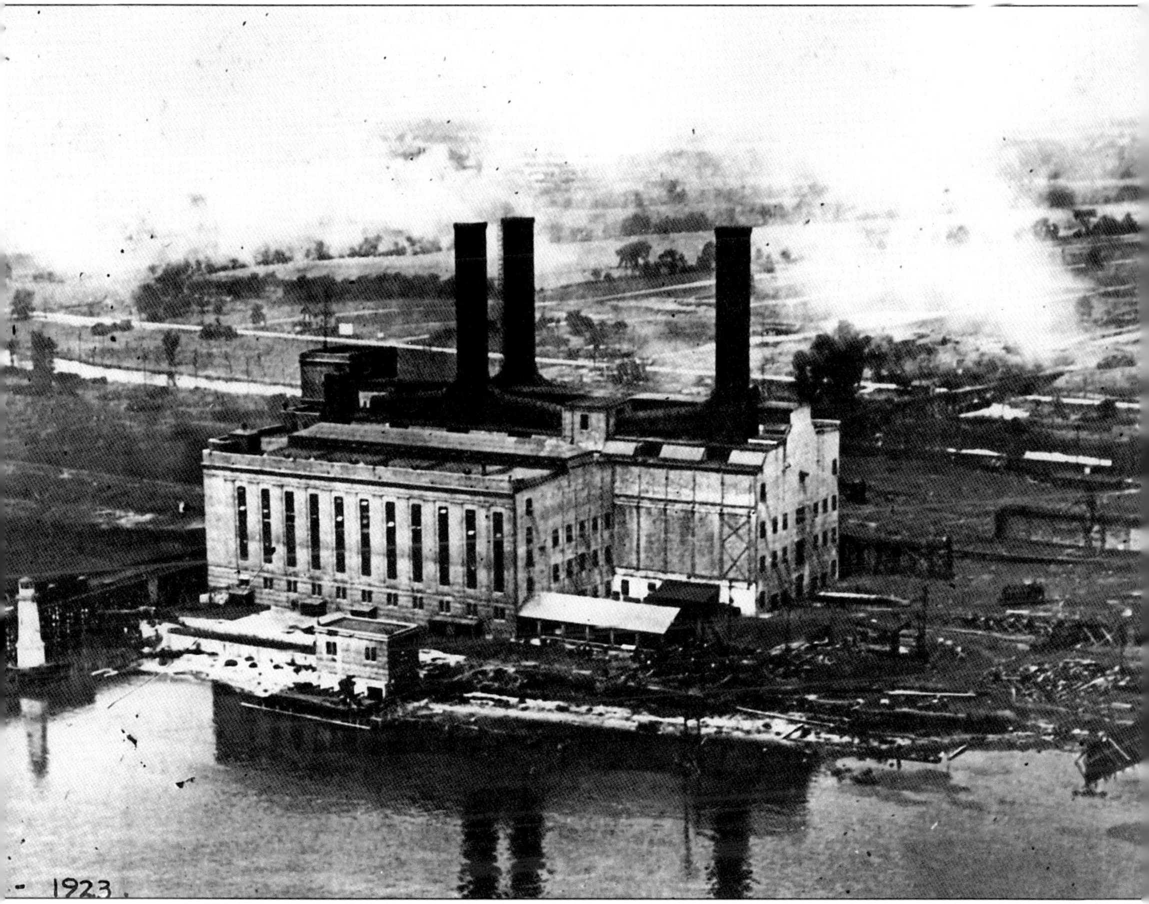

Buffalo General Electric Company's River Station (now the Charles R. Huntley Station) as seen from an "aeroplane" in 1923. River Road farmland and the abandoned Erie Canal are in the background. A small lighthouse aided the nighttime navigation of canal boats docking at the station. (WNYHI)

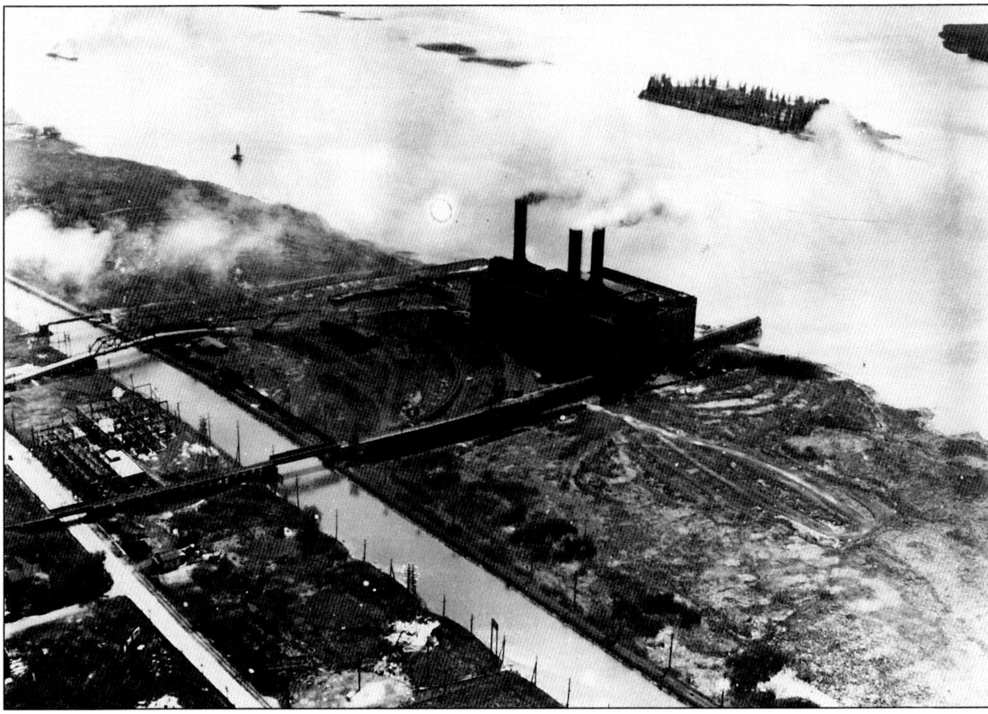

Buffalo General Electric's River Road steam generating station in 1923. River Road and the abandoned Erie Canal are at lower left; the Niagara River is at top. Note the tracks for trains which delivered coal for the boilers (coal was also delivered by boat). The building on Motor Island at top burned many years ago in a spectacular fire.

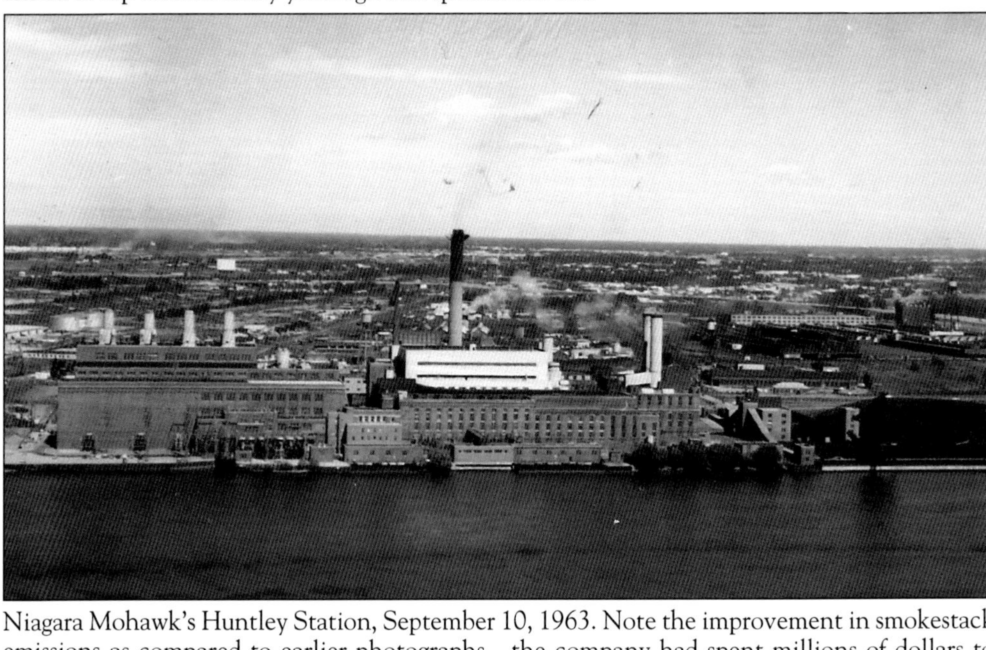

Niagara Mohawk's Huntley Station, September 10, 1963. Note the improvement in smokestack emissions as compared to earlier photographs—the company had spent millions of dollars to meet modern environmental standards. The Dupont rubber products factory with its familiar water tower is at right. (WNYHI)

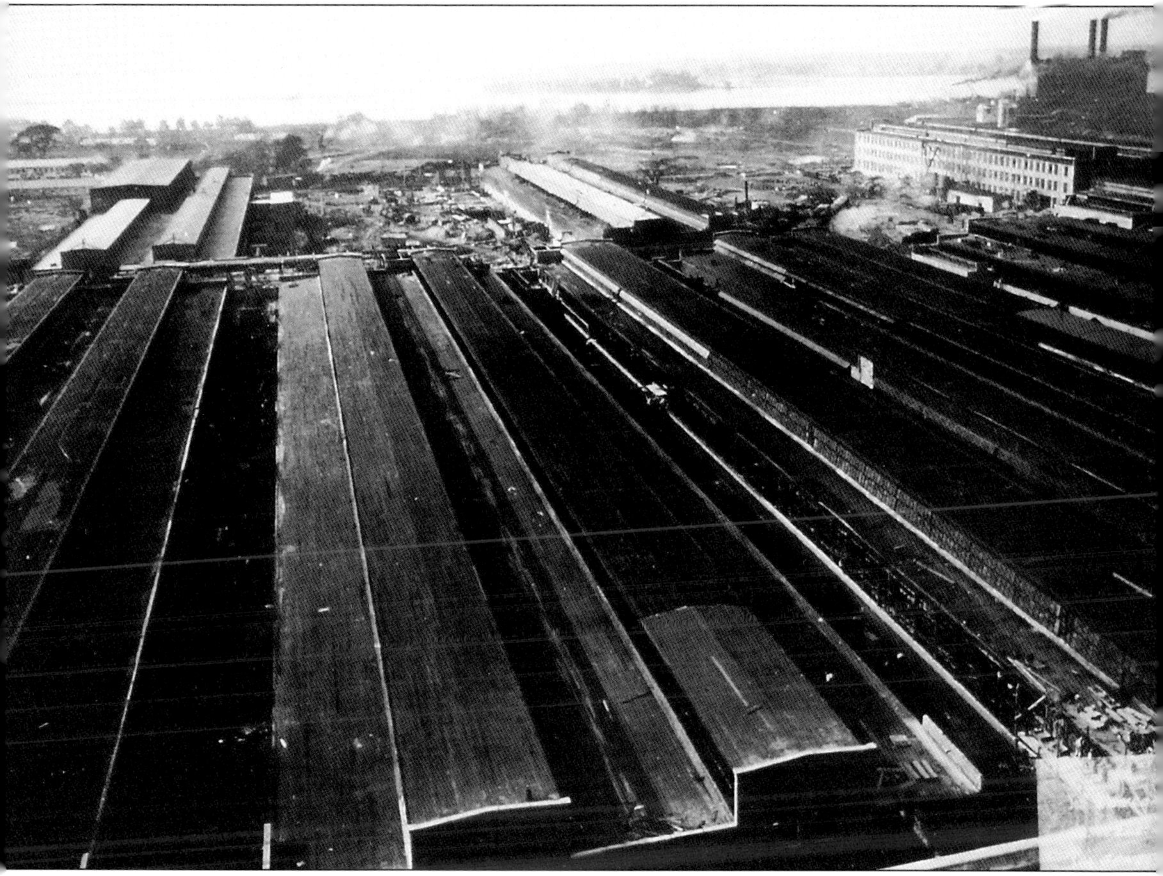

Looking southwest from the top of Dunlop's water tower in 1921. The British company began construction of the new facility in the Town of Tonawanda in 1920. Tires have been produced in the long buildings for seventy-five years. For many years Dunlop turned out tennis balls and golf balls in the factory as well. Today all of Dunlop's North American-produced motorcycle tires and a large share of its truck tires come from this plant, which is now part of the worldwide Sumitomo Corporation.

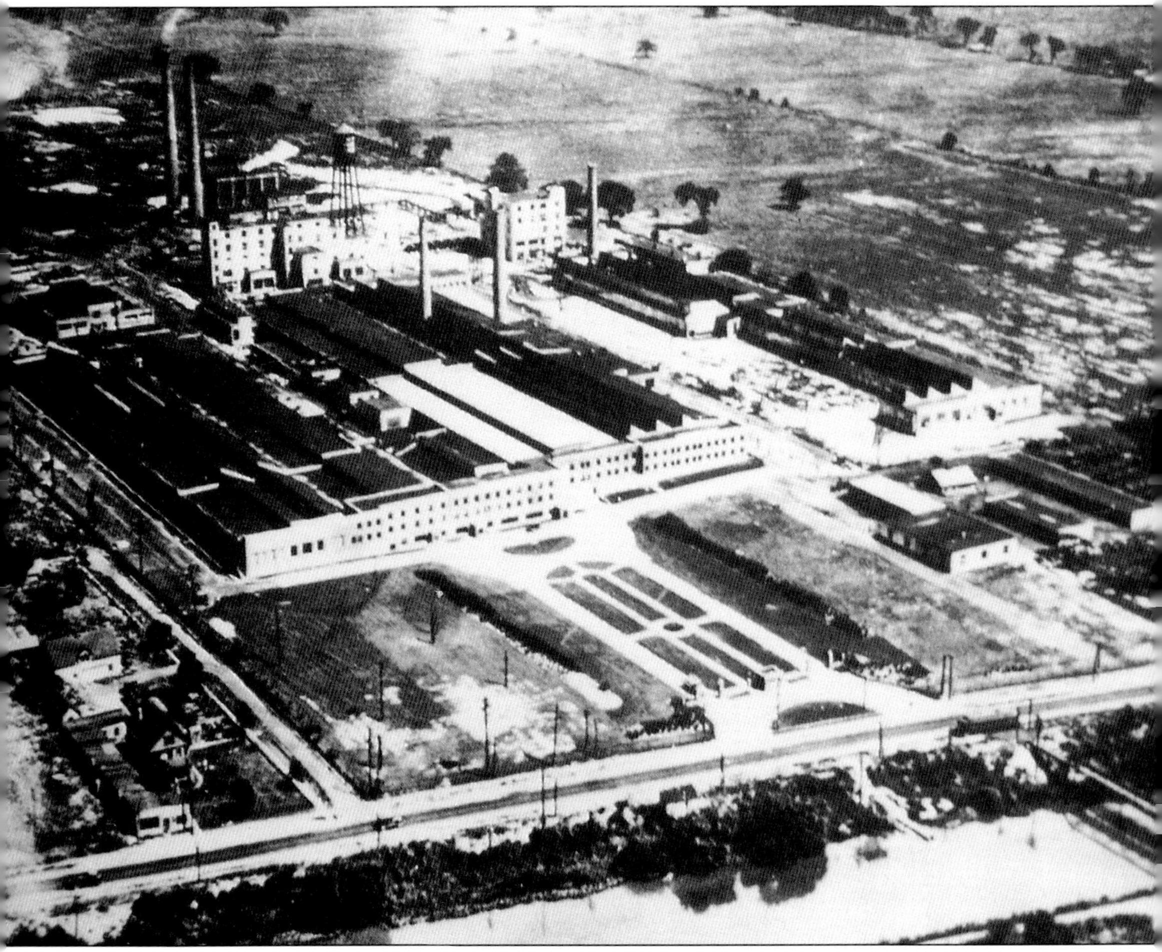

The DuPont Fibersilk plant on River Road in 1926. "Fibersilk," first produced in 1921, became well-known as rayon. This plant also pioneered the production of cellophane. Many other DuPont products manufactured worldwide were researched and developed in this Yerkes plant. Today it is a major producer of the company's "Tedlar" and "Corianne" products.

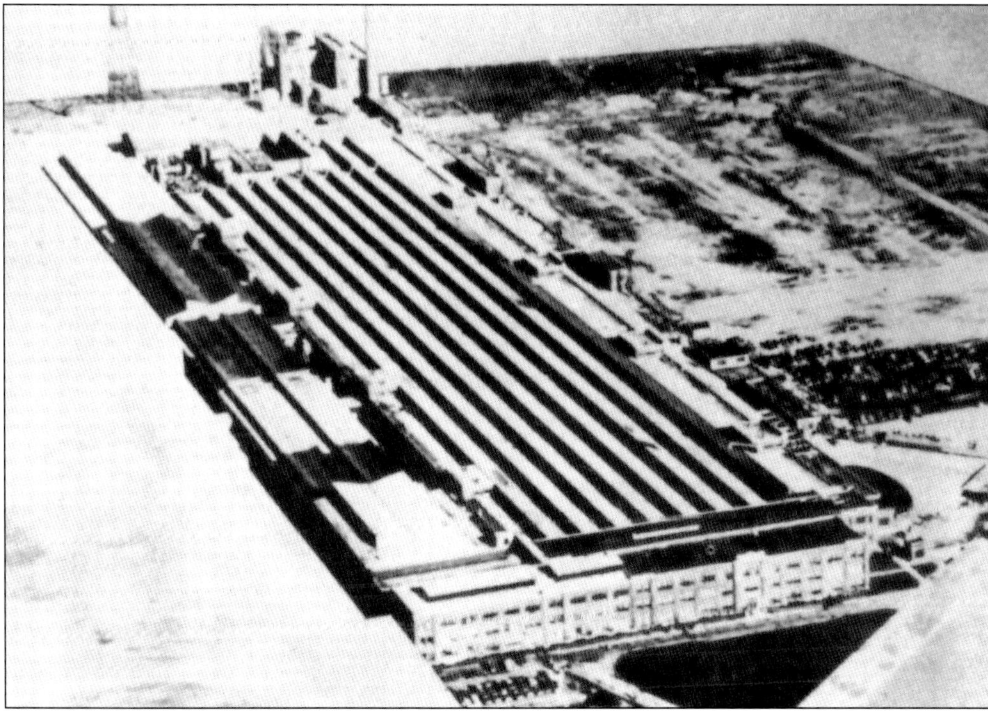

The Western Electric Company's factory on Kenmore Avenue in 1948. Western Electric manufactured telephone equipment here. The plant was built in 1929 by the Curtiss-Wright Corporation, which manufactured warplanes, including the famous P-40, until the end of World War II. The building is now a warehouse and recycling operation.

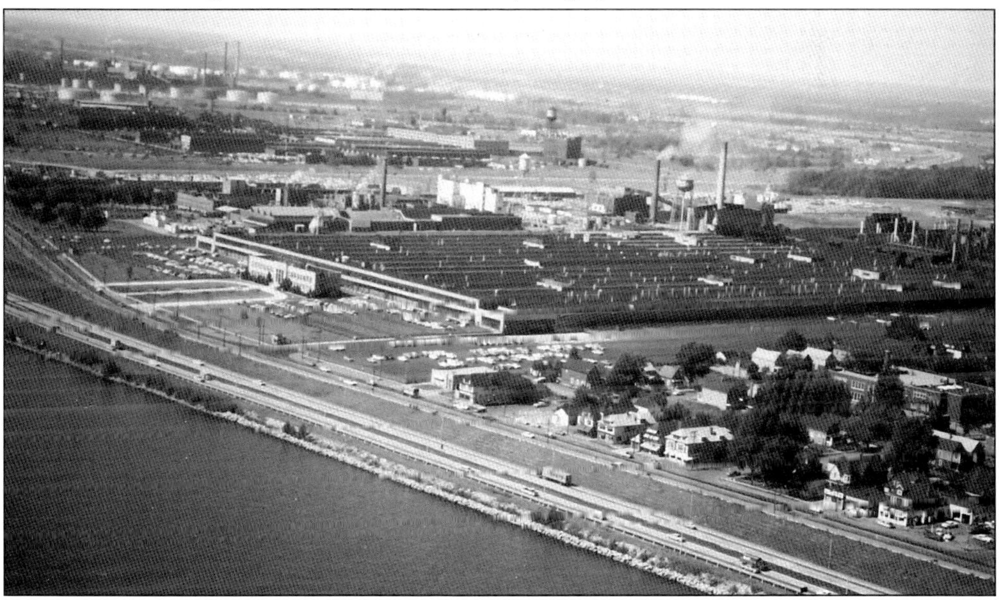

The town's industrial waterfront, August 15, 1962. The Riverside neighborhood is in the foreground, with the Chevrolet-Tonawanda and Dupont-Yerkes plants beyond. Huntley Station is on the river. Beyond the tank farm is the Wickwire-Spencer steel plant which closed in 1964. (WNYHI)

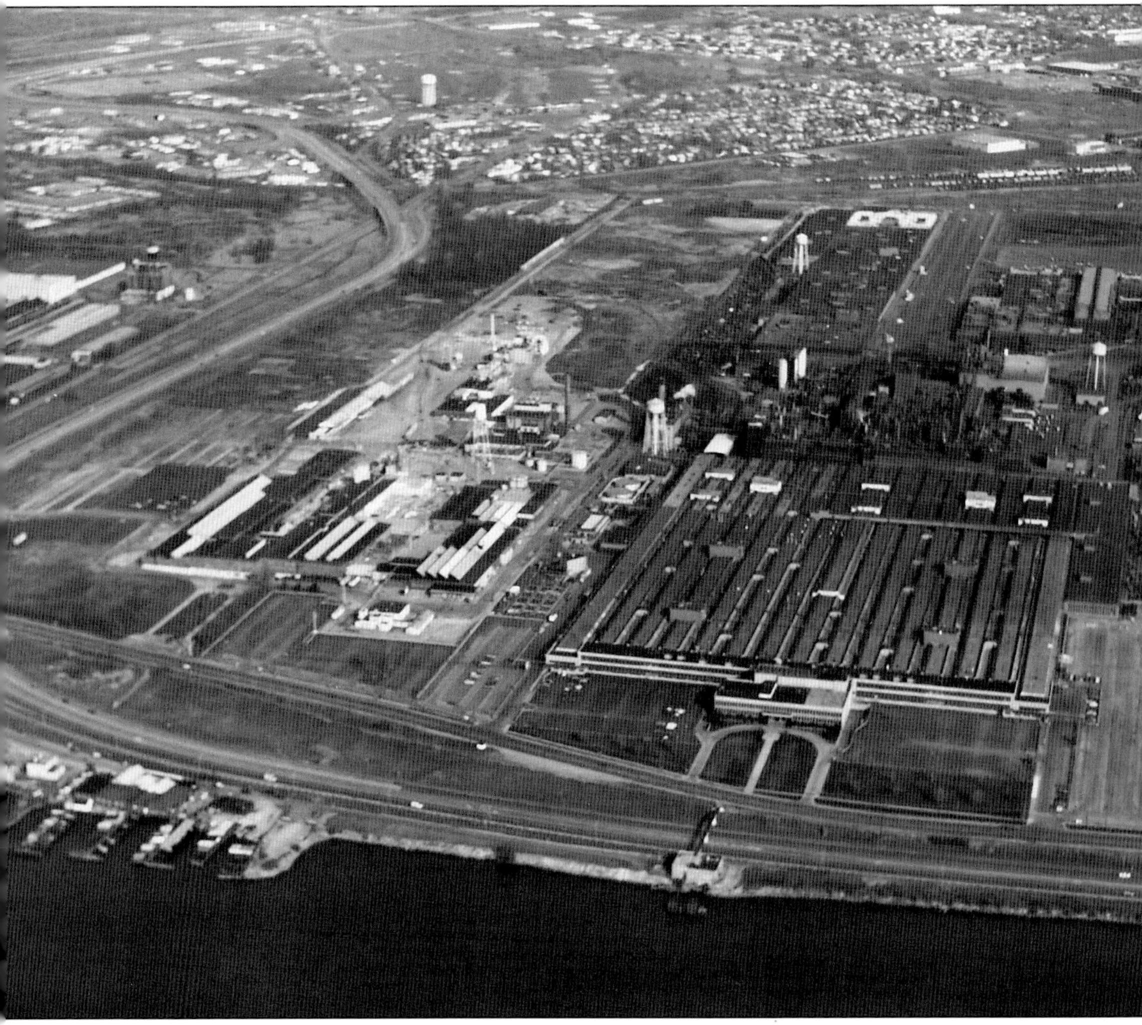

The General Motors River Road automobile engine plant (at right). First opened in 1938, it is now the largest engine factory in the world. Left of center is the Dupont-Yerkes plant, where several everyday products, including cellophane and rayon, were first developed.

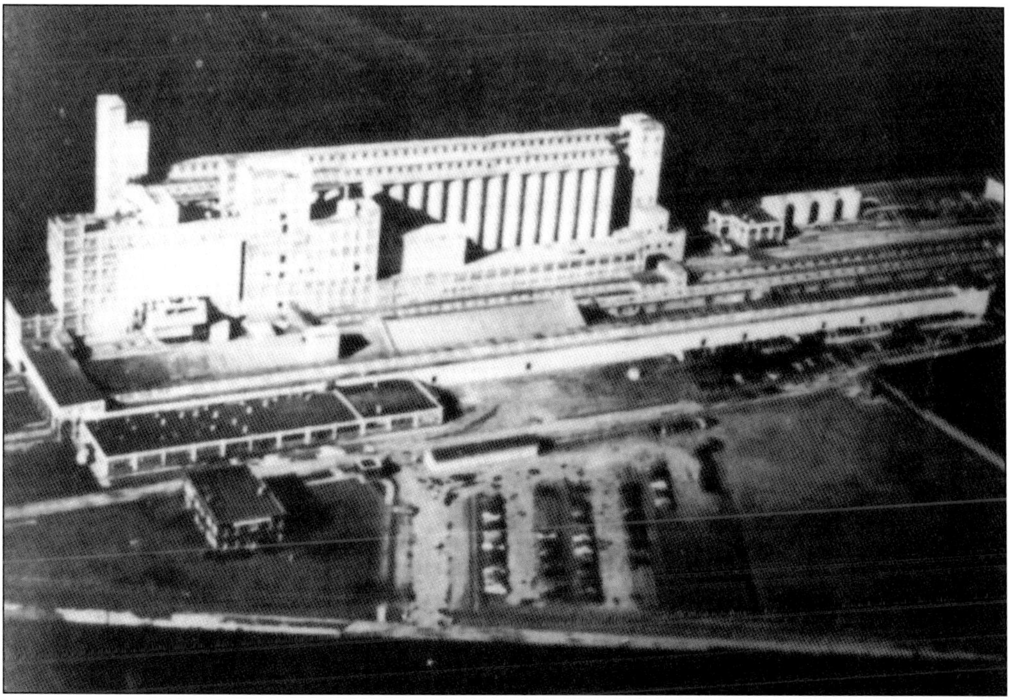

The Eastern States Farmers' Exchange in 1948. The plant was built alongside the New York Central Railroad in the 1920s as the Eastern States Milling Company. Like so many other grain elevators in the Buffalo area, this one lies broken and abandoned today. The Town of Tonawanda is actively seeking demolition of this complex.

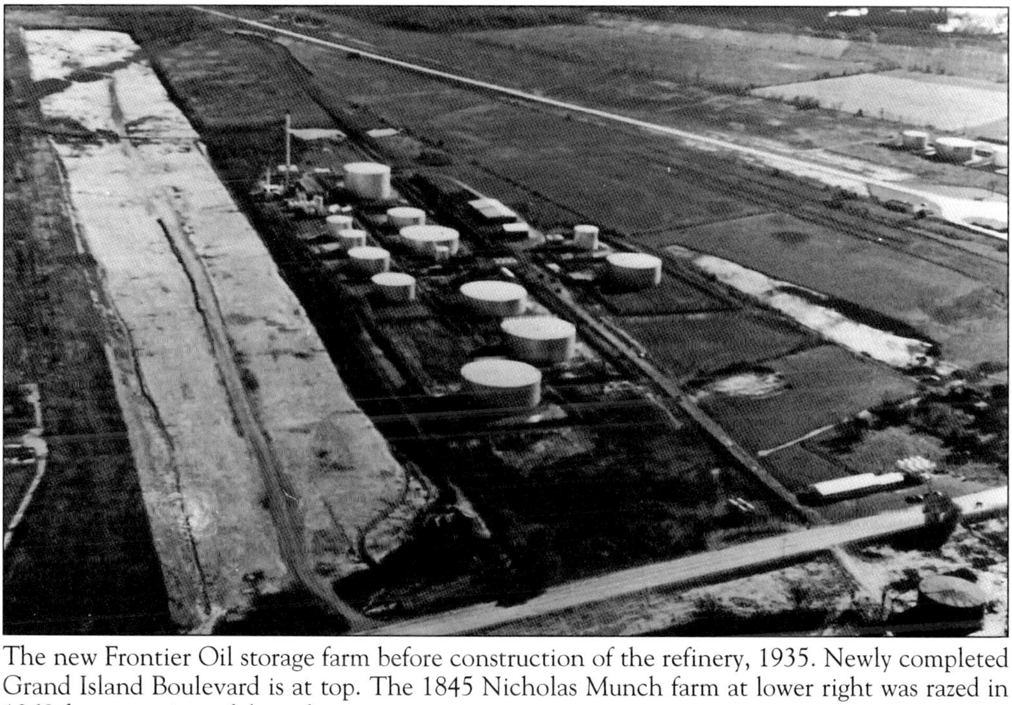

The new Frontier Oil storage farm before construction of the refinery, 1935. Newly completed Grand Island Boulevard is at top. The 1845 Nicholas Munch farm at lower right was razed in 1968 for expansion of the refinery.

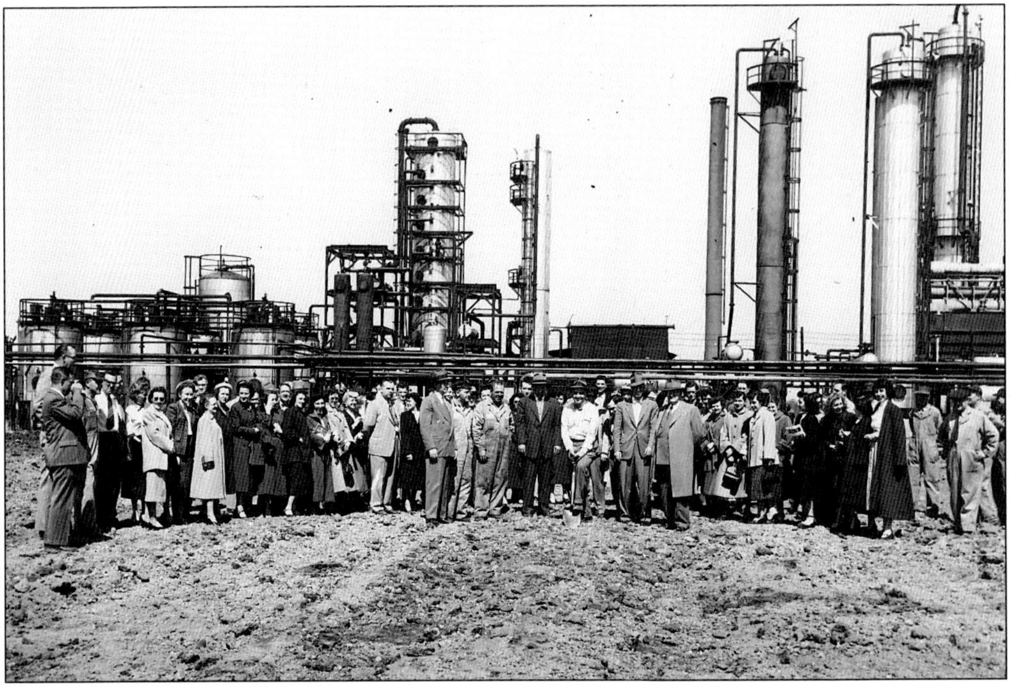

Employees of the former Frontier Oil Refinery at River Road and Grand Island Boulevard at a ground-breaking ceremony for an addition to the refinery, April 29, 1952. The refinery was acquired by the Ashland Oil Company a few years later. (WNYHI)

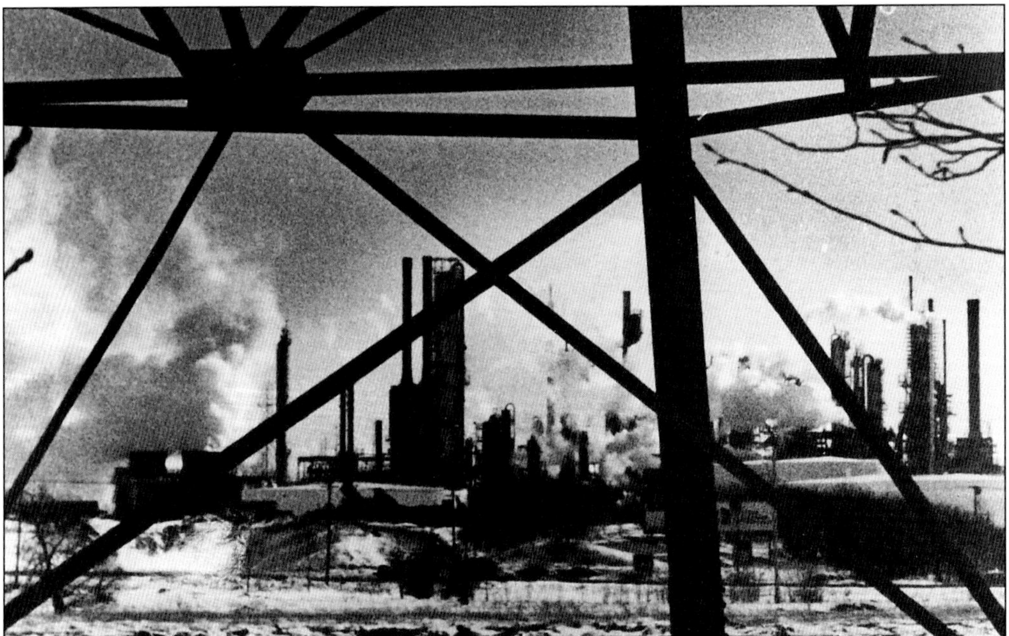

The busy Frontier Oil Refinery as seen through the legs of an electric transmission line tower on Grand Island, *c.* 1953. This was one of only two oil refineries in all of New York State, the other being Socony on Elk Street in South Buffalo. (WNYHI)

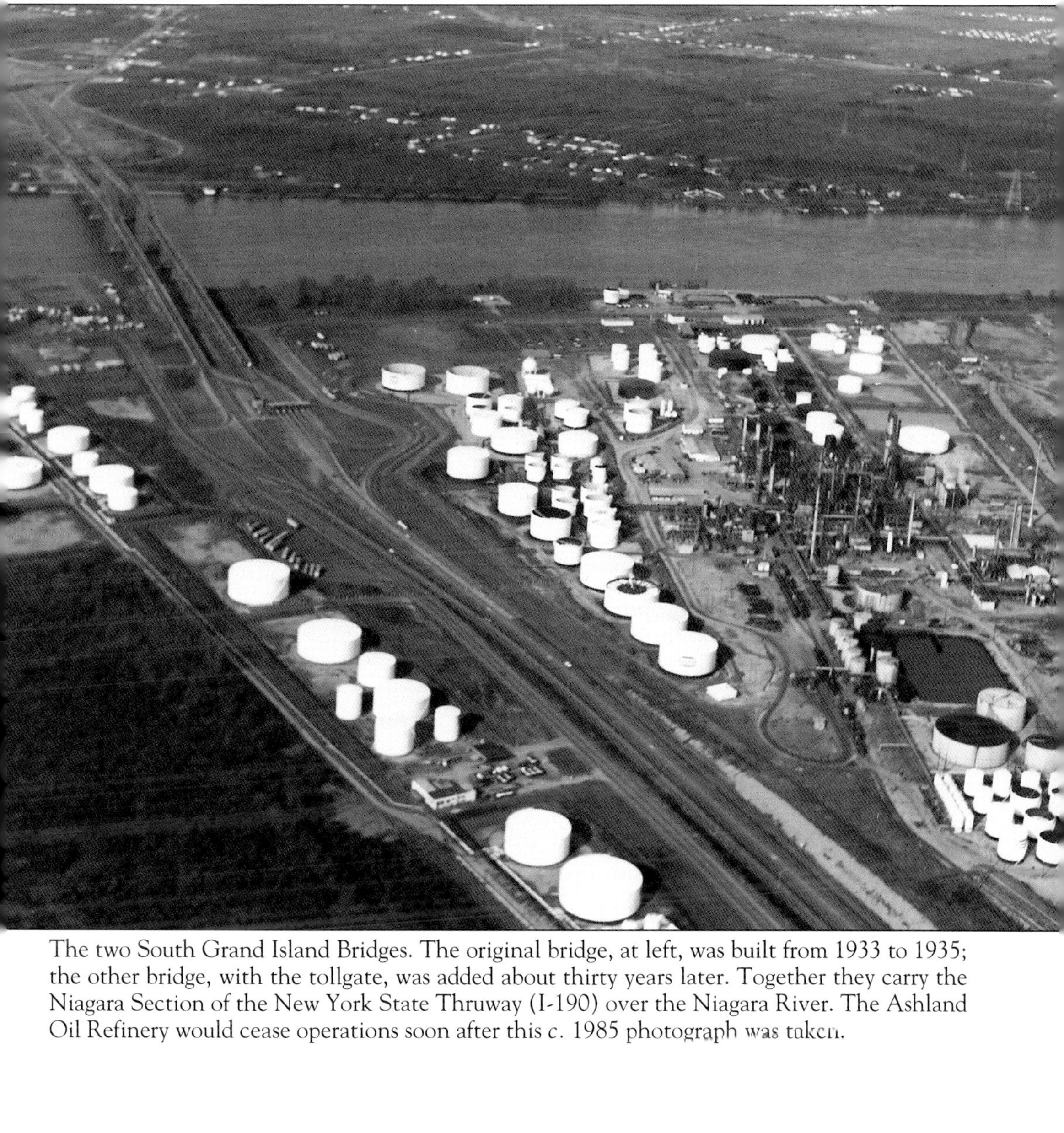

The two South Grand Island Bridges. The original bridge, at left, was built from 1933 to 1935; the other bridge, with the tollgate, was added about thirty years later. Together they carry the Niagara Section of the New York State Thruway (I-190) over the Niagara River. The Ashland Oil Refinery would cease operations soon after this c. 1985 photograph was taken.

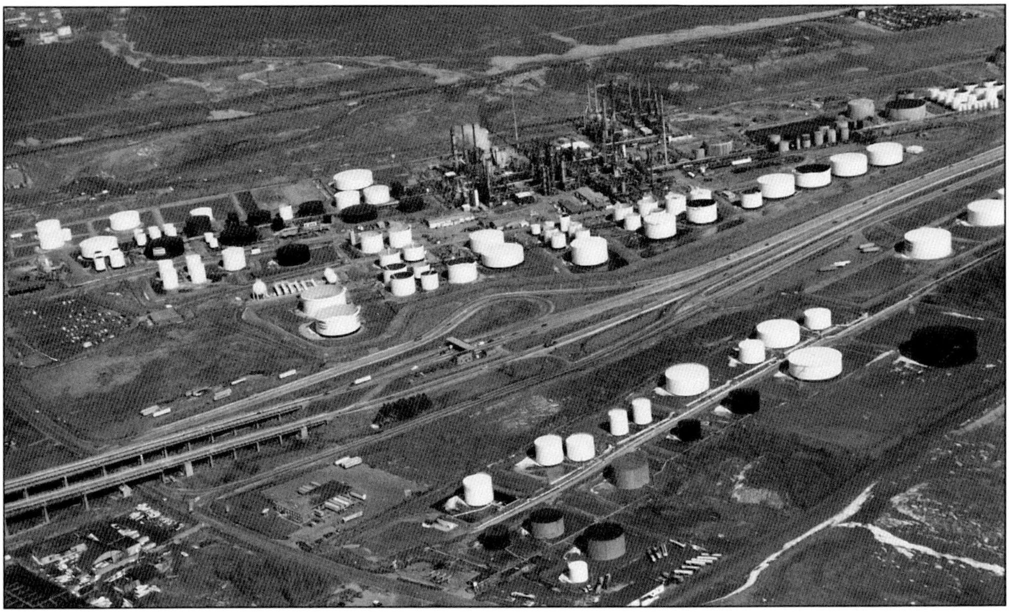

A *c.* 1985 view of the Ashland Oil Refinery shortly before it ceased operations. The business began as the locally owned Frontier Oil Corp. before World War II. The entrance to the South Grand Island Bridges on I-190 is at center.

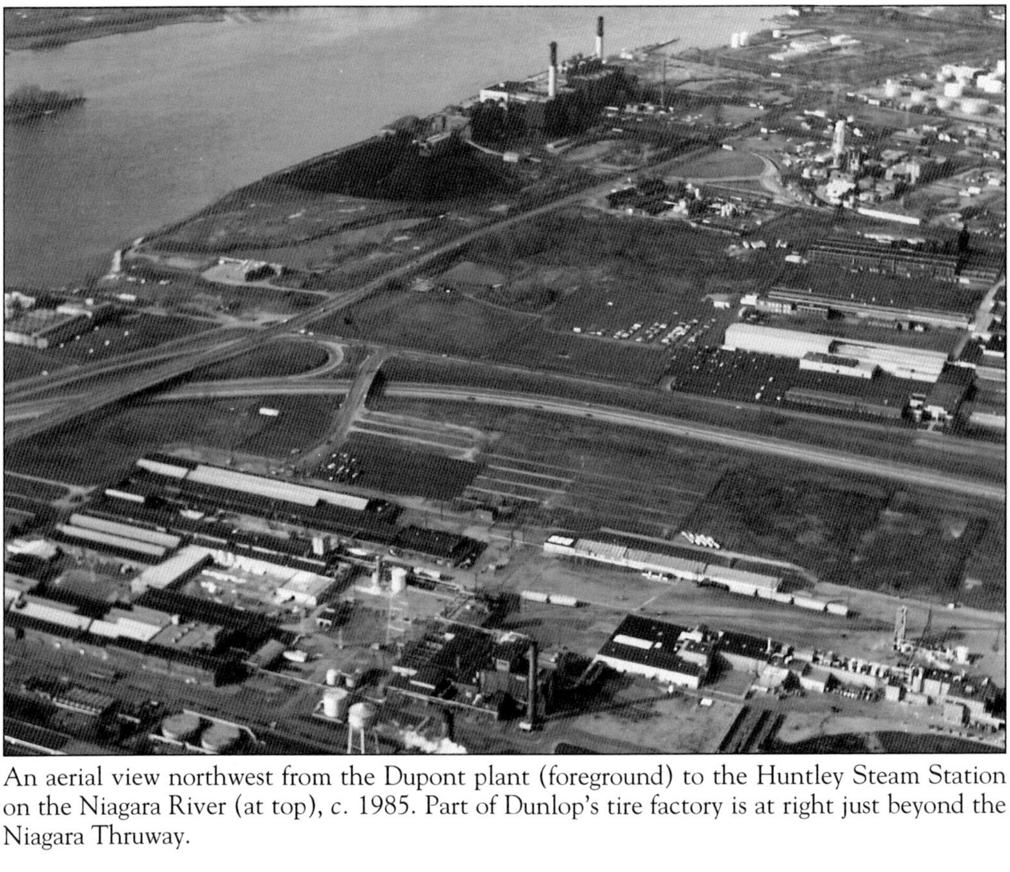

An aerial view northwest from the Dupont plant (foreground) to the Huntley Steam Station on the Niagara River (at top), *c.* 1985. Part of Dunlop's tire factory is at right just beyond the Niagara Thruway.

Four

Kenmore, the Pioneer Suburb

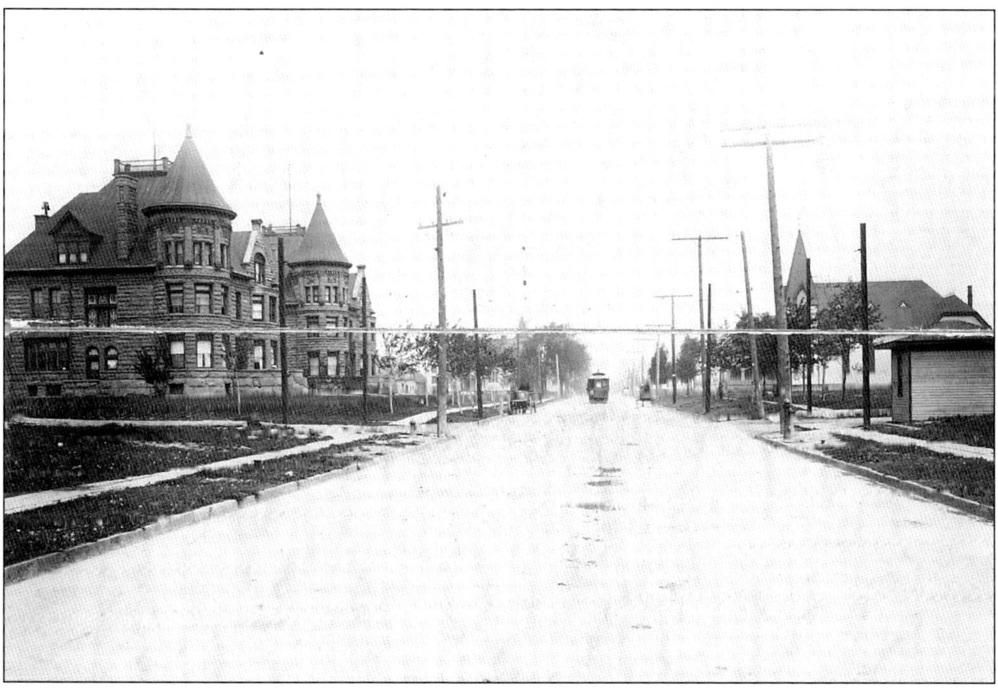

Delaware Avenue at Kenmore Avenue, *c.* 1899. Kenmore's "twin sentinels" were erected by Fred and L.P.A Eberhardt in 1893. Fred's home (left) still stands today as the Jack Hunt Coin Mansion. The original wooden Kenmore Presbyterian Church stands at Hazeltine Avenue on the right. The "Kenmore" trolley ran between Buffalo and Tonawanda from 1893 to 1926.

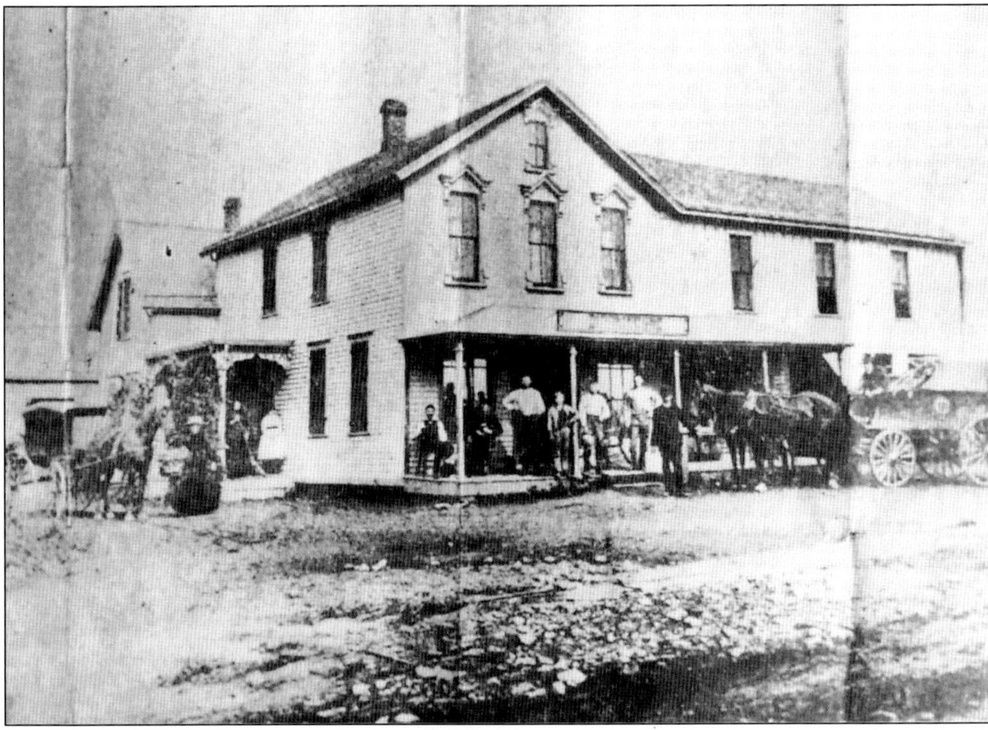

The Winfield Mang store and tavern on the northwest corner of Delaware and Kenmore Avenues. Kenmore citizens bought out the saloon and converted it into a residence and pharmacy which was occupied by Dr. J.J. Drake. L.P.A. Eberhardt then bought the property and erected the "twin sentinels" there in 1894. The old tavern was divided and moved, and part of it still stands at 12 Warren Avenue. The Saratoga Restaurant at Ramsdell Avenue in North Buffalo utilizes another portion.

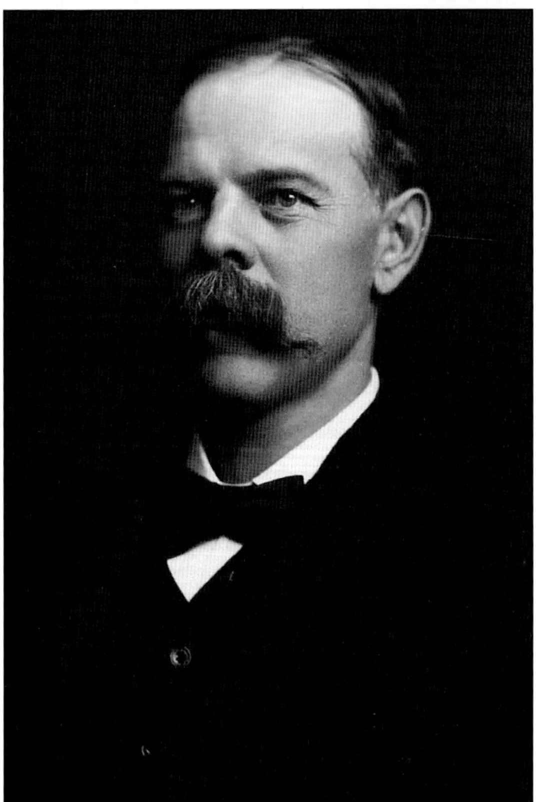

Louis Phillip Adolph Eberhardt (1860–1939) in his thirties, when he established Kenmore in the 1890s as Buffalo's pioneer suburb. LPA Eberhardt entered the real estate business at age twenty-two with a purchase of land in North Buffalo. His first Kenmore house was erected in 1888–1889 just north of Kenmore Avenue.

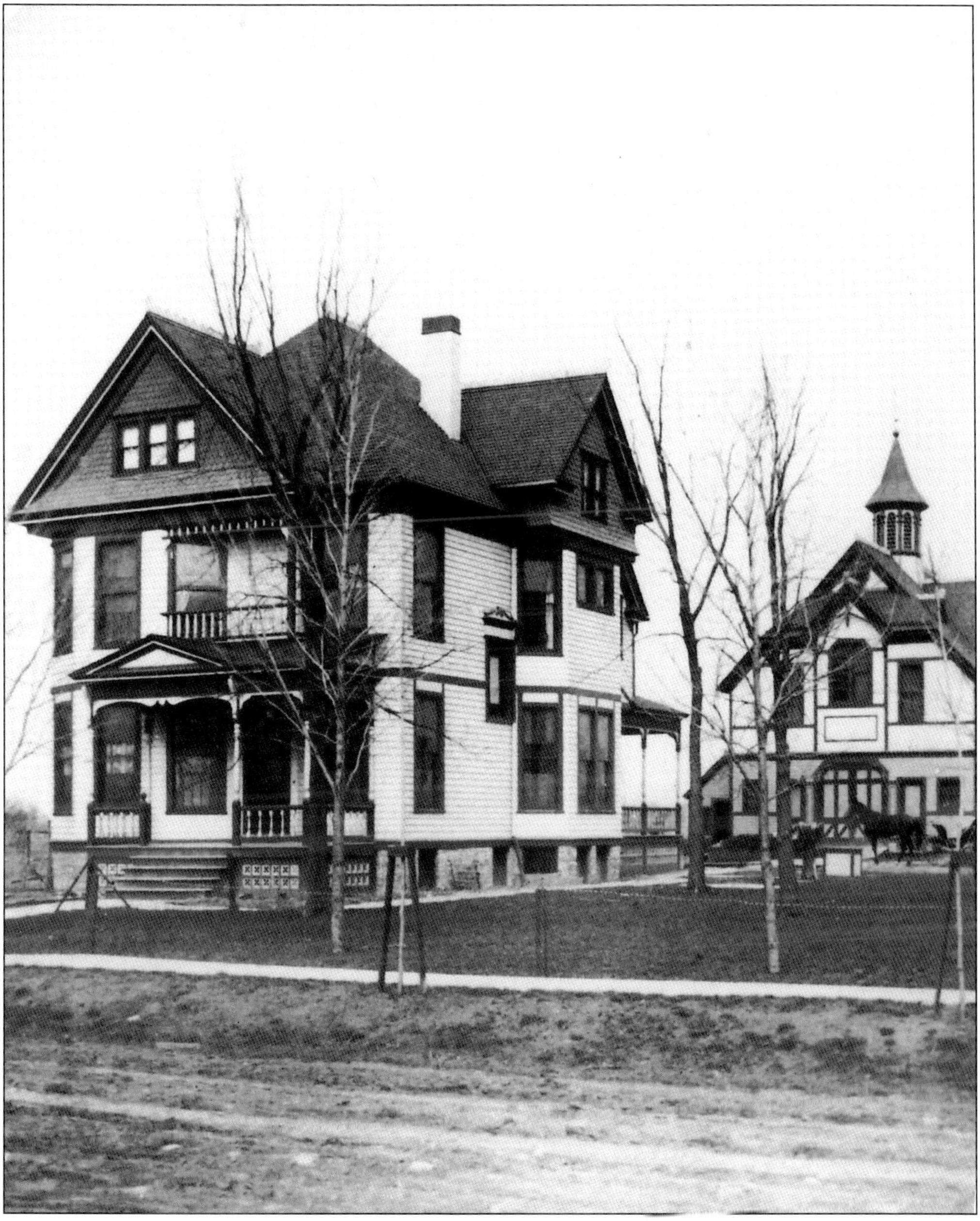

The carriage house (at right) of LPA Eberhardt's first home. LPA built his first house at 2749 Delaware Avenue in 1888–1889. When it burned in 1894, the carriage house was moved across the street behind LPA's new stone mansion at 2756 Delaware; it stood there until it was demolished in 1977.

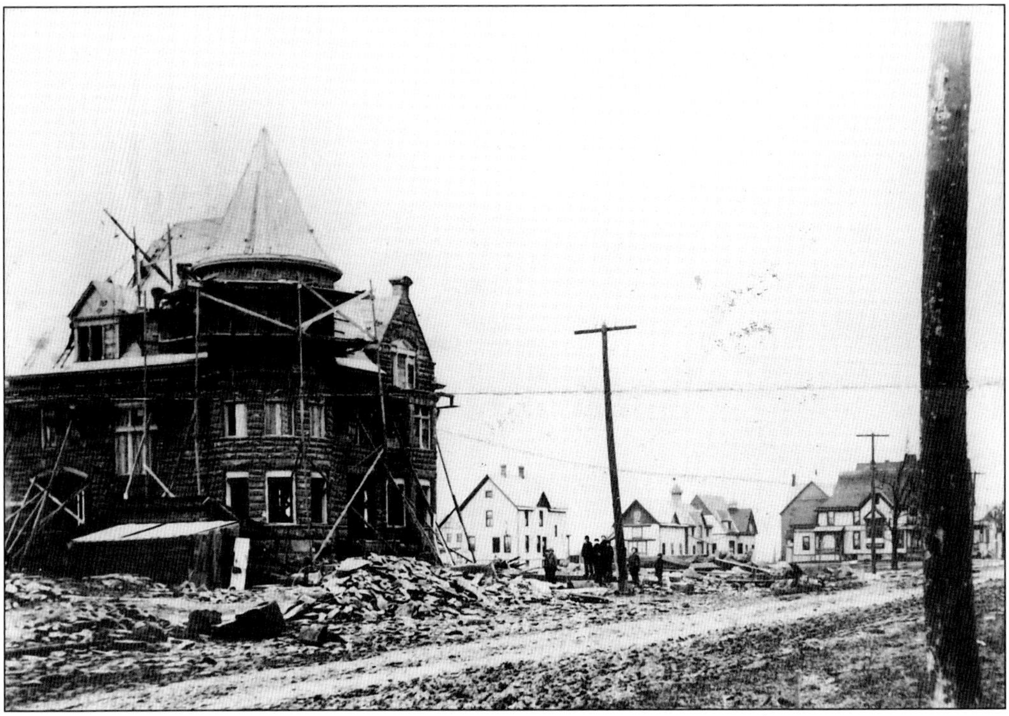

The erection of LPA Eberhardt's home in 1893. The home was built for $15,000, as was its twin next door. The Myron Phelps home is at far right. Delaware was paved with brick in 1894 when the trolley line was built.

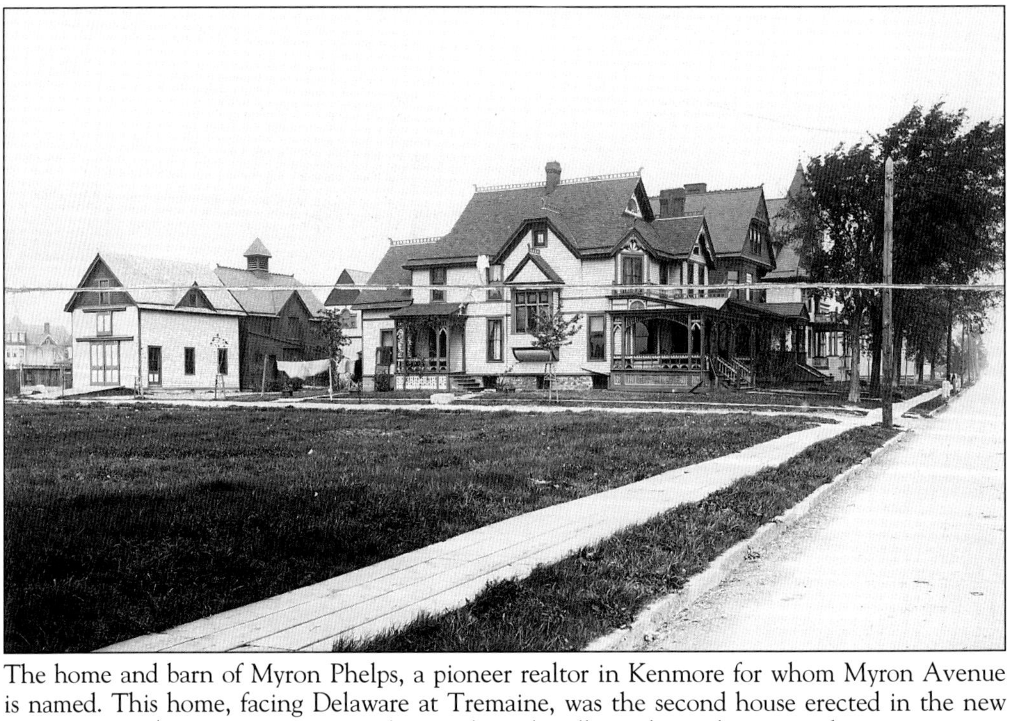

The home and barn of Myron Phelps, a pioneer realtor in Kenmore for whom Myron Avenue is named. This home, facing Delaware at Tremaine, was the second house erected in the new suburb. It cost $4,500 in 1889. Note the wooden sidewalks in this early-twentieth-century view.

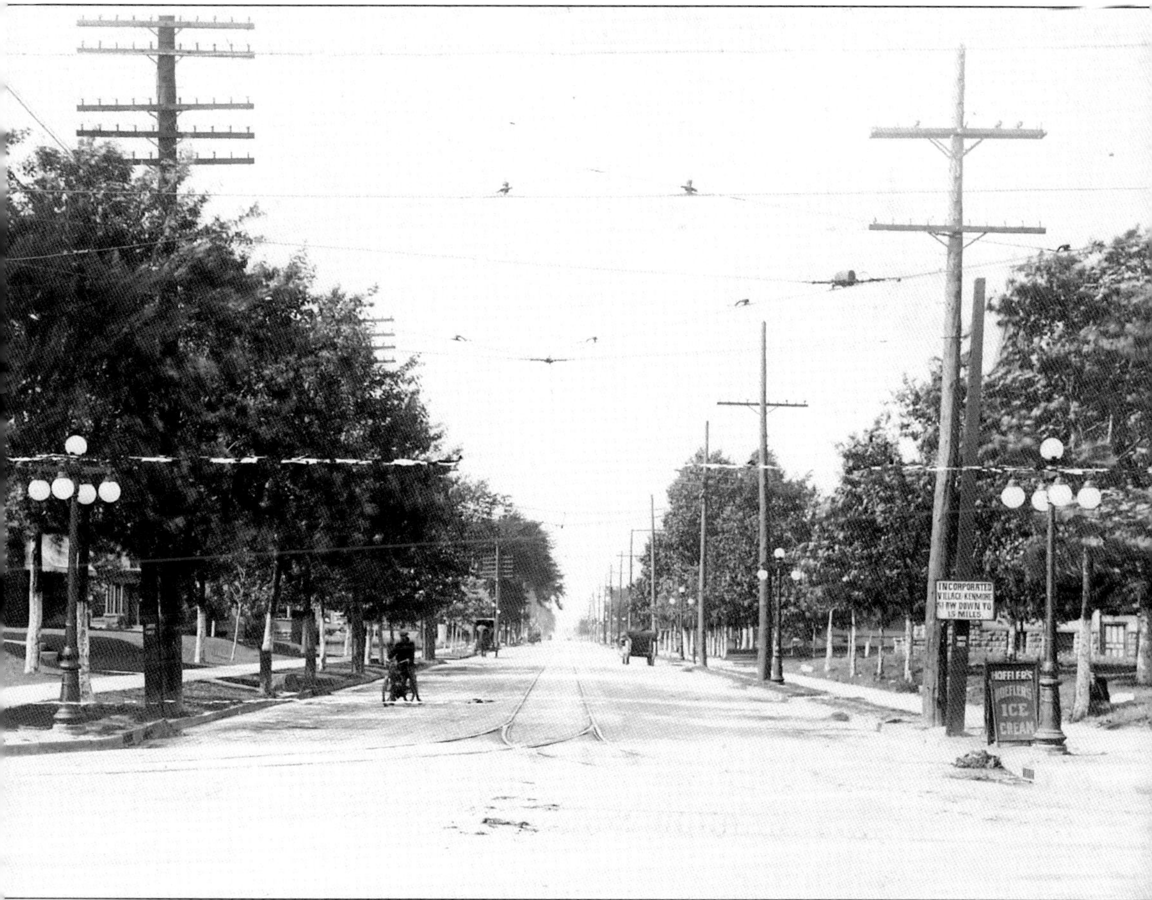

Delaware Avenue at Kenmore Avenue in 1920. Note the 15 mph speed limit, which was strictly enforced. Kenmore police even pulled over a trolley car for going 35 mph in 1922, when the speed limit had been raised to 18. Later, Chief Yochum shot at a speeder's tires to get him to stop. Except for the motorcycle and automobile in the picture, horse-drawn vehicles were still the rule, necessitating regular street sweeping. The trolley ran to Tonawanda until June 27, 1926.

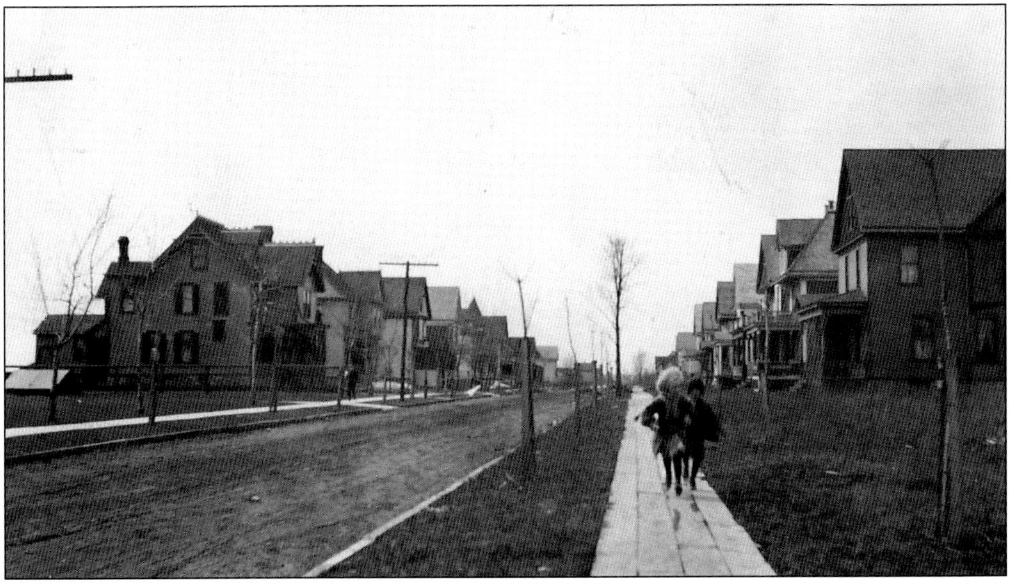

West Hazeltine Avenue from Delaware, *c.* 1900. Early Kenmore had wooden sidewalks which were gradually replaced with concrete walks as the village matured. Trees were planted and curbs installed before residential streets were paved.

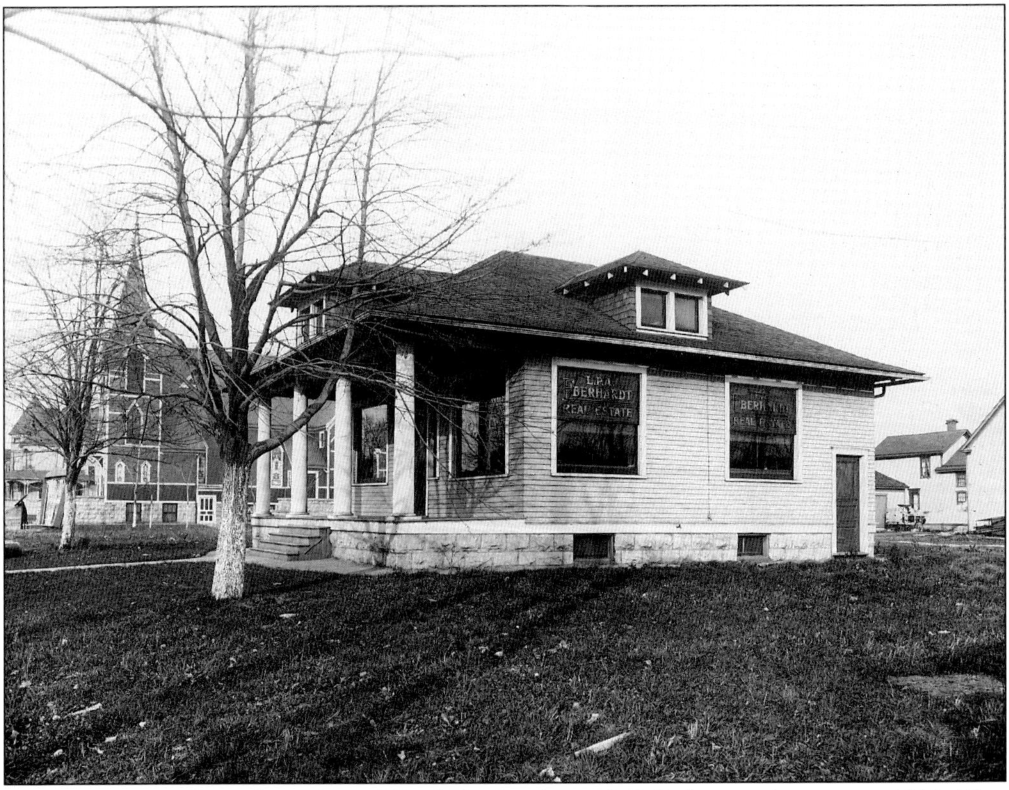

The real estate office of L.P.A. and Fred Eberhardt at 2749 Delaware Avenue, *c.* 1910. This building stood until 1978 when it was demolished to make a parking area. At left is the original wooden Kenmore Presbyterian Church, which stood until 1926.

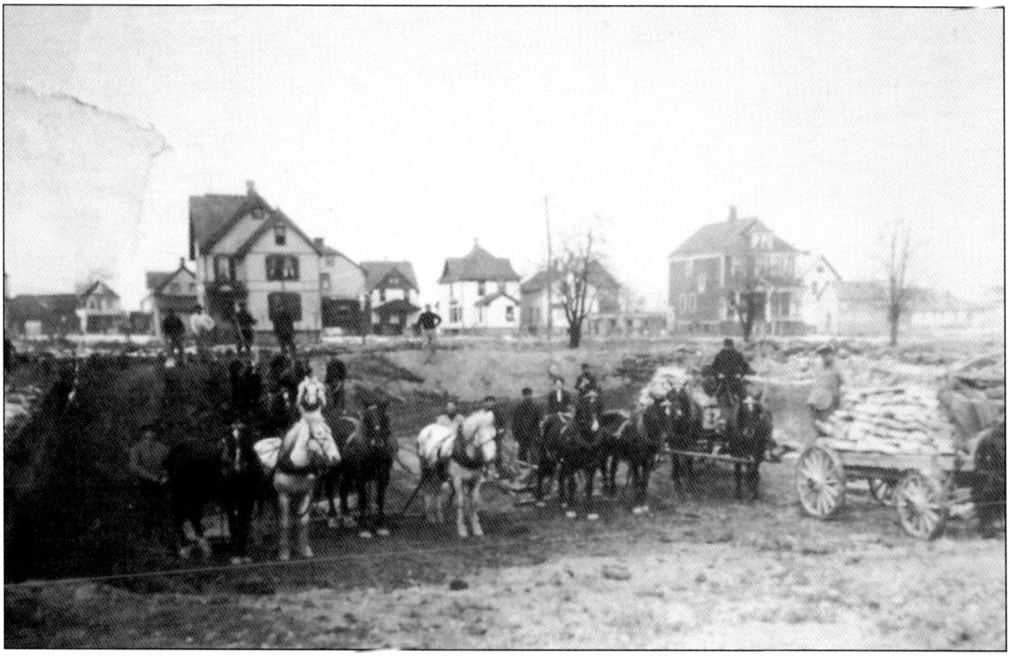

Excavation for the Elite Theater and gymnasium addition at the rear of the Kenmore Presbyterian Church, 1907. This age was still powered by horses and men. Later excavations were done with steam shovels. The homes in the background are on East Tremaine (Parkwood) and East LaSalle (Euclid) Avenues.

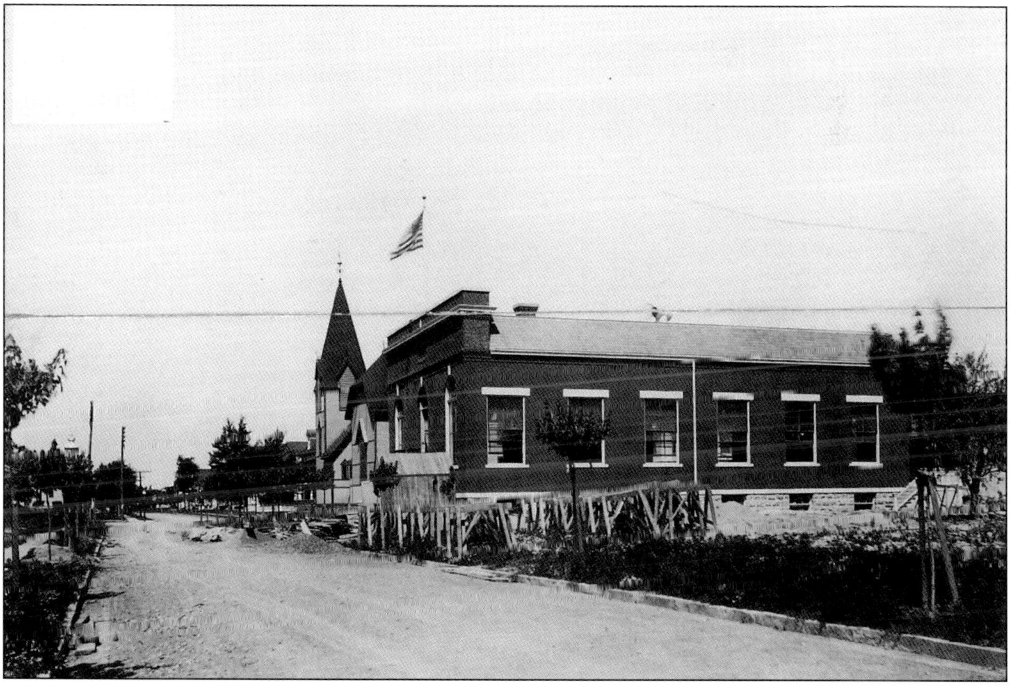

The Elite Theater behind the Kenmore Presbyterian Church on East Hazeltine Avenue as it was nearing completion in 1907. The building cost $26,000, a civic donation of LPA Eberhardt. It had a gymnasium, auditorium, and swimming pool; later, bowling alleys were added.

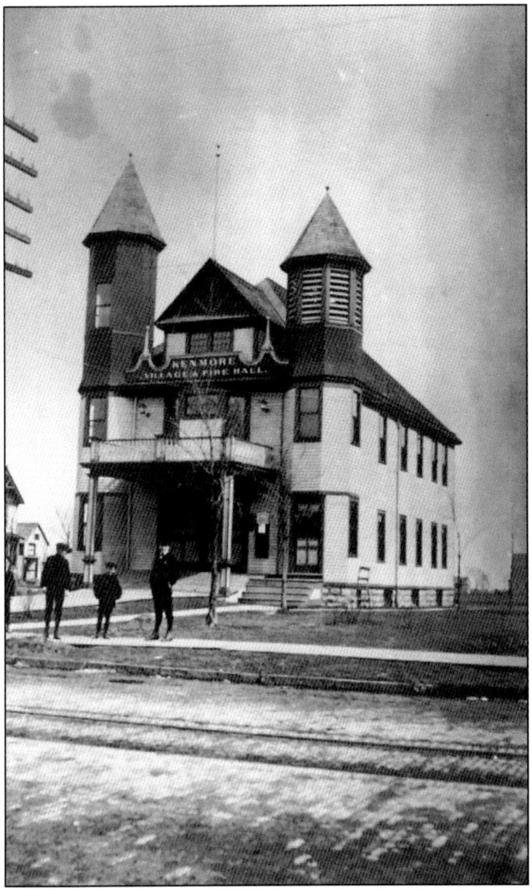

The original Kenmore Village and Fire Hall, erected in 1903 on Delaware Avenue between Warren and Euclid Avenues. The taller tower was for drying hoses, and the shorter tower held the fire bell, which is on permanent display in front of the 1929 Nash Road Fire Hall.

District School No. 6 (the Kenmore Union School) shortly after it opened in 1892. Fruit trees from the old Winter family farm were left standing for a few years. The schoolhouse became the Village and Town Hall in 1911. The municipal building was erected on this site in 1936.

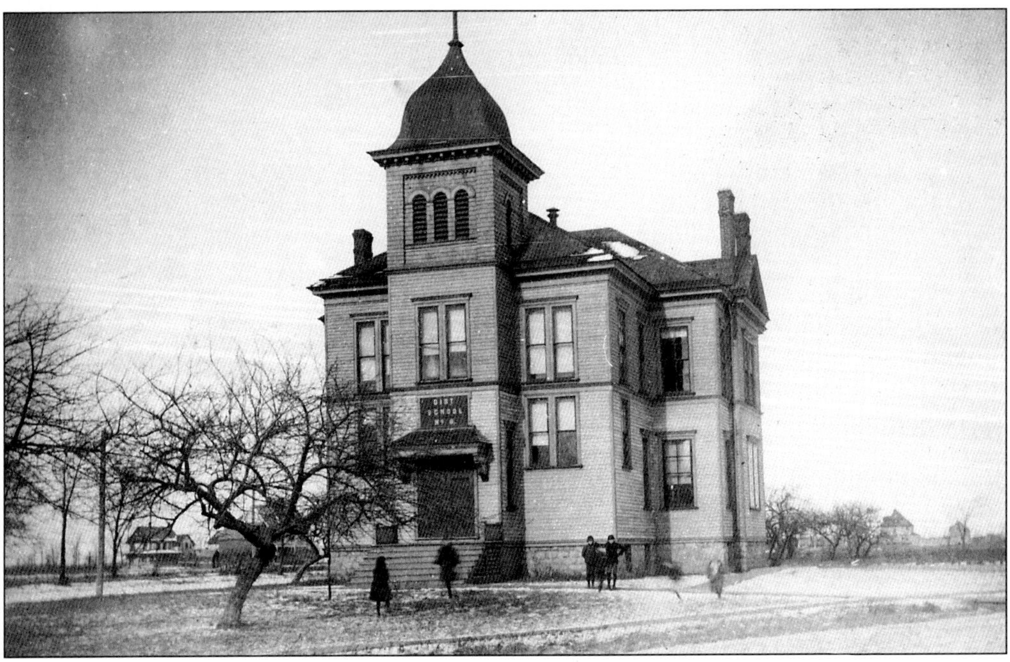

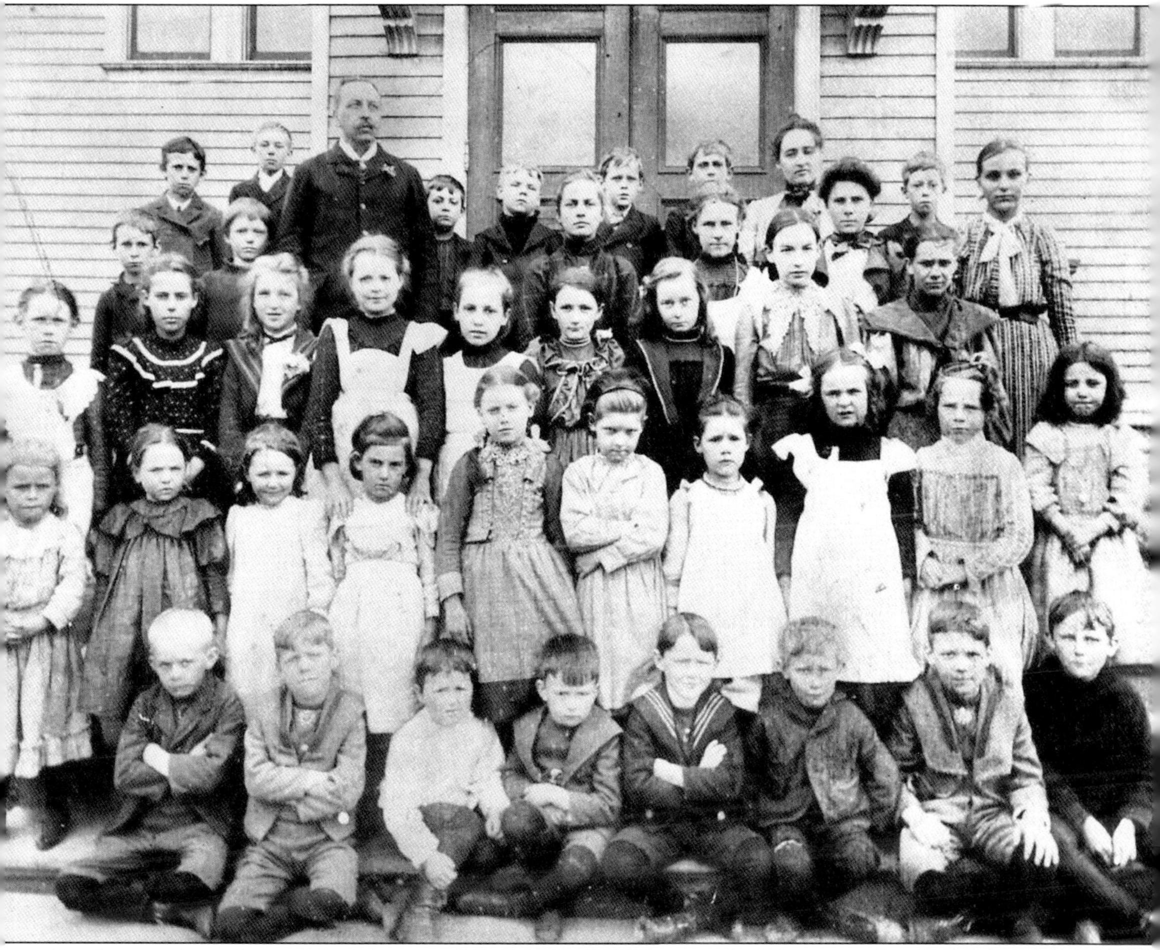

Students and teachers of the Kenmore Union School (District #6). The new school at Delaware Road and Delaware Avenue opened in the autumn of 1892. Children hiked across open fields and along muddy lanes to get to and from school. Those some distance away might arrive by horse-drawn wagons. This photograph was reprinted in 1924 as part of the village's 25th anniversary celebration of incorporation in 1899.

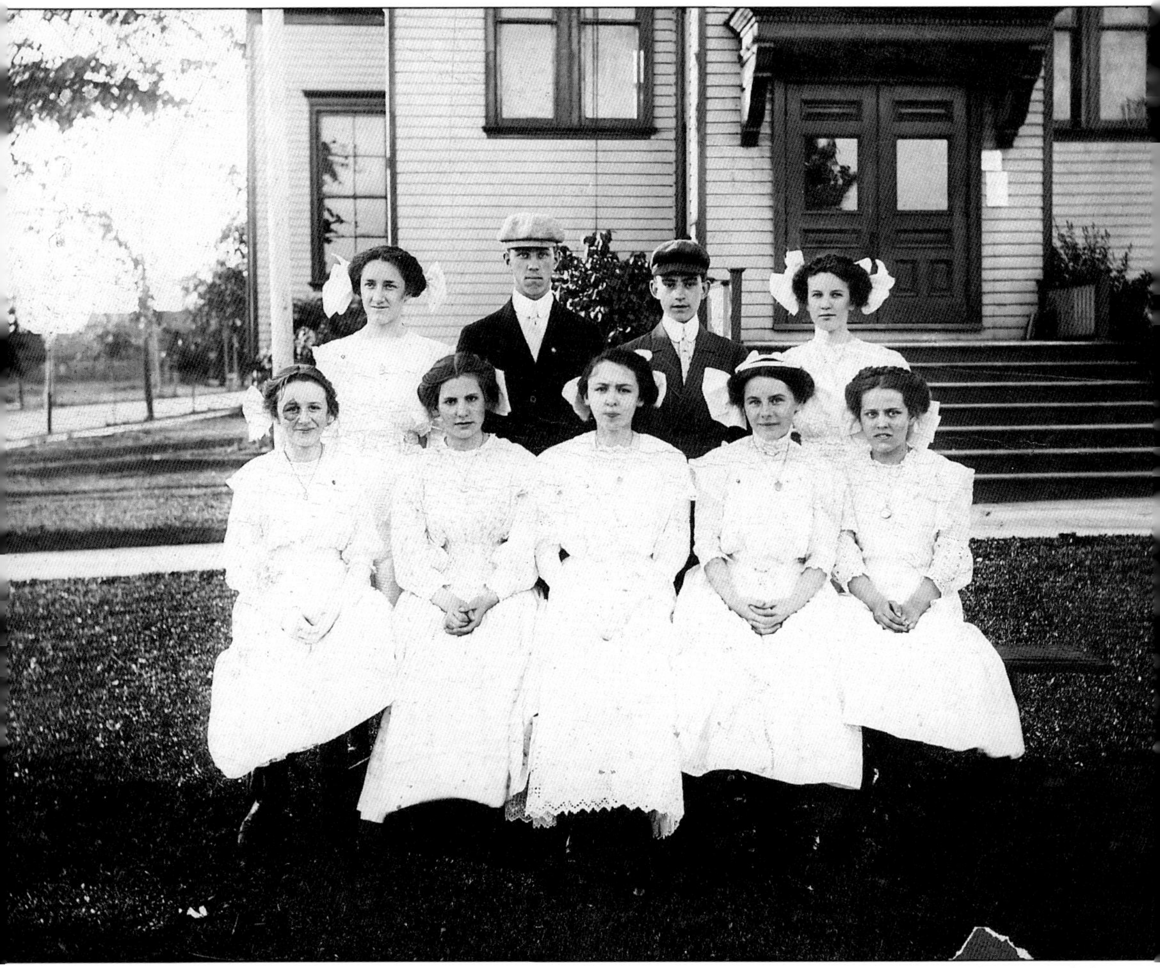

The 1910 eighth-grade graduating class of old District School No. 6, located on the site of the present-day Municipal Building. From left to right are as follows: (front row) Esther Lauderdale, Florence Wilson, Jane Towne, Gladys Hider, and Edna Avery; (back row) Emily Schunk, Edward Wiseman, Rowland Barker, and Agnes Kiernan. Jane V. Towne went on to become the first and sole graduate of Kenmore High School's "Class of 1913."

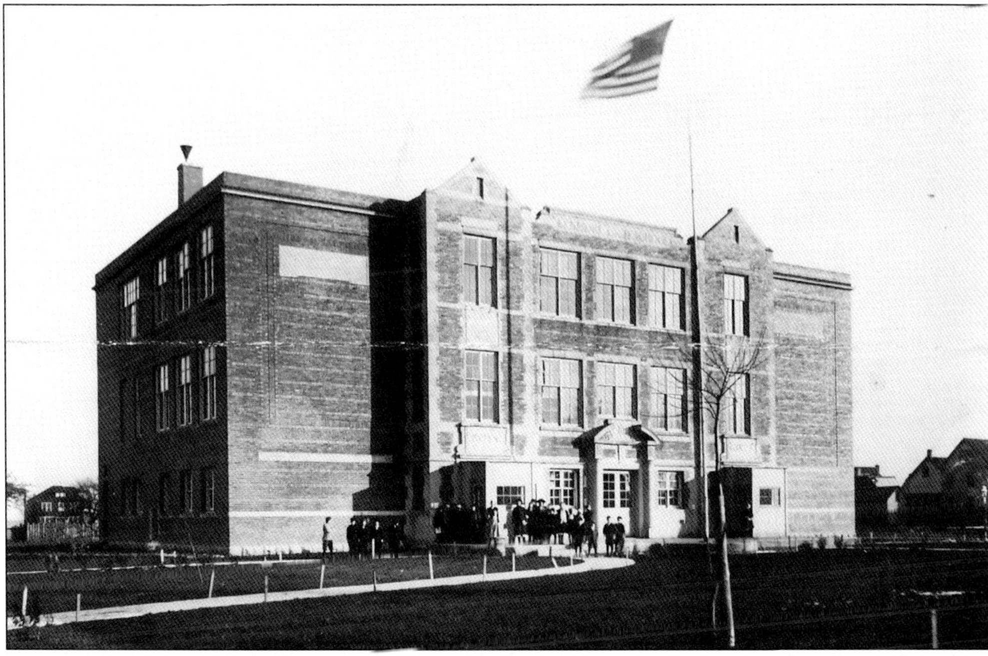

Kenmore's first high school. Opened as Kenmore High School (grades 1–12) in 1911, the school cost $50,000 to build. It was renamed Washington Elementary School in 1924 when a larger junior-senior high school was built at 155 Delaware Road.

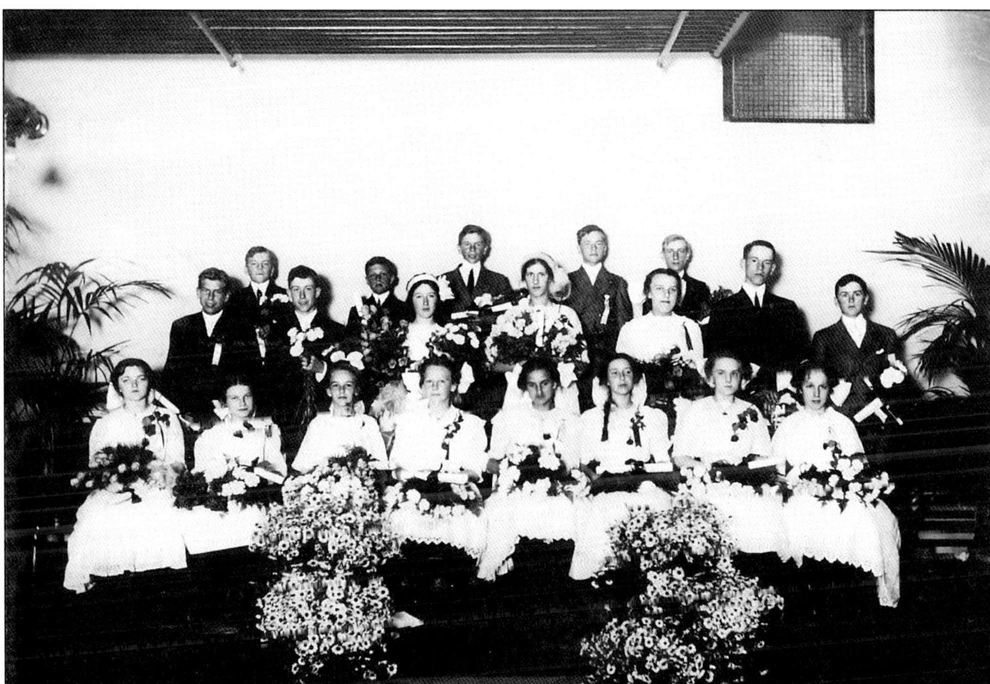

The first eighth-grade class to graduate from grammar school in the new Kenmore High School building, 1911. Grammar school graduation was important at a time when many children never completed high school due to work demands.

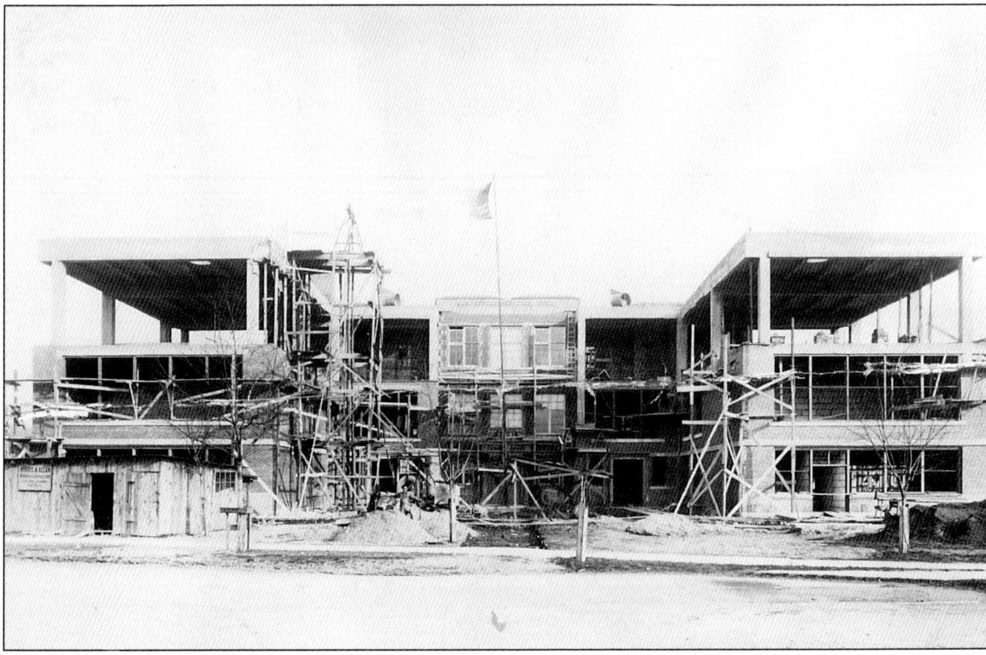

The $46,000, twelve-room addition to the front of Kenmore High School in 1916–1917. The village's rapid growth due to expanding wartime job opportunities soon made even this enlarged school inadequate.

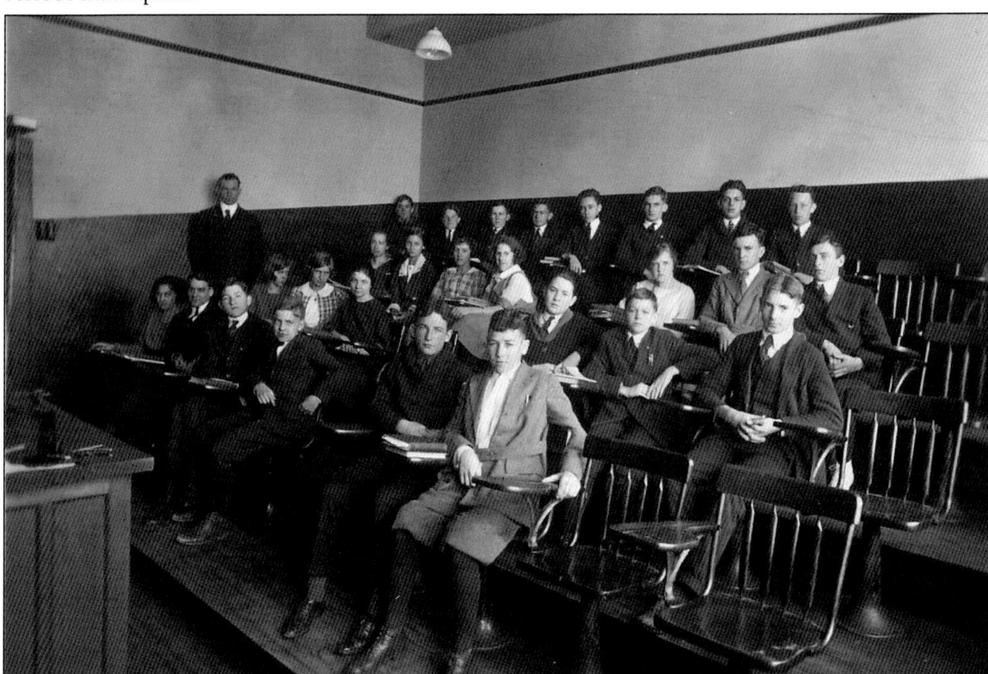

Mr. Carl Baisch's chemistry class in Kenmore High School, 1924. This science lecture room was located on the Wardman Road side of the third floor. The picture is from the files of Alfred F. Smith, the third student from the left in the front row. Mr. Baisch became superintendent of schools many years later.

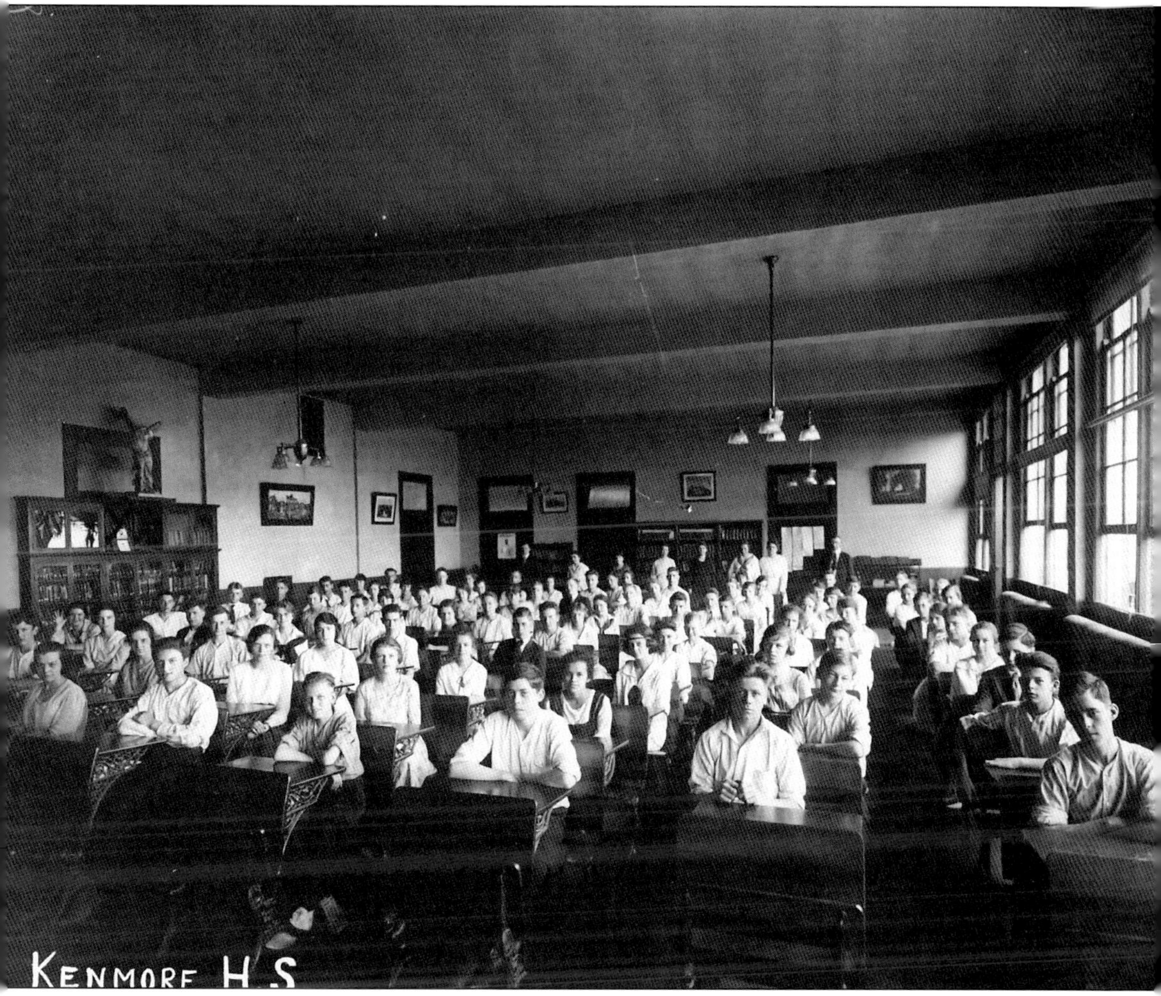

Kenmore High School students and faculty in the large third-floor study hall at the rear of the school, probably June 1924. Note the "modern" electric lighting and reference library. Frank C. Densberger, principal, became the first superintendent of schools for Union Free School District #1.

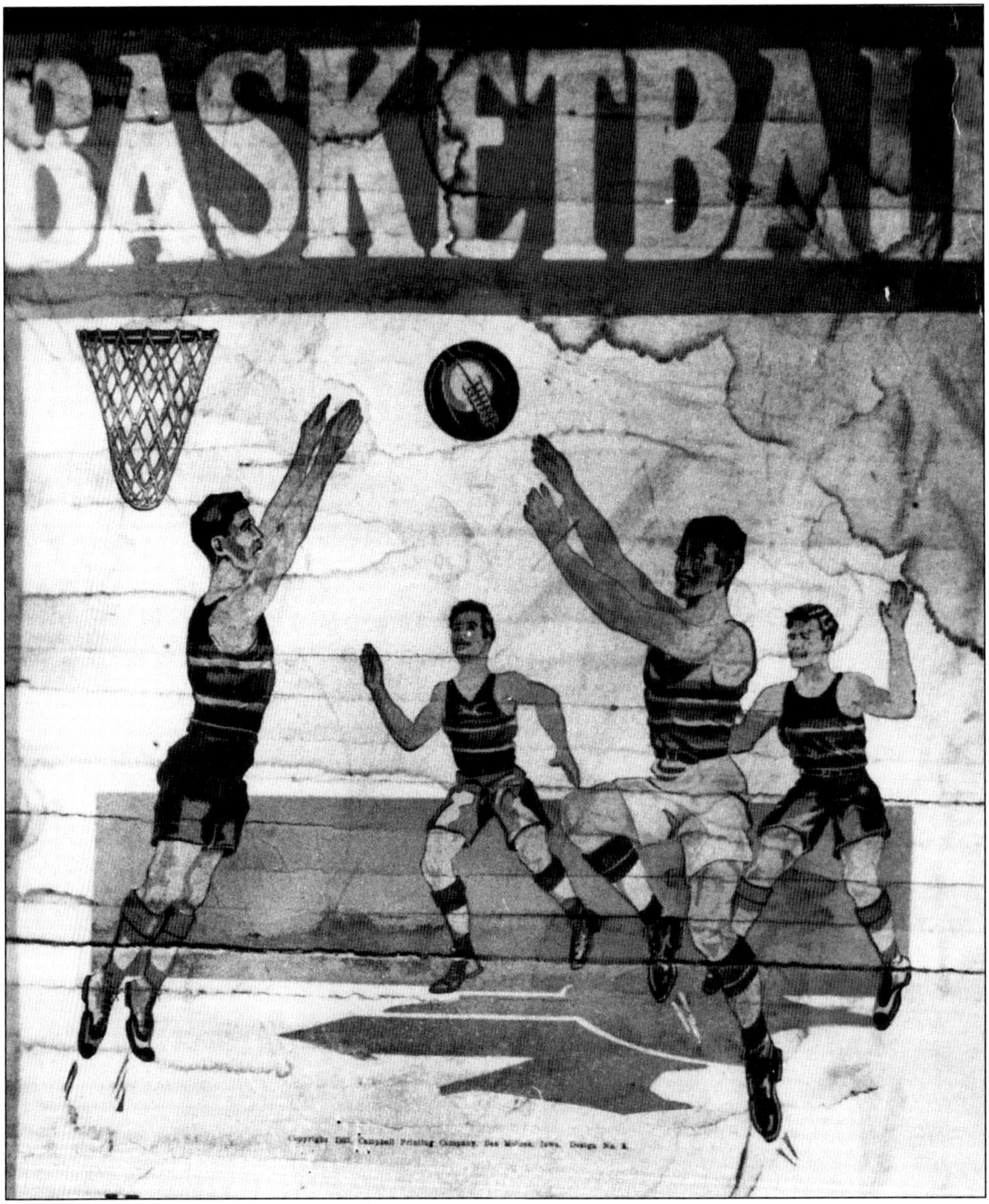

A community of good sports. Kenmore High School, still in its original building in 1923, played its basketball games in the East Hazeltine gymnasium because the old school's basement gymnasium had low ceiling beams. Kenmore's athletic teams were very successful during the 1920s. The Kenmore team was undefeated in 1927 until mastered in the sectionals by Lafayette High School. True to its reputation as a community of good sports, the Lafayette players were guests at a luncheon hosted by the Kenmore Rotary Club. This is part of a poster advertising an Erie County League game between Kenmore and Springville on Friday, March 2, 1923. General admission was 25¢.

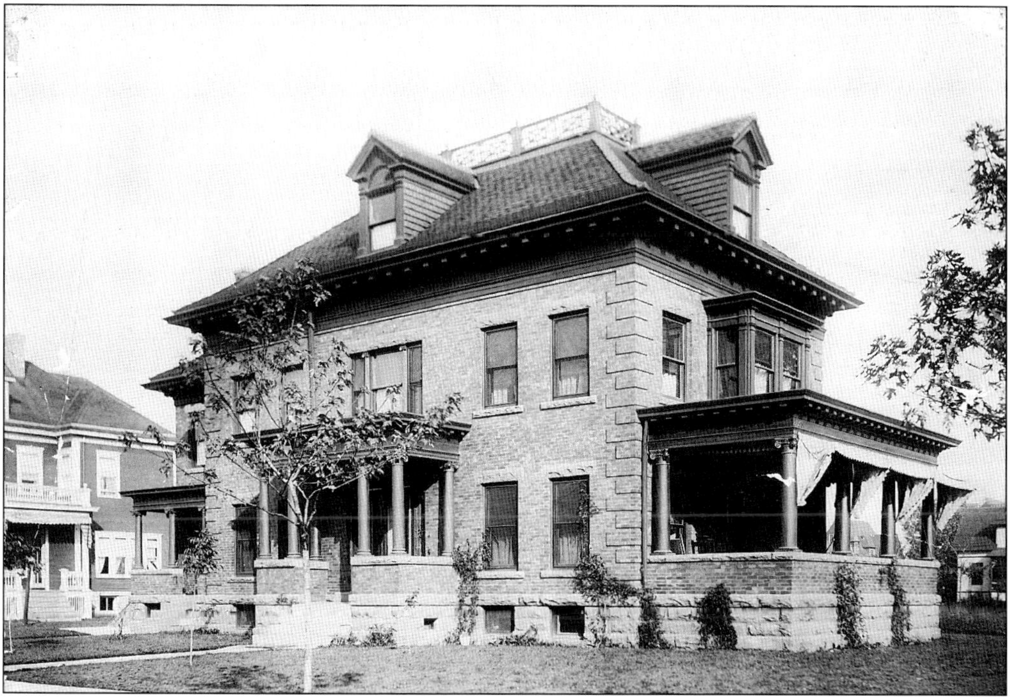

The home of George V. Eberhardt on West Hazeltine at Delaware, *c.* 1910. The home was a wedding gift from his father, L.P.A. In 1934 the side porch and west wing were removed and the home was moved one lot west to make room for business development on Delaware Avenue.

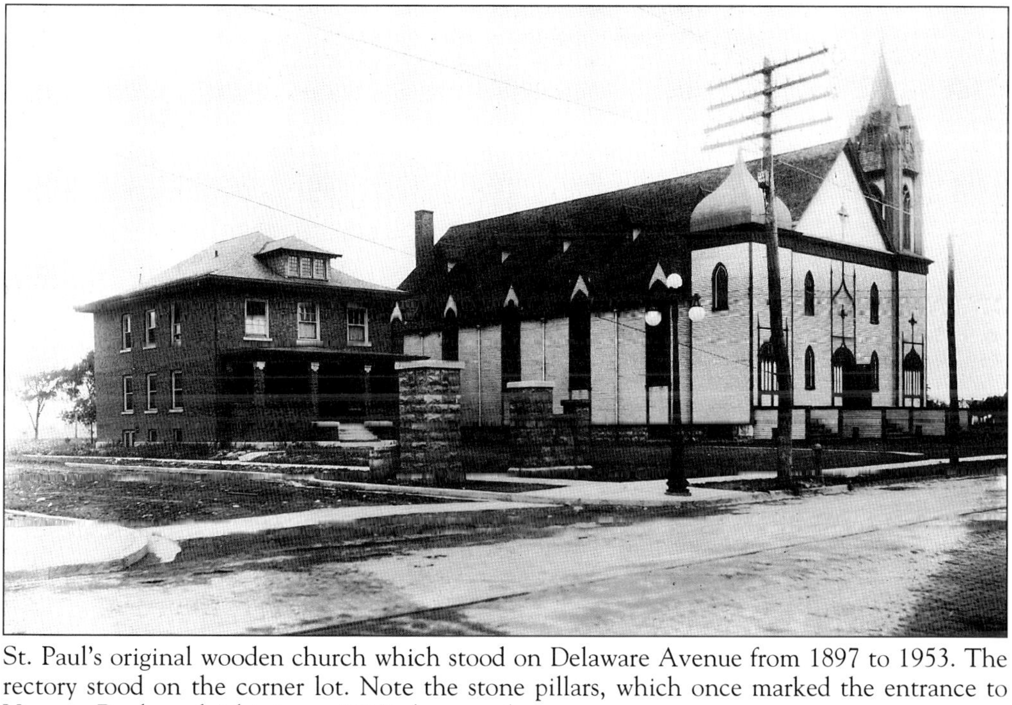

St. Paul's original wooden church which stood on Delaware Avenue from 1897 to 1953. The rectory stood on the corner lot. Note the stone pillars, which once marked the entrance to Victoria Boulevard. This is a *c.* 1910 photograph.

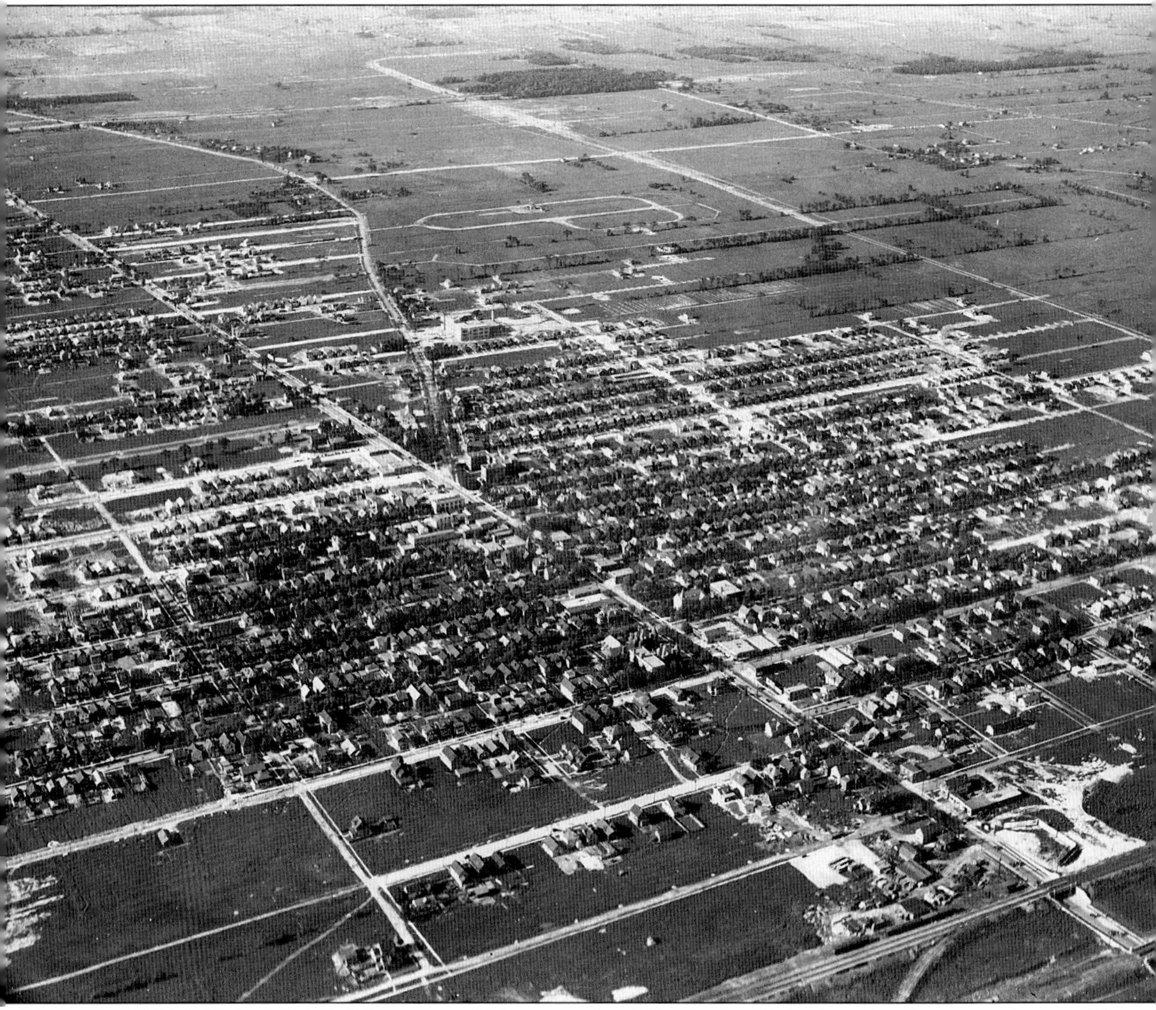

A 1924 Ronne & Washburn aerial photograph of Kenmore. Delaware Avenue runs diagonally from top left to bottom right. Note Colvin Avenue and Sheridan Drive under construction at the top of the photograph. Between Colvin and Delaware Road is the beginning of Deerhurst Park. Bridges for the DL&W and Erie Railroads over Delaware Avenue, at bottom right, replaced grade crossings in 1913. A Kenmore boy was killed in 1911 at one of the crossings.

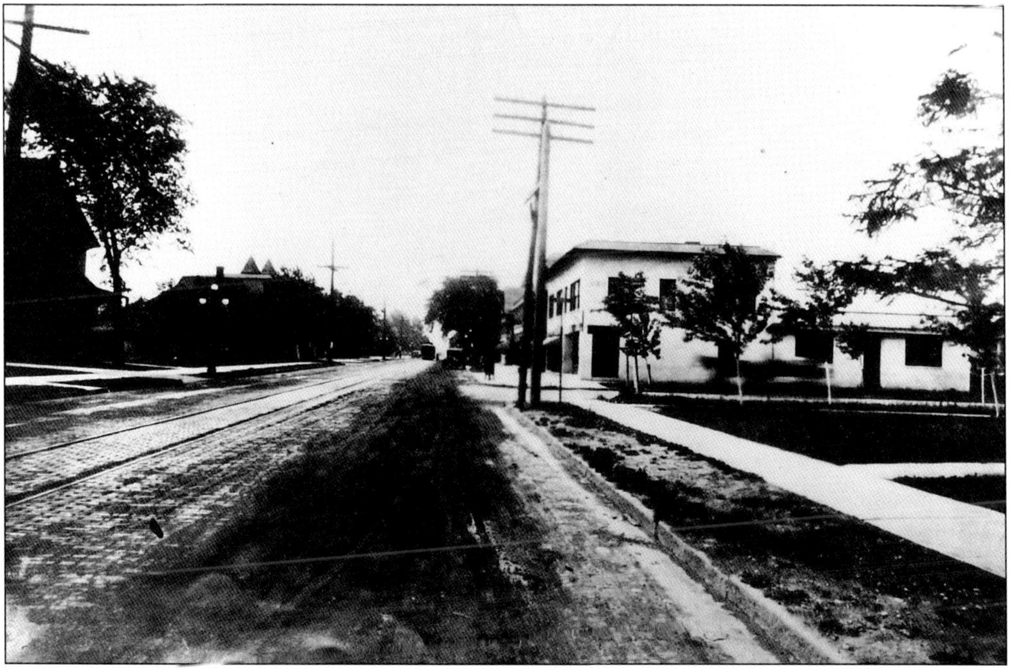

A view south on Delaware Avenue at Mang in 1913. Kenmore's first bank, the State Bank of Kenmore, opened in the white building the following year. Kenmore's "Big Tree" can be seen in the middle of the sidewalk near the corner of Sanborn (now LaSalle). One of the oldest trees in the area, it was taken down in 1929 as a public hazard. (WNYHI)

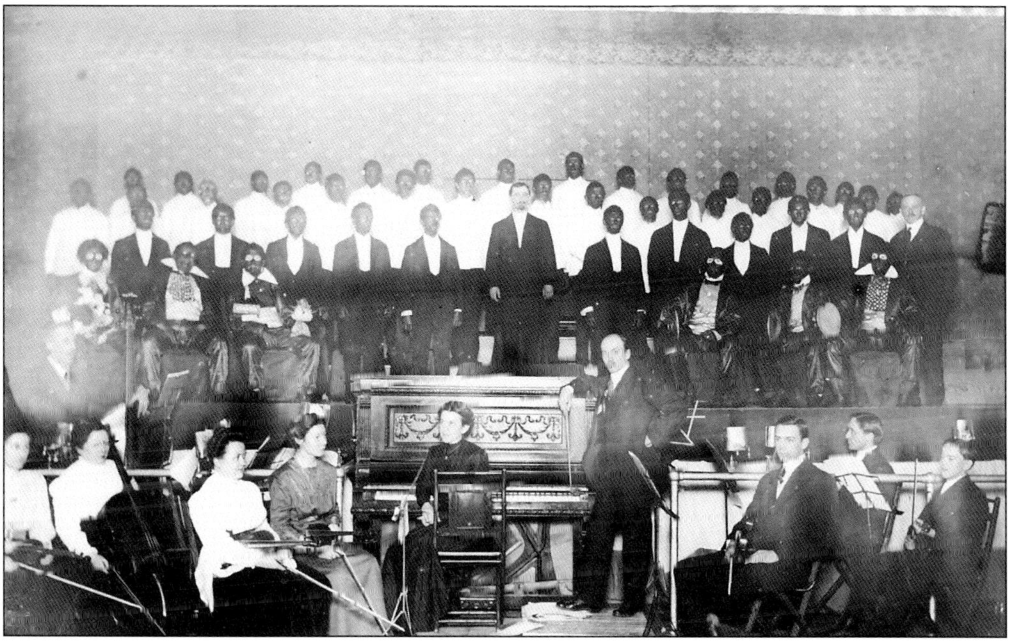

A 1910 minstrel show. How times have changed! The annual minstrel show was a highlight of Kenmore's social calendar early in the twentieth century. A traveling group of whites dressed in blackface sang, danced, told jokes, and performed comic skits. This performance was given at one of the local churches.

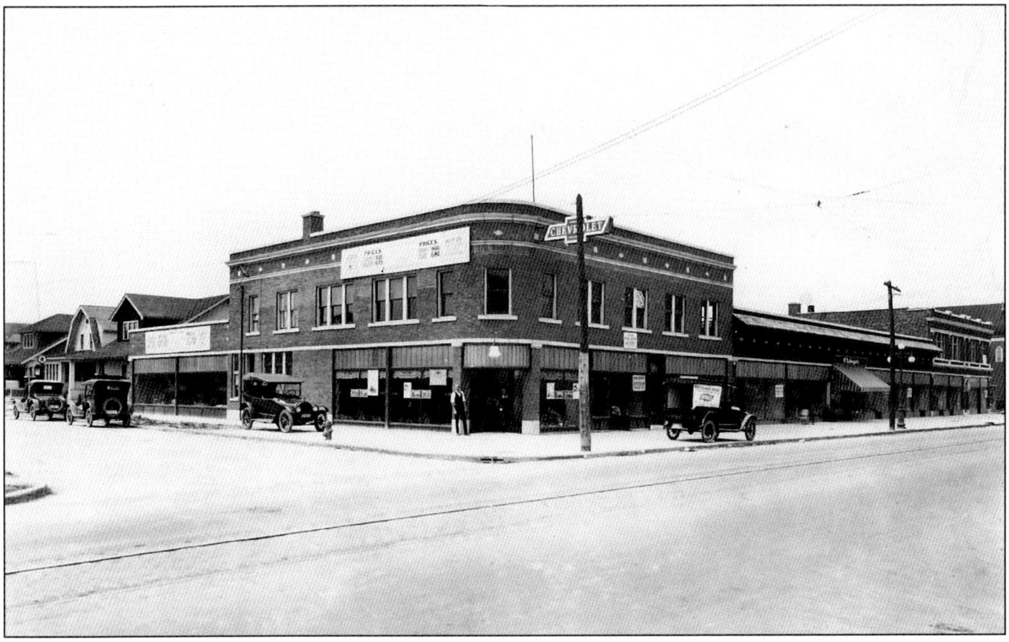

North Delaware Motors, the first Chevrolet dealer in town. This building, located at Delaware Avenue and Lincoln Boulevard, is presently a CVS Pharmacy. Prices, *c.* 1920, ranged from $510 for a roadster to $860 for a sedan.

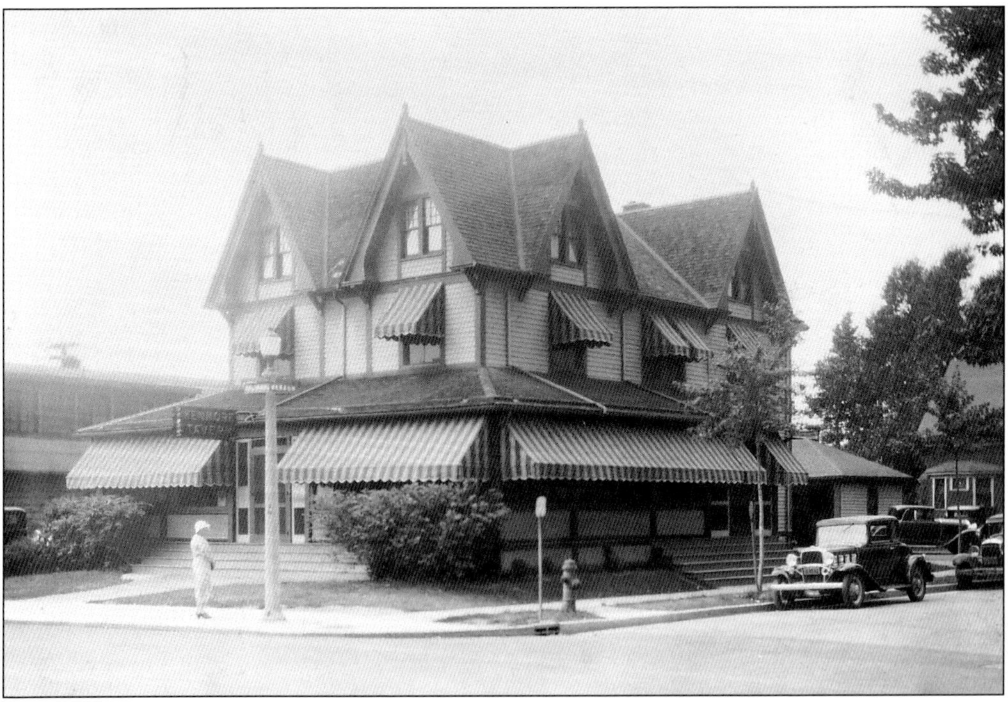

The "Kenmore Tavern" at Delaware and Wabash, *c.* 1930. Originally Bleyle's "Kenmore Hotel," the building was erected in 1893 as a "half-way house" between Tonawanda and Buffalo to serve travelers along newly paved Delaware Avenue.

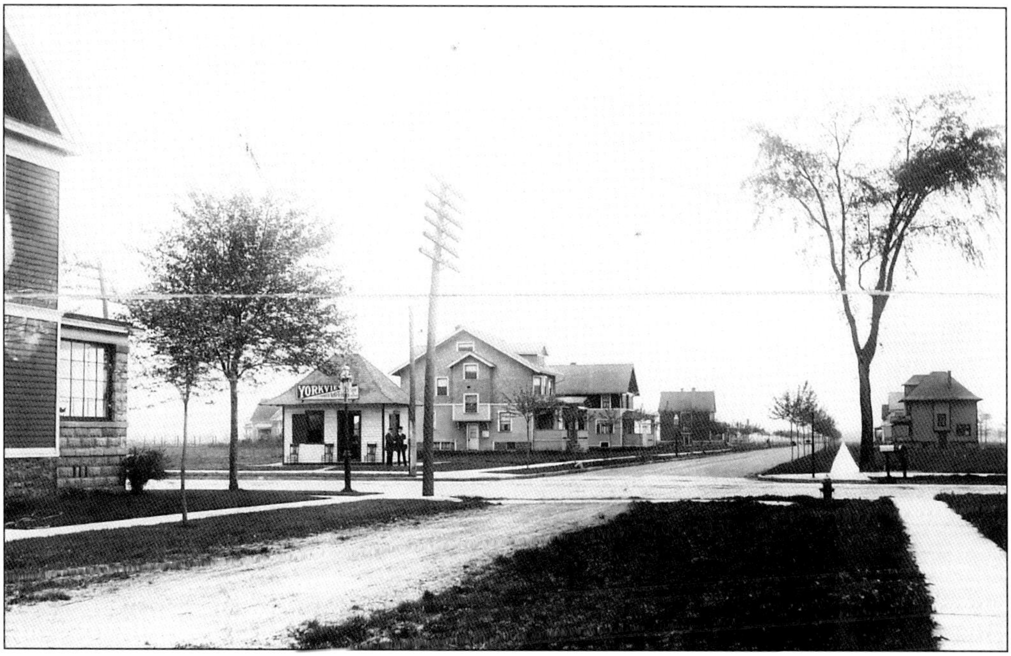

Kinsey Avenue across Delaware Avenue from Allegany Avenue. Kinsey was being developed by Yorkview Improved Lots and had new curbs and sidewalks but was not yet paved. Real estate offices were a common sight throughout the village, *c.* 1920.

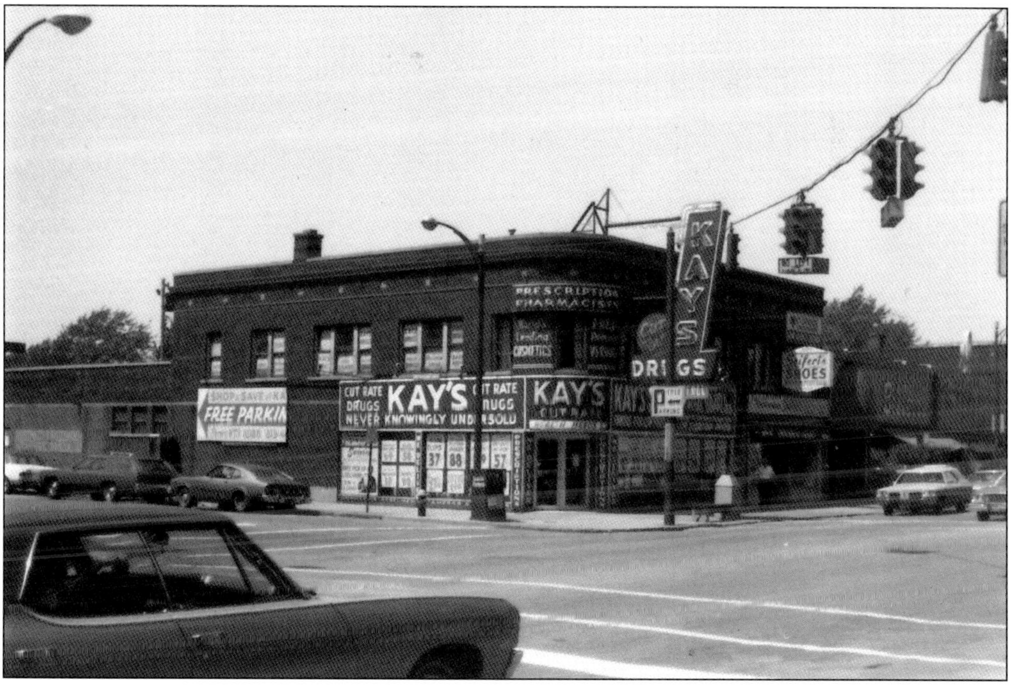

Kay's Cut Rate Drugs in 1975. Located on the northwest corner of Lincoln Boulevard and Delaware Avenue, this was a landmark for generations of Kenmorites. Originally a Chevrolet agency, the building now houses a CVS pharmacy. At the right was Brownbitt Shoes, Moeloth & Hofert Jewelers, and the W.T. Grant Company's variety store.

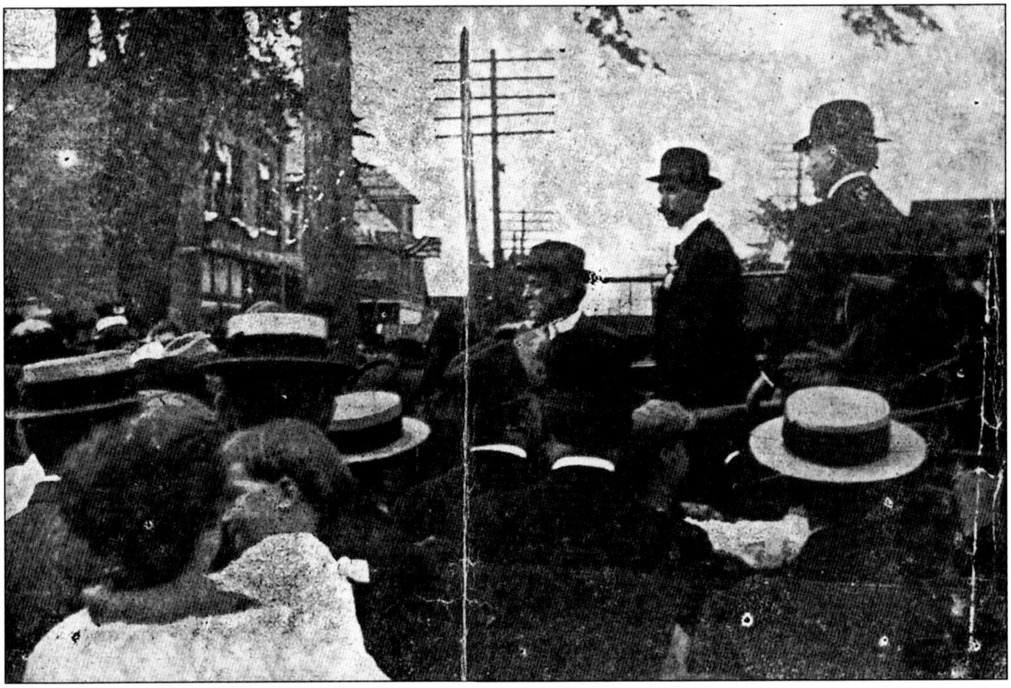

Woodrow Wilson (center) at Delaware and LaSalle Avenues on Labor Day, 1912. The Democratic presidential nominee was invited to speak by Village President Matthew Young (behind Wilson) along with the Democratic national chairman, owner of the *Buffalo Times*. Wilson defeated Republican President Taft and "Bull Moose" candidate Theodore Roosevelt.

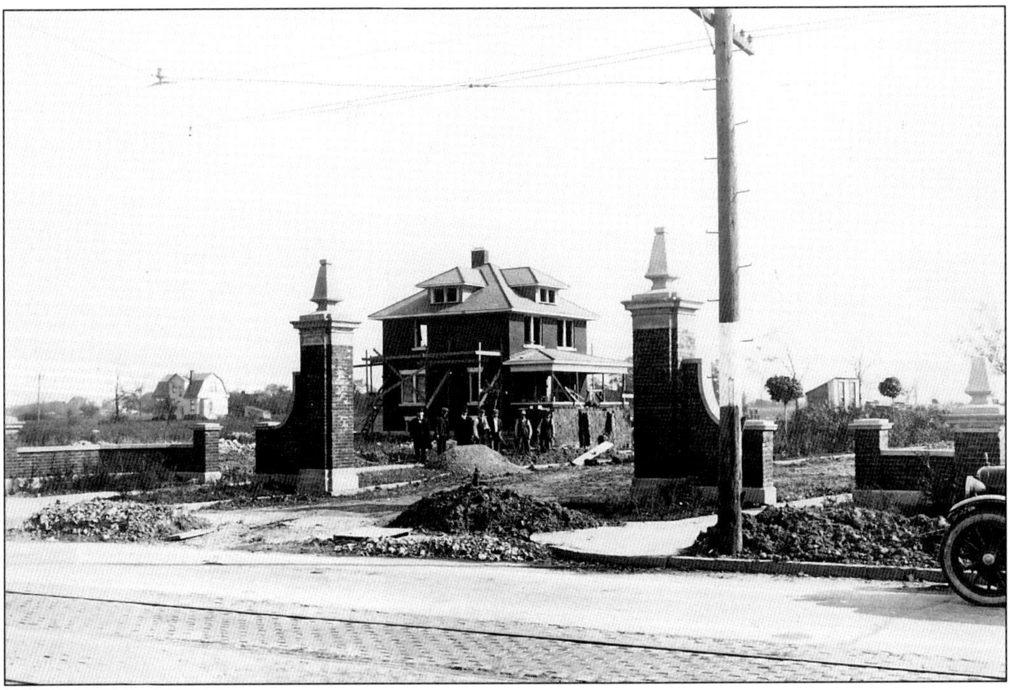

East Girard Boulevard and Delaware Avenue, *c.* 1924. In front of #12 East Girard are LPA Eberhardt (the "Daddy of Kenmore," at left) and William F. Squire (third from left).

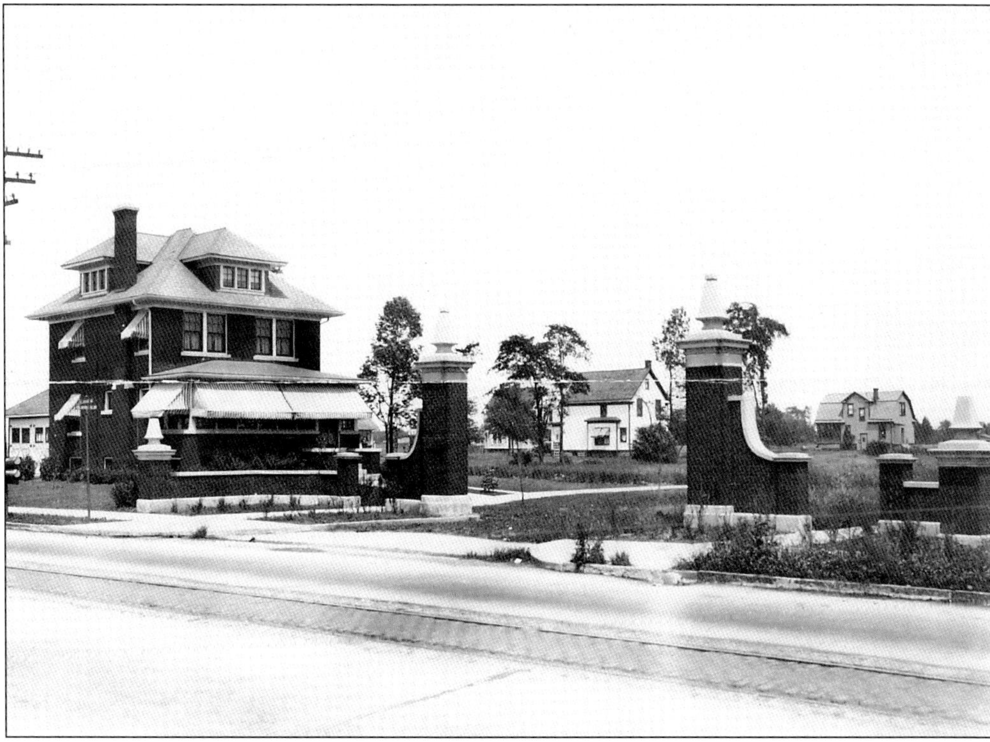

The northeast corner of Columbia Boulevard and Delaware Avenue. The street was not yet paved when this c. 1924 photograph was taken. The brick house was built in 1919 and now serves as part of the D. Lawrence Ginnane Funeral Home. The distant home with the gambrel roof stands at 49 Enola Avenue. The brick pillars were removed in later years when Columbia was widened. The tracks for the Kenmore-Tonawanda trolley were in use until 1926.

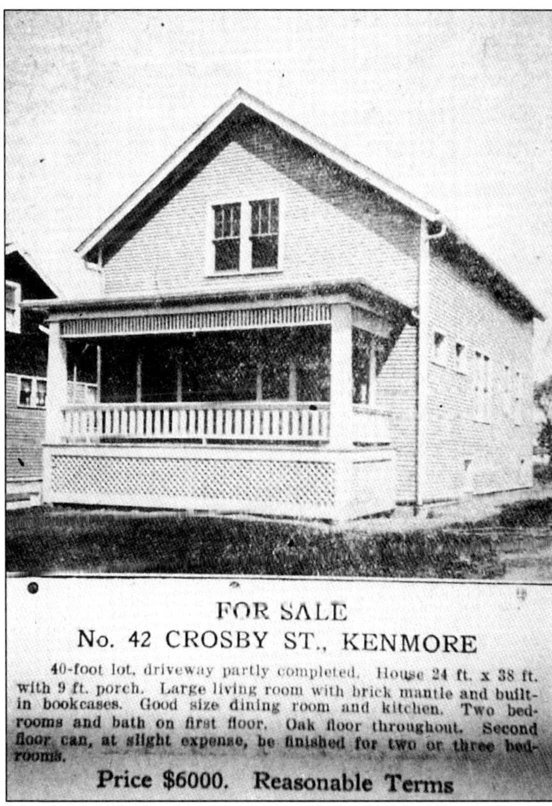

FOR SALE

No. 42 CROSBY ST., KENMORE

40-foot lot, driveway partly completed. House 24 ft. x 38 ft. with 9 ft. porch. Large living room with brick mantle and built-in bookcases. Good size dining room and kitchen. Two bedrooms and bath on first floor. Oak floor throughout. Second floor can, at slight expense, be finished for two or three bedrooms.

Price $6000. Reasonable Terms

A 1921 advertisement in the *Kenmore Record* for a new home in rapidly growing Kenmore. The village grew from 3,160 to 16,482 residents during the decade of the 1920s. Crosby, previously called East Wabash Avenue, was named for Harry E. Crosby, who gave his life for his country in World War I.

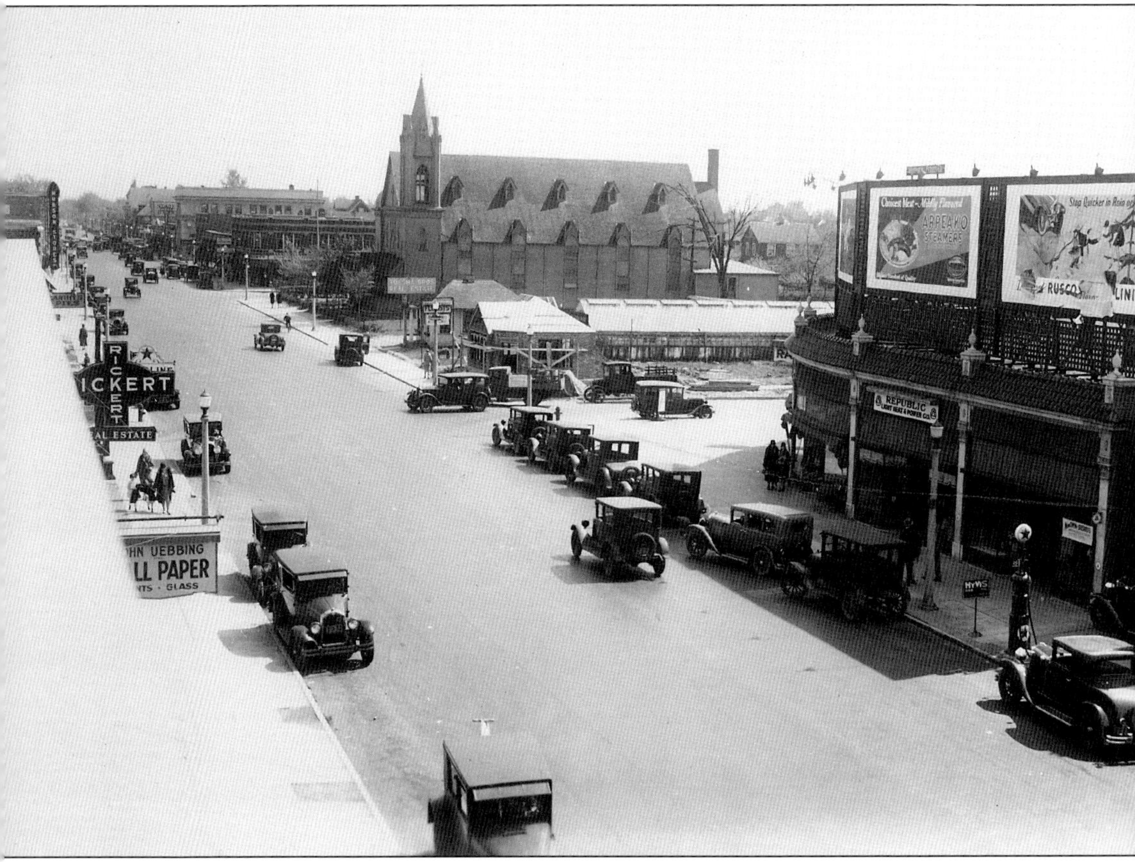

Delaware Avenue at Westgate in 1929. The "Circle Building" on the right burned in 1930. "The Flower Houses" florist and the original wooden St. Paul's Church (1897–1953) can be seen. At the corner a new "Deco" restaurant is under construction. Deco boasted "Buffalo's Best Nickel Cup of Coffee." The greenhouse was replaced by Henel Dairy in the 1930s which, in turn, yielded to Hector's Hardware store four decades later.

Five

Roads and Runways

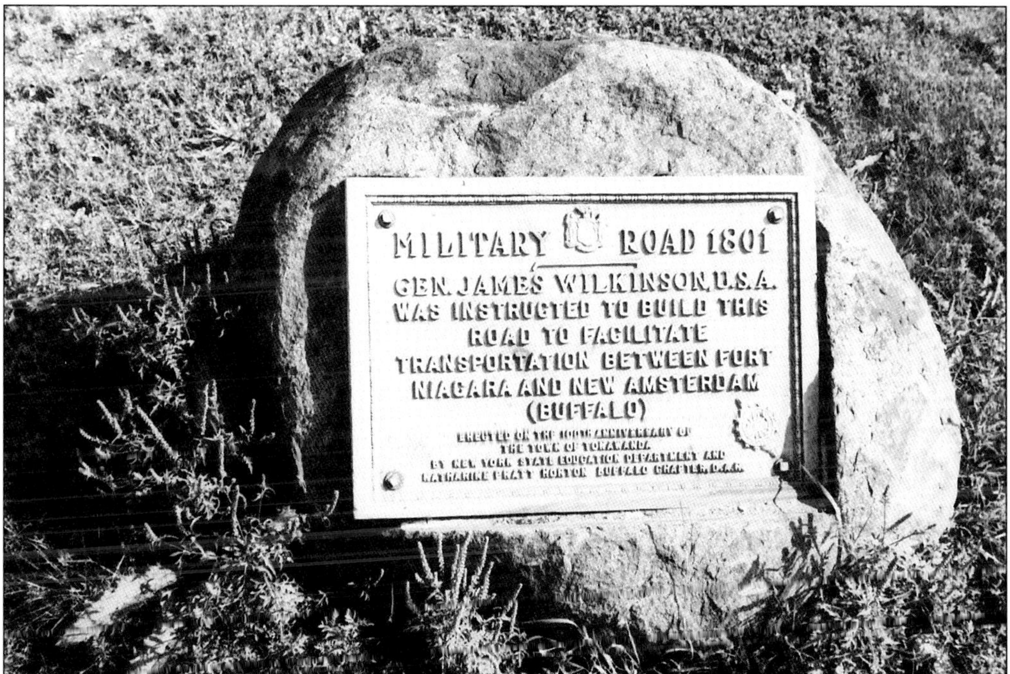

The stone placed at the intersection of Sheridan Drive and Military Road in July 1936 as part of the town's centennial celebration. The stone has been moved several times as the roads were widened. Military Road was constructed through the town by soldiers from Fort Niagara in 1802, but the muddy track was not passable year-round until 1832.

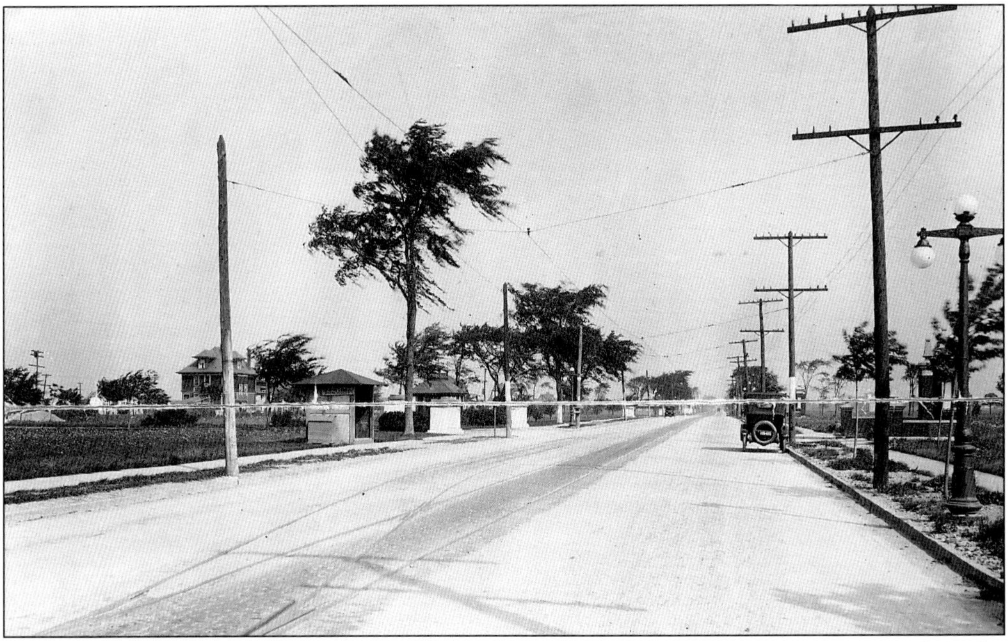

Delaware Avenue south of Girard in 1924. The entrance to "Kenmore Estates" was at left; the East Girard pillars are on the right. Trolleys passed on this turnout, one of three along the line to Tonawanda. There was no problem finding a parking place in 1924.

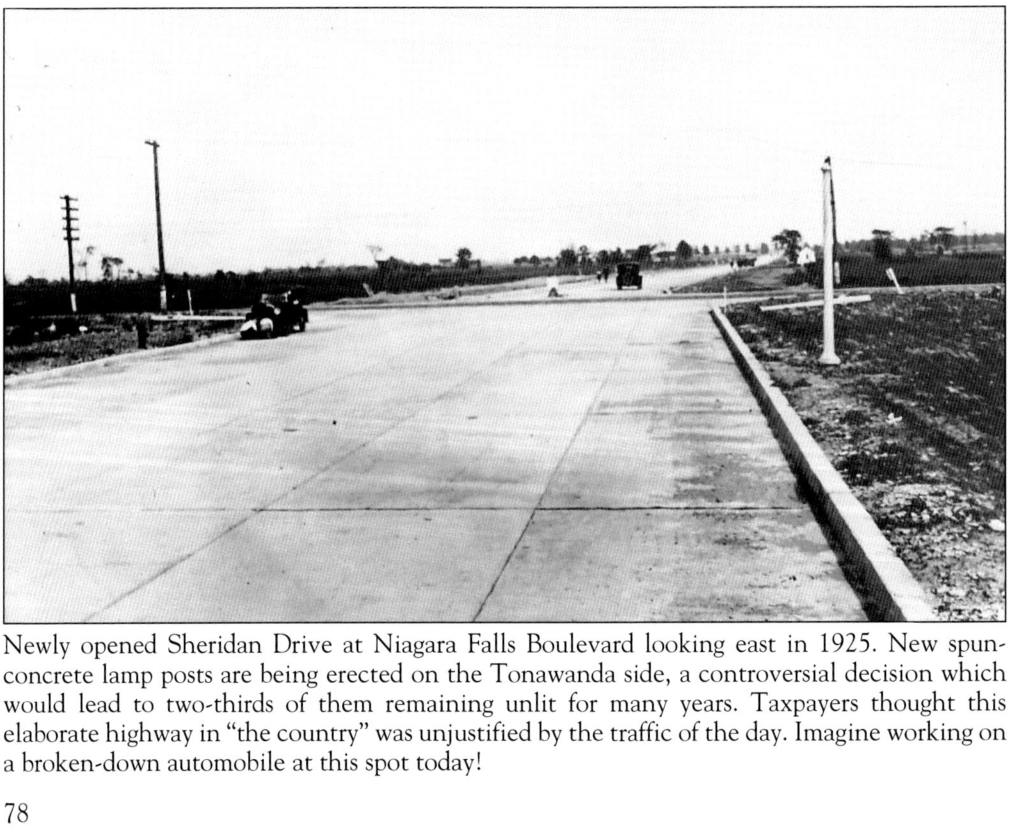

Newly opened Sheridan Drive at Niagara Falls Boulevard looking east in 1925. New spun-concrete lamp posts are being erected on the Tonawanda side, a controversial decision which would lead to two-thirds of them remaining unlit for many years. Taxpayers thought this elaborate highway in "the country" was unjustified by the traffic of the day. Imagine working on a broken-down automobile at this spot today!

One of the original traffic signals erected along Sheridan Drive. This 1934 photograph was taken looking west at Elmwood Avenue. Note the "No Horses Allowed" sign in the median. It doesn't appear that automobile drivers paid much attention to the "Keep To Right" sign on the signal base.

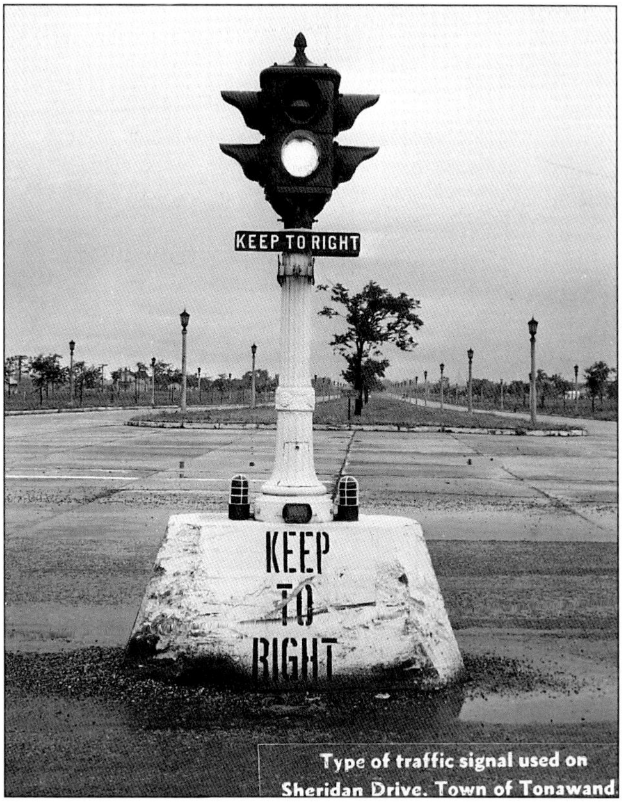

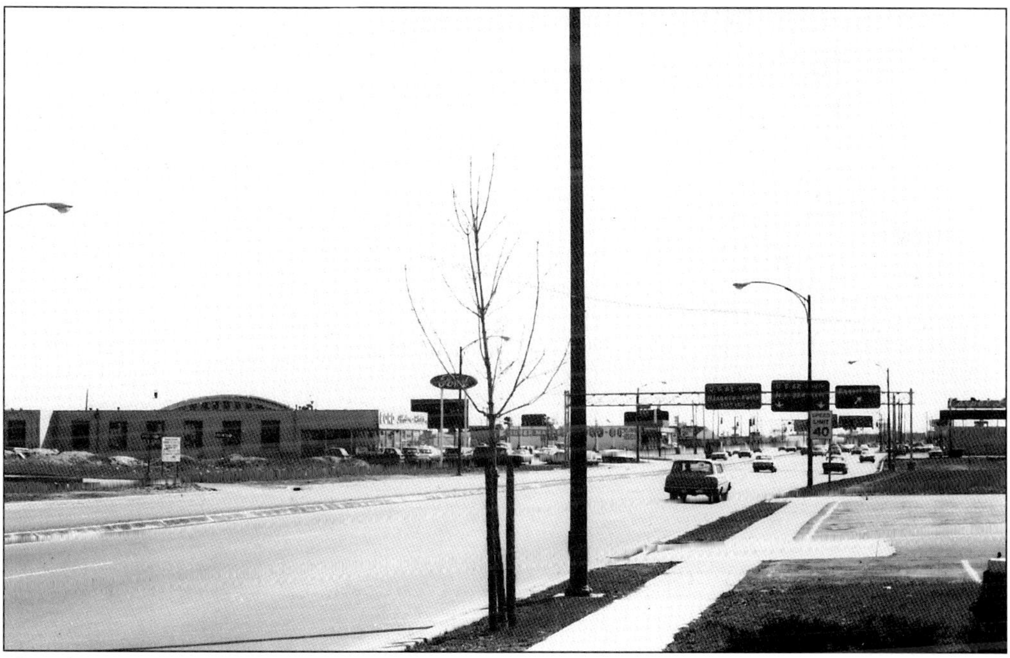

Sheridan Drive west of Eggert Road, May 5, 1965. The former Ibbotson-Ritchie Ford agency is at left. The curved roof beyond it is part of the former Park-Edge Super Market. The recently closed Carpet Land store is at right. (WNYHI)

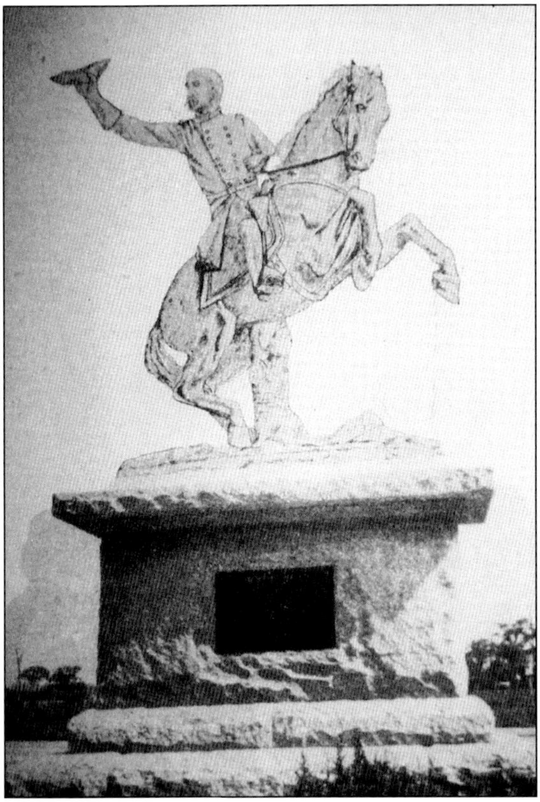

The statue that never was! Civil War hero General Philip Sheridan had no direct connection with the Town of Tonawanda. Sheridan Drive, according to old-timers who built the highway in 1925, was named after Chicago's famous Sheridan Drive. A statue of Sheridan does stand on the steps of the State Capitol building in Albany, but never on this pedestal. Taxpayers thought too much money had been spent already on what they considered an unnecessarily fancy highway through rural lands.

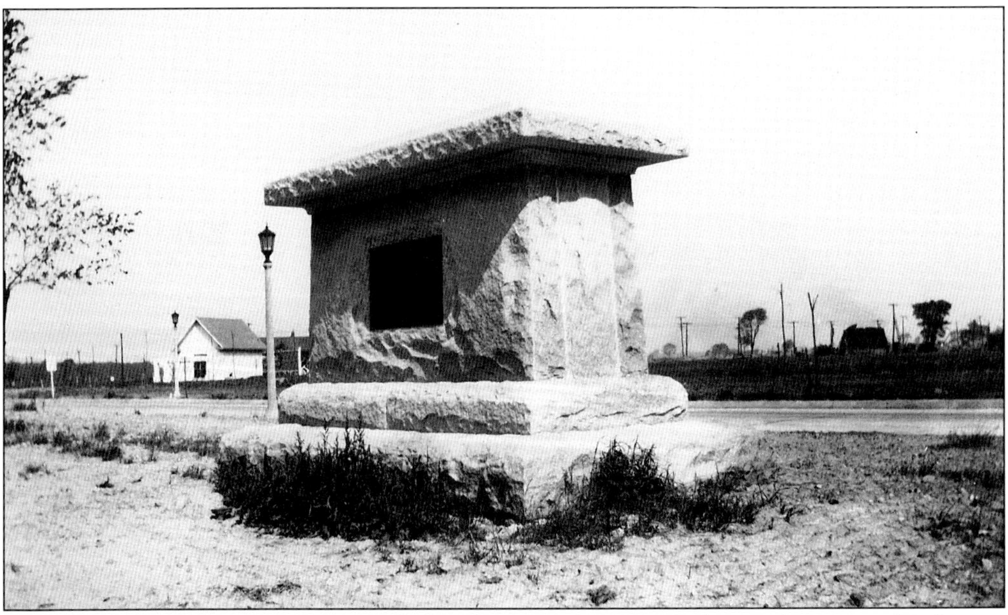

The 1925 monument on newly opened Sheridan Drive between Delaware Avenue and Delaware Road. The white building in the background is a gas station where Burger King is now located. The vacant land across Sheridan Drive was the site of the town's Centennial Park in 1936. That land was developed as Sheridan Plaza in 1950.

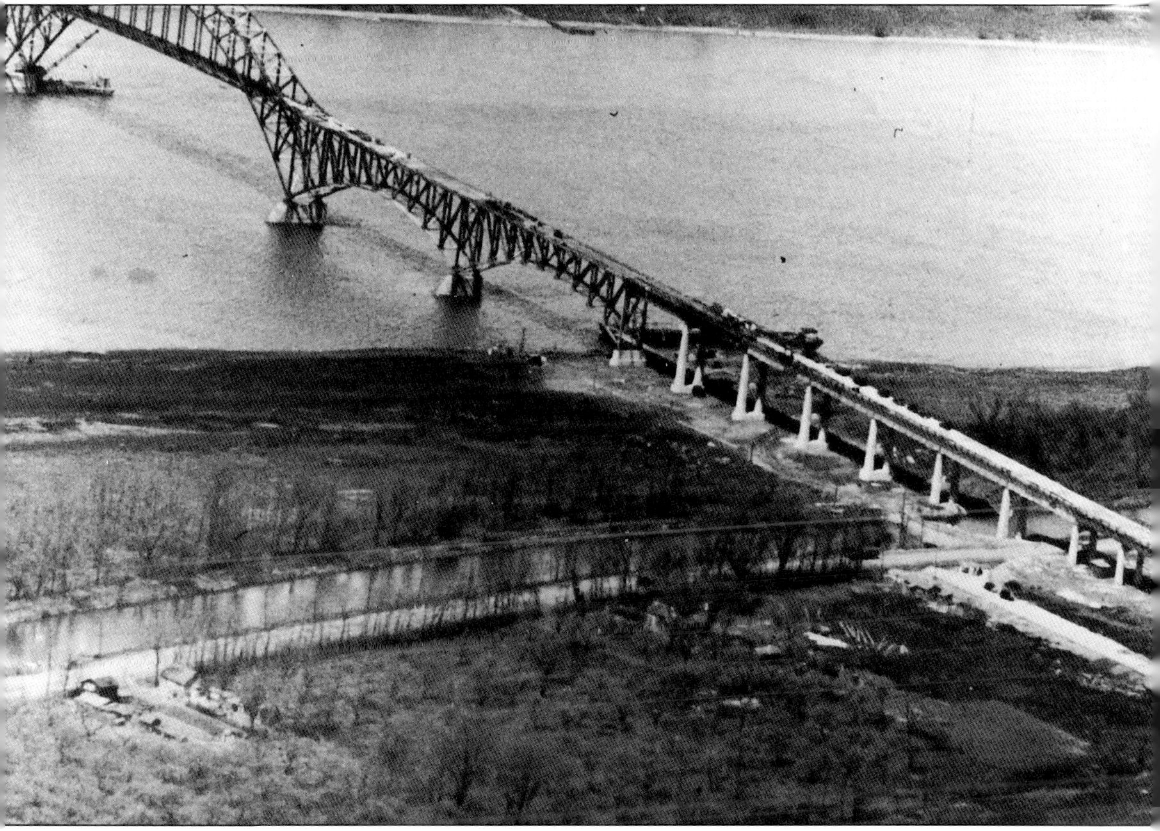

The original South Grand Island Bridge under construction early in the spring of 1935. The bridge approach was built directly over old Schoolhouse #2. The buildings along River Road are part of the old Cherry farm. The abandoned Erie Canal is alongside River Road. (WNYHI)

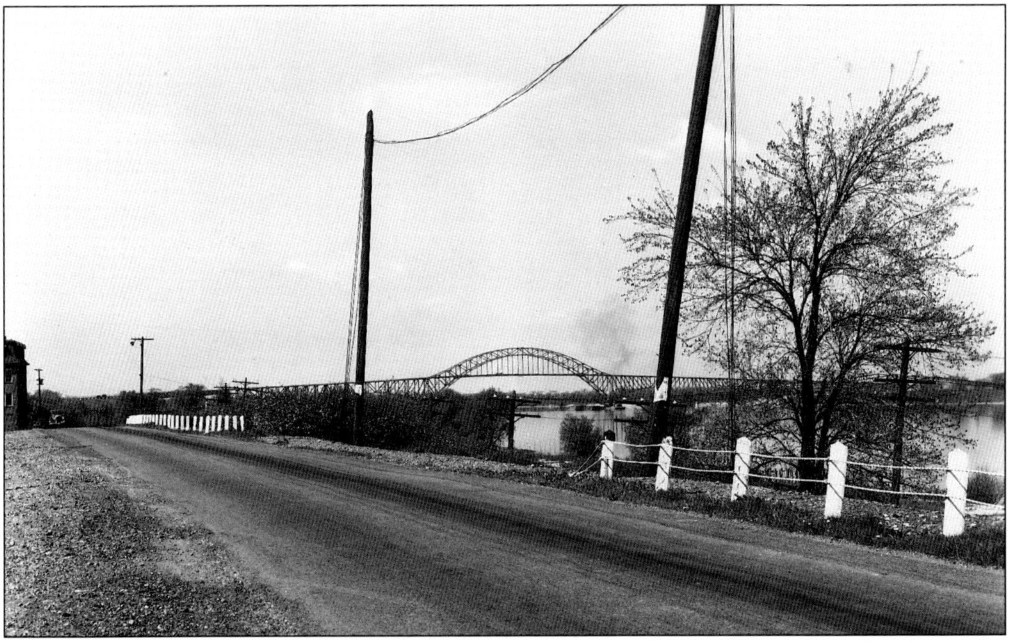

A view of the new South Grand Island Bridge from River Road on May 22, 1935. The old Sunset Inn (at left) was a popular "watering hole" again after prohibition ended in 1933. (WNYHI)

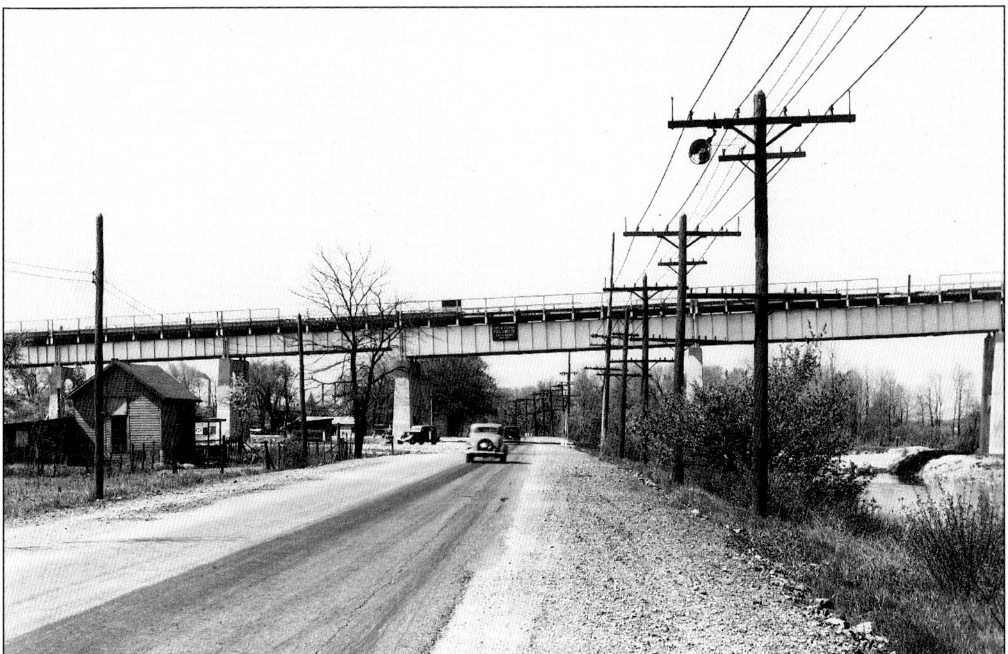

Looking south on River Road at the South Grand Island Bridge, May 22, 1935. Steelwork is being done by the Taylor Fichter Company of New York City. Note the abandoned Erie Canal bed at right. Much of the old canal bed was used as a landfill. (WNYHI)

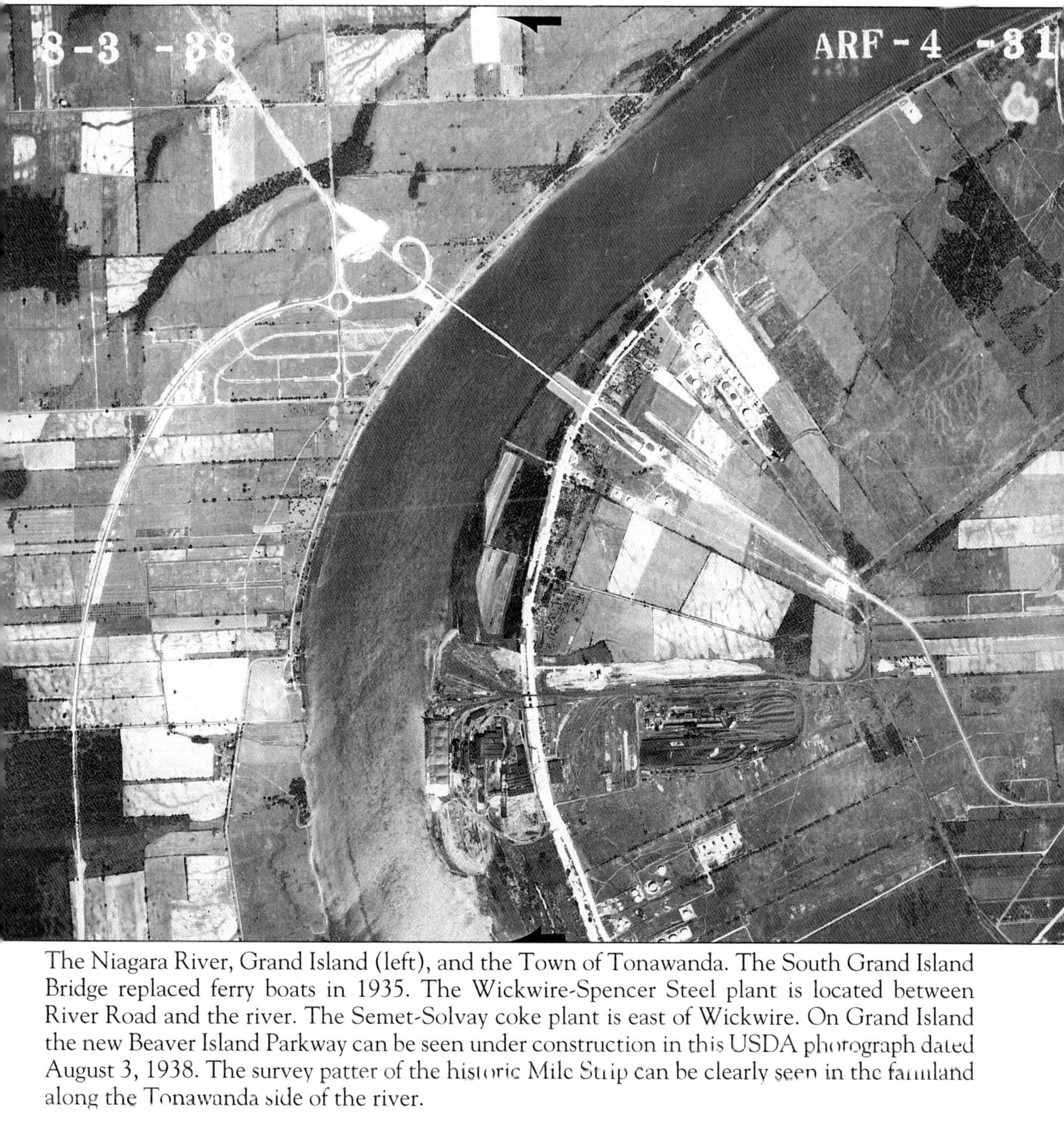

The Niagara River, Grand Island (left), and the Town of Tonawanda. The South Grand Island Bridge replaced ferry boats in 1935. The Wickwire-Spencer Steel plant is located between River Road and the river. The Semet-Solvay coke plant is east of Wickwire. On Grand Island the new Beaver Island Parkway can be seen under construction in this USDA photograph dated August 3, 1938. The survey patter of the historic Mile Strip can be clearly seen in the farmland along the Tonawanda side of the river.

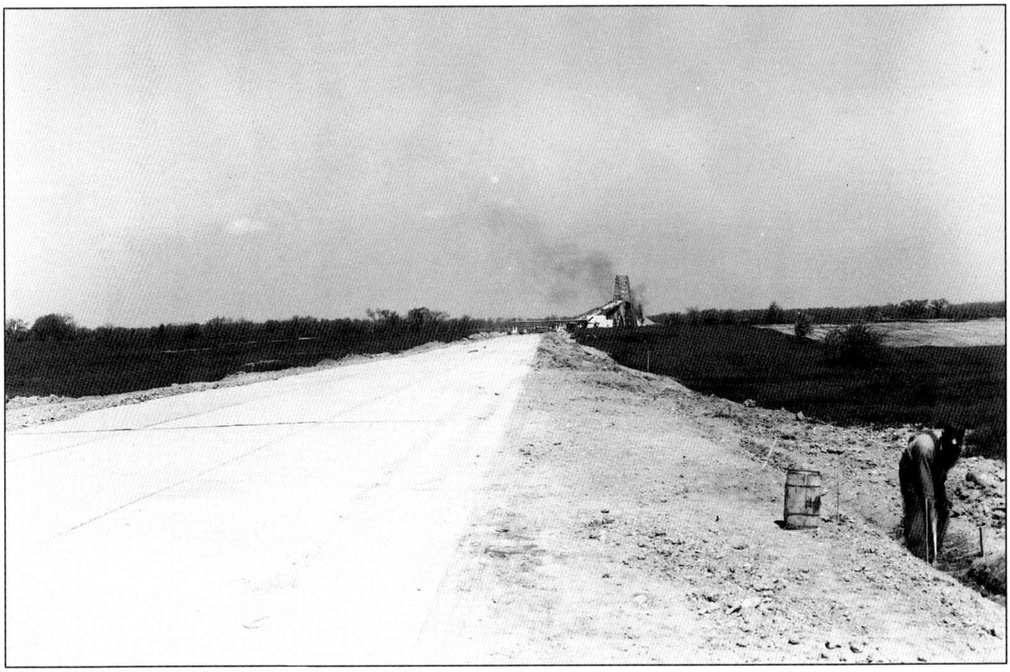

Grand Island Boulevard nearing completion at the approach to the original South Grand Island Bridge, May 22, 1935. Until its official opening in July, only ferries offered regular access to the island. Kenmore, Brighton, Sheridan-Park, and Buffalo fire equipment responded to a fire at the Bedell House on June 30 by way of the new bridge. (WNYHI)

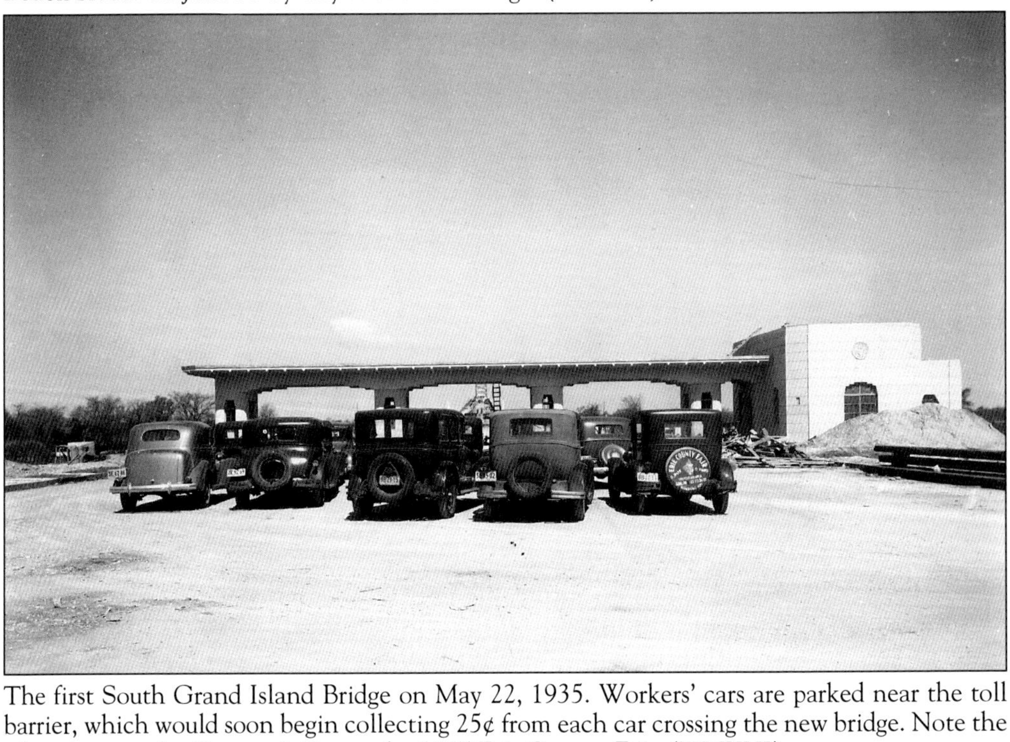

The first South Grand Island Bridge on May 22, 1935. Workers' cars are parked near the toll barrier, which would soon begin collecting 25¢ from each car crossing the new bridge. Note the advertisement for Firemen's Day at the 1935 Erie County Fair. (WNYHI)

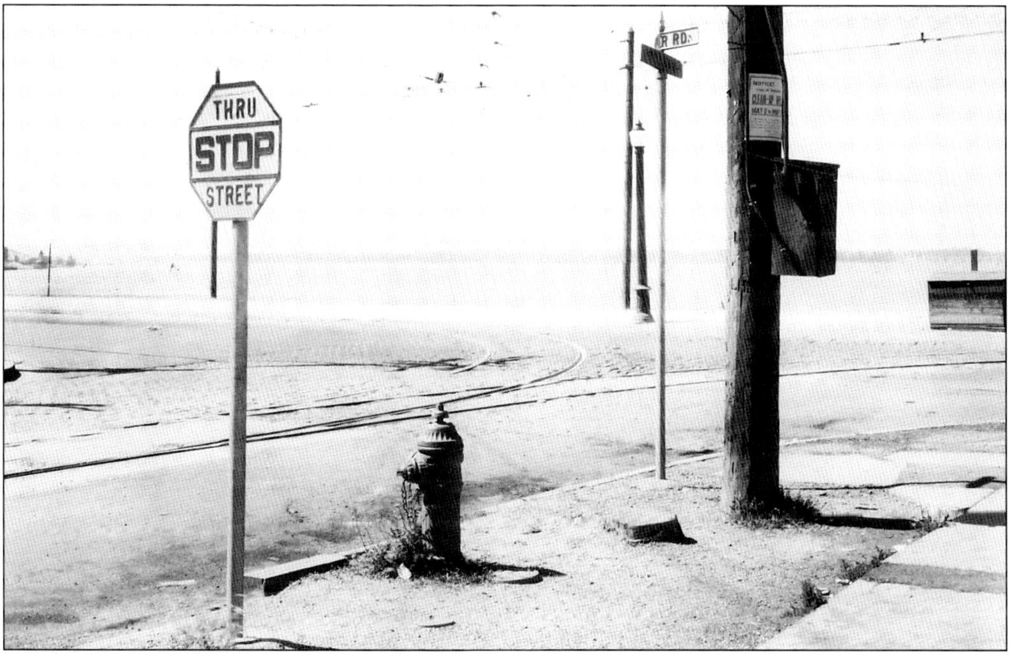

The intersection of Vulcan Street and River Road, July 5, 1933. Trolleys ran down Niagara Street into Buffalo and north along River Road to the Wickwire Steel plant. This photograph was taken from the entrance of Sully's, a long-standing tavern at that corner. Note the town's "Clean-up Week" sign for the week of May 8–15 still posted in July.

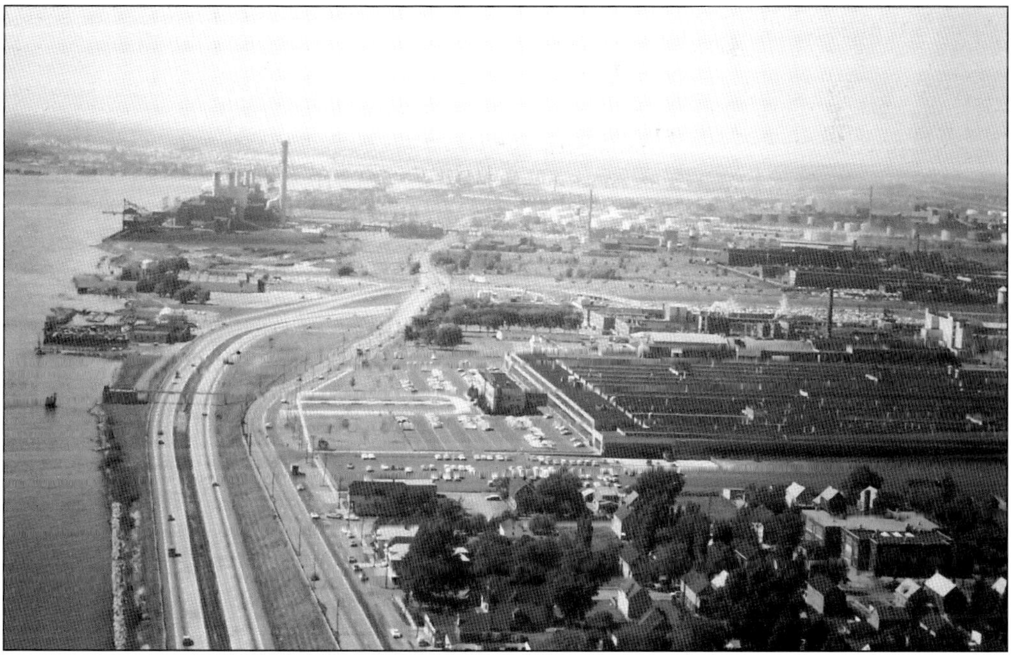

Tonawanda's Riverside neighborhood, centered around the former Harding Elementary School, now the Boys' Club. The giant Chevrolet-Tonawanda engine plant and Dupont-Yerkes plant lie to the north. The Niagara Thruway follows the bed of the old Erie Canal in this August 15, 1962 photograph. (WNYHI)

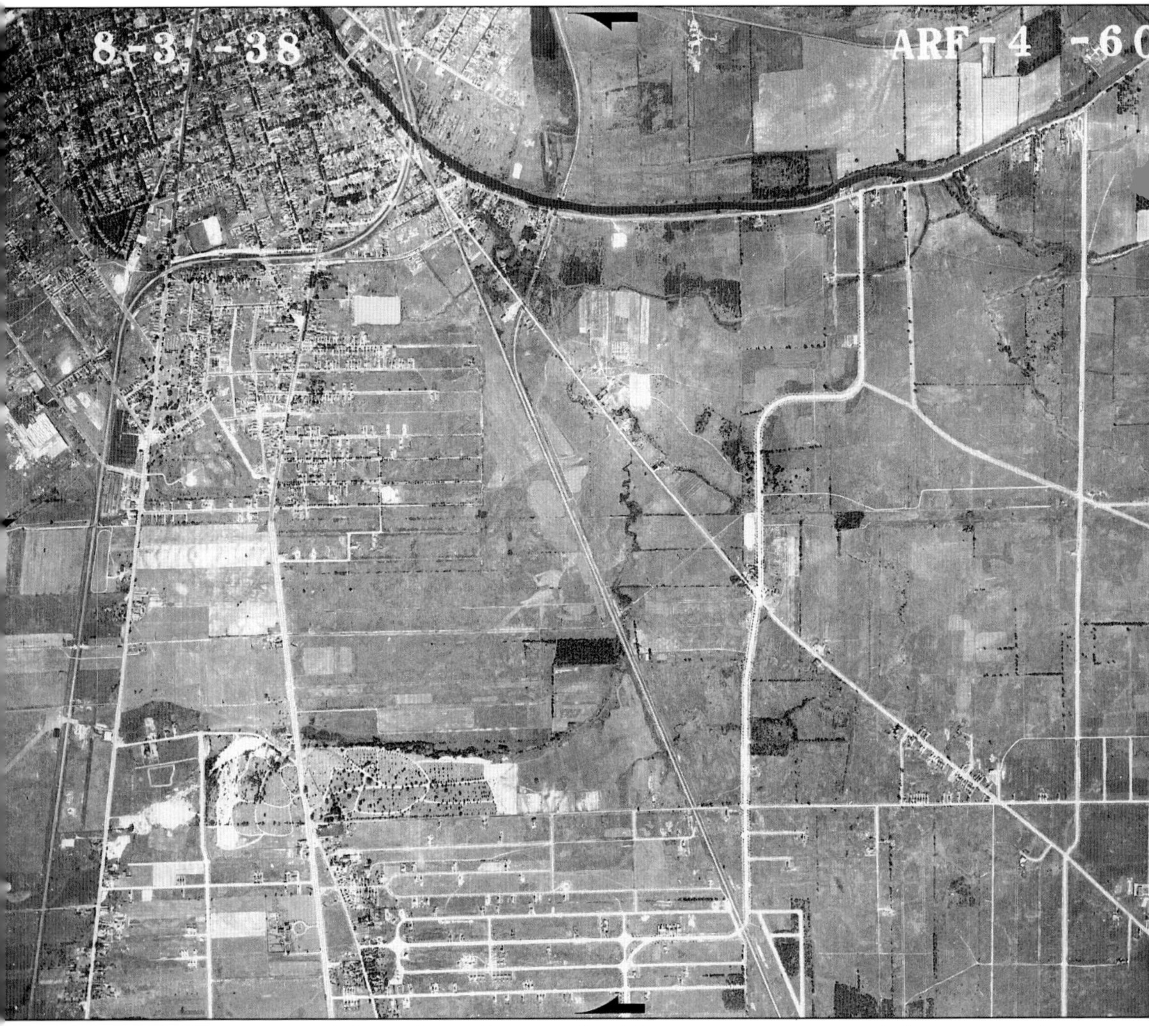

A US Department of Agriculture photograph of the northeast portion of the town on August, 3, 1938. Ellicott Creek curves at the top of the photograph, while Black Creek drains the upper right section. Colvin Boulevard, with its a prominent "S" curve, ended at Ellicott Creek Road for nearly fifty years. Paramount Parkway, Northwood, and Southwood are newly paved at bottom center. The City of Tonawanda is at upper left. Guideboard Road (Eggert Road) runs diagonally from Tonawanda to the southeast.

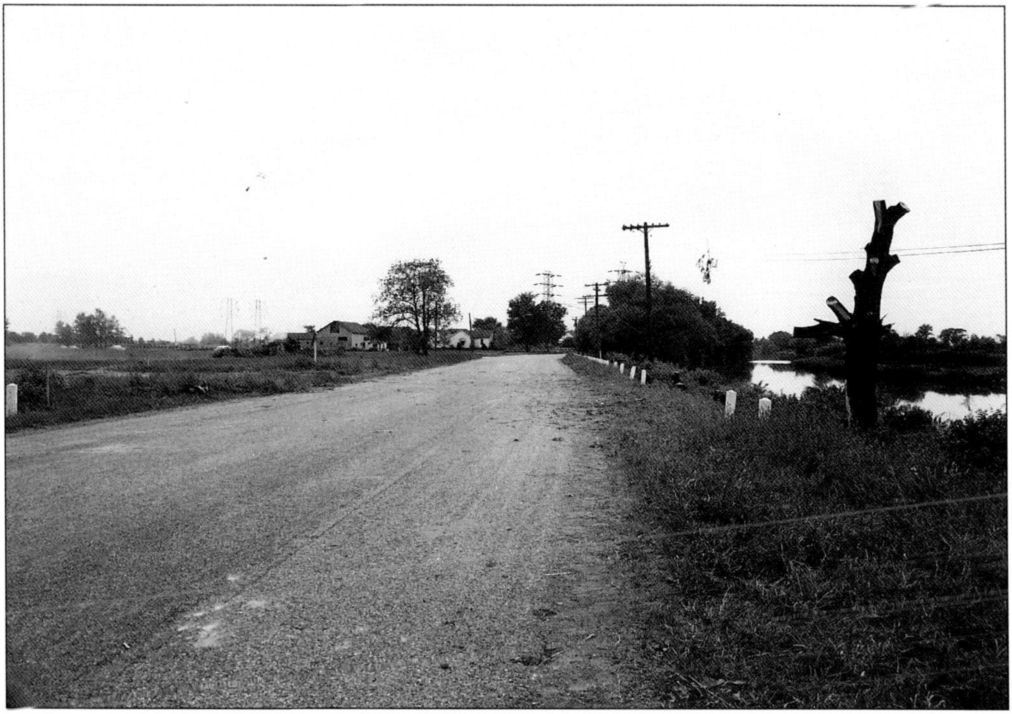

Looking southwest on Ellicott Creek Road, June 1, 1952. The farm just beyond Parker Boulevard had a stable where horses could be rented to ride the miles of trails through the woods and fields where Brighton Park was later developed.

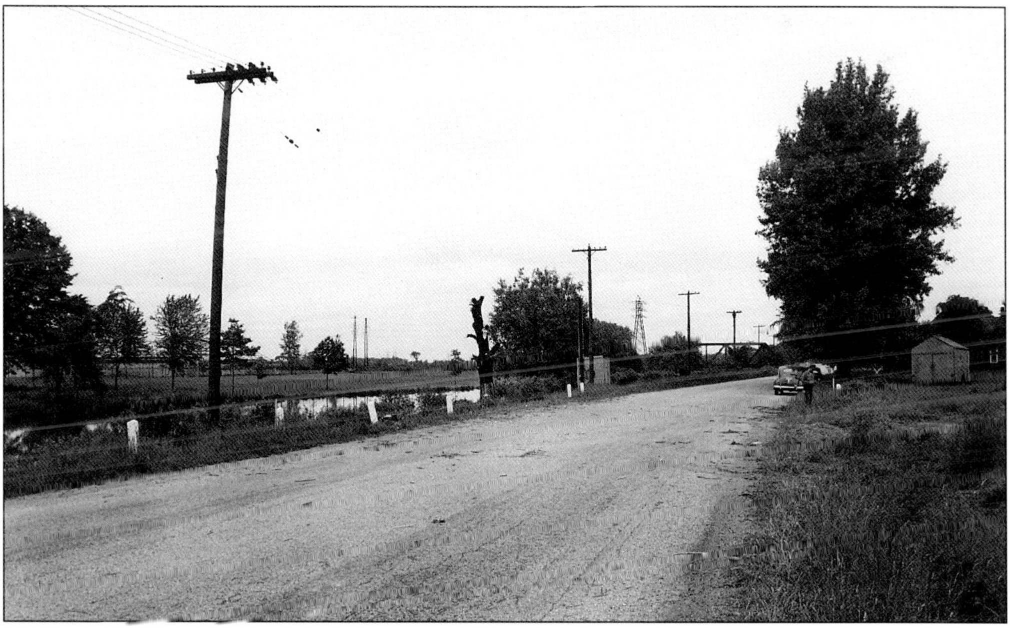

Ellicott Creek Road looking northeast from Parker Boulevard on June 1, 1952. Land is being cleared for a trunk sewer line to the pump station that was eventually built on the north side of Ellicott Creek. In the distance can be seen the former Lehigh Valley Railroad bridge over Ellicott Creek.

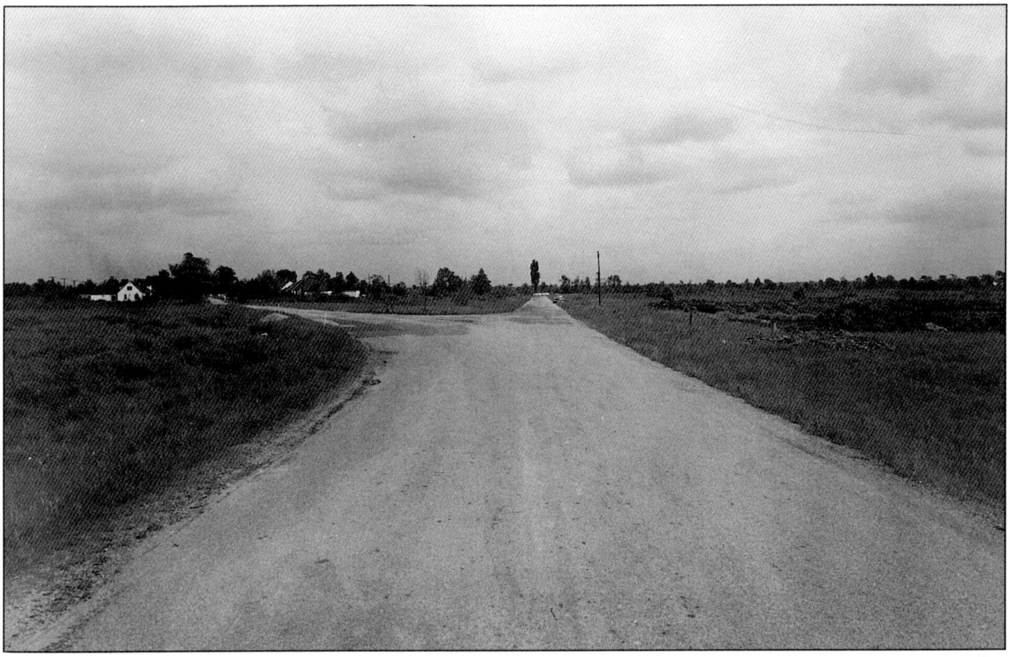

Fries Road looking southeast from Parker Boulevard, June 1, 1952. Koenig Road angles to the left. Today the site of this photograph is located just north of the bridge which carries the Elmer Youngmann Highway (I 290) over Parker Boulevard.

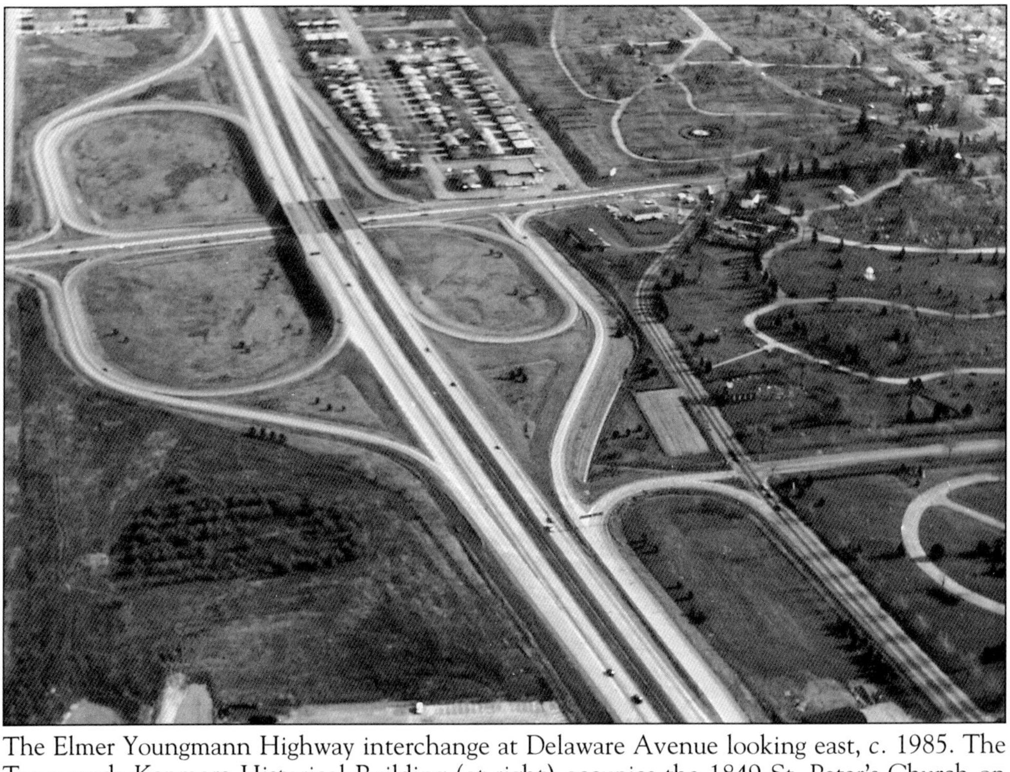

The Elmer Youngmann Highway interchange at Delaware Avenue looking east, *c.* 1985. The Tonawanda-Kenmore Historical Building (at right) occupies the 1849 St. Peter's Church on Knoche Road. The Mt. Olivet Cemetery is at right, and the Elmlawn Cemetery is at top right.

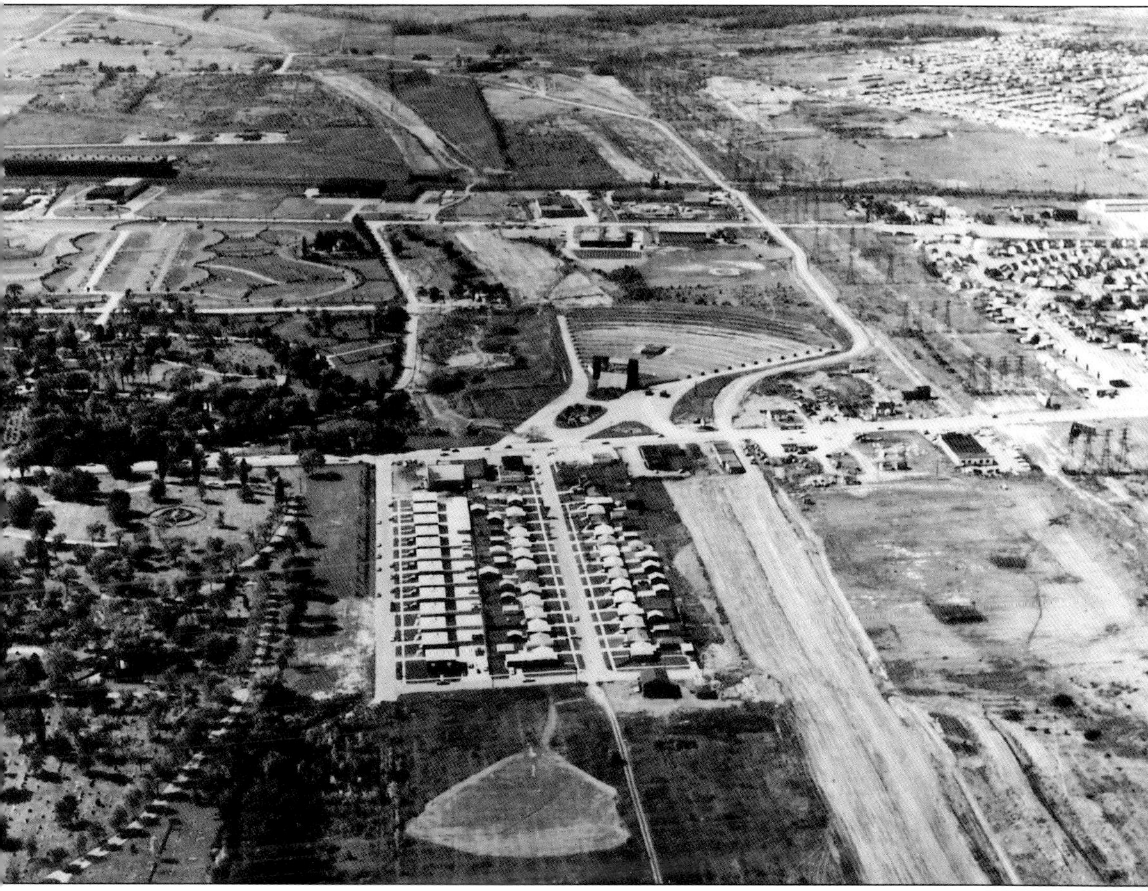

The view west across Delaware Avenue in 1963. The Elmer Youngmann Highway is under construction. The old Delaware Drive-In Theater is still intact. Mallory Road and Bonnett Avenue have new homes at center, and the Elmlawn and Mt. Olivet Cemeteries are at left. Part of "Pretzel Park" is at right. At top left the remains of the former Consolidated Airport runway can be seen. (WNYHI)

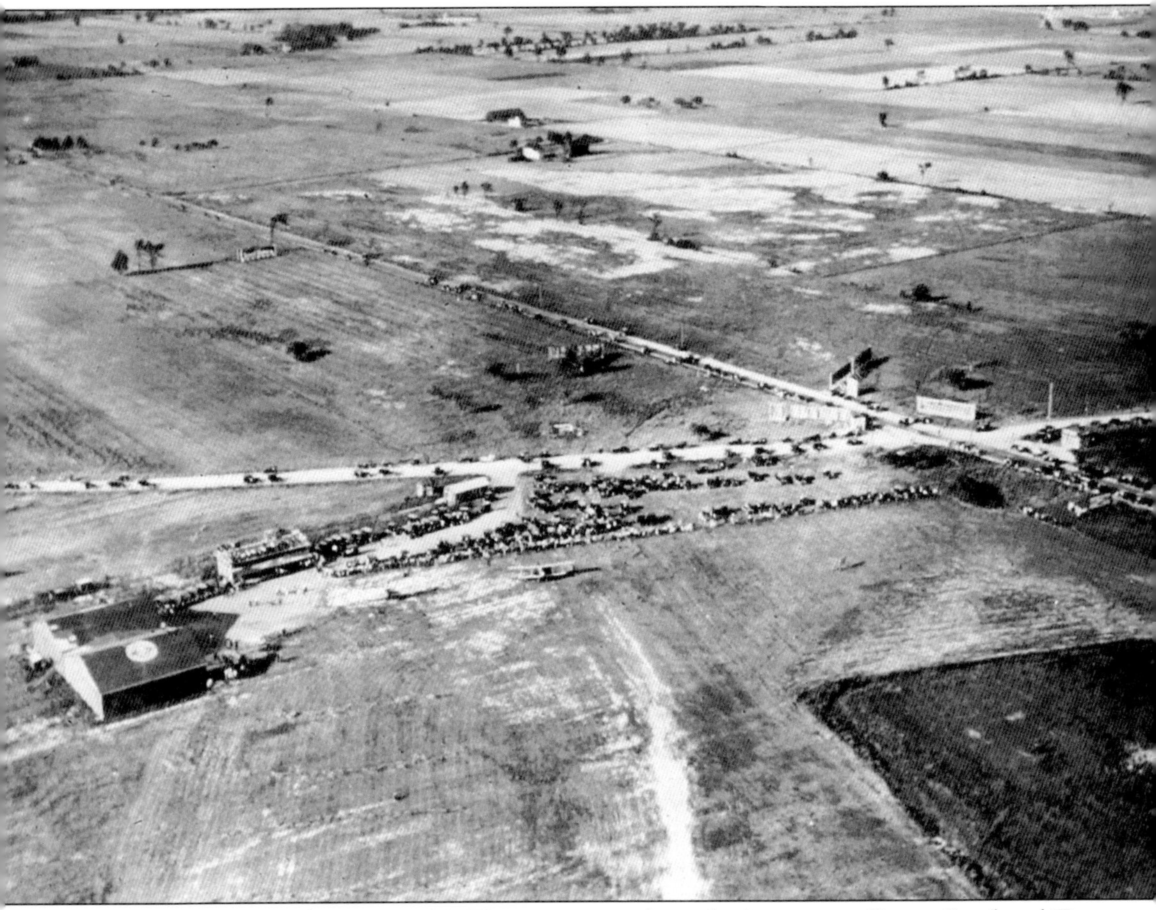

The Curtiss Aerodrome in 1920. The view is northeast looking across Eggert Road and Town Line Road (now Niagara Falls Boulevard). The cars parked near the hangar area have brought eager western New Yorkers here for an air show. This was Buffalo's first commercial airport, replaced in 1926 by the present facility in Cheektowaga. Boulevard Mall now occupies the land at the top of the photograph.

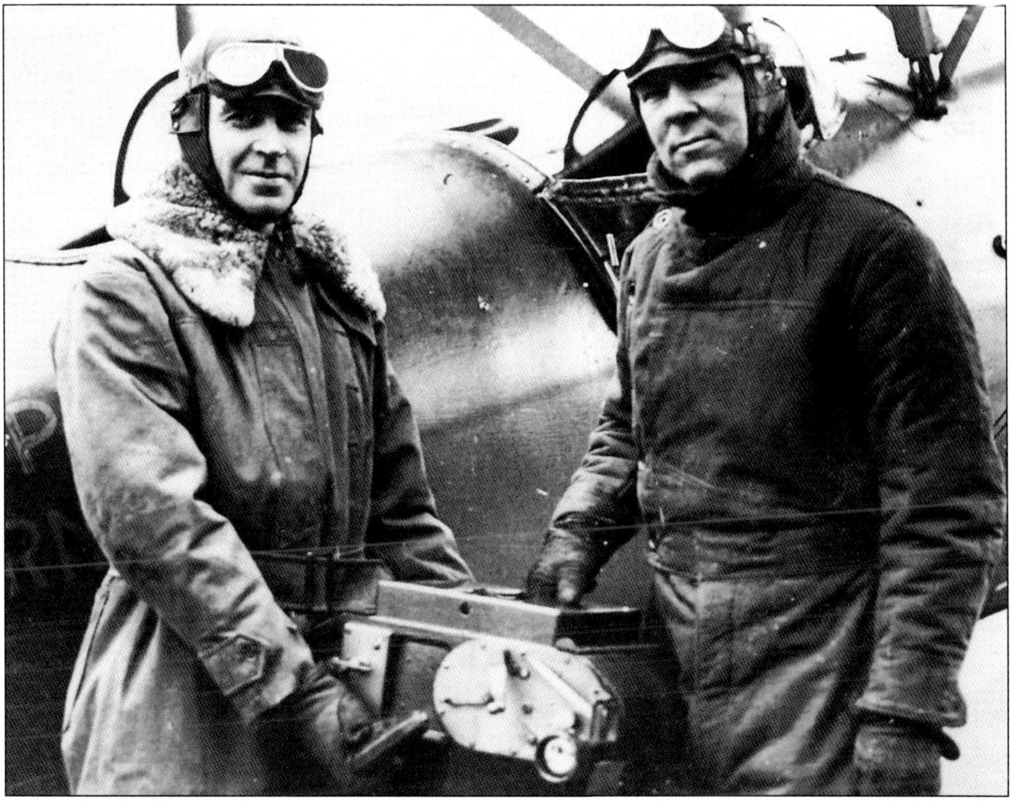

Edwin M. Ronne and Milton J. Washburn with the aerial camera they developed, *c.* 1924. Ronne did the flying, usually from Curtiss Field, while Washburn did the photography. Ronne became the first manager of the new Buffalo airport in 1926.

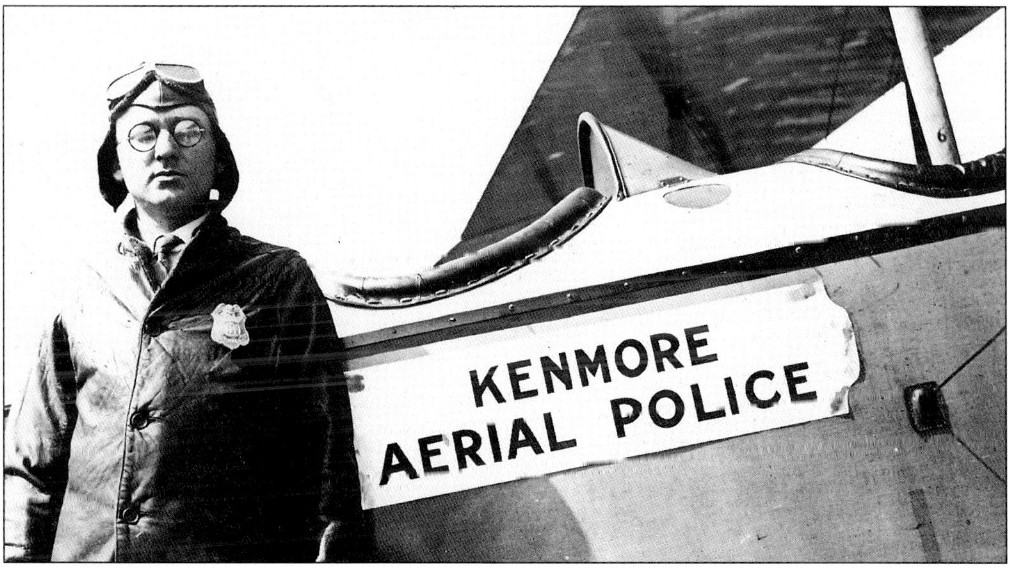

Les Irvin of Landers Road, inventor of the modern parachute, at Curtiss Field, *c.* 1920. Irvin and Roy Brockett, later the mayor of Kenmore and town supervisor, "policed" the town and village using this Curtiss JN-4, "Jenny."

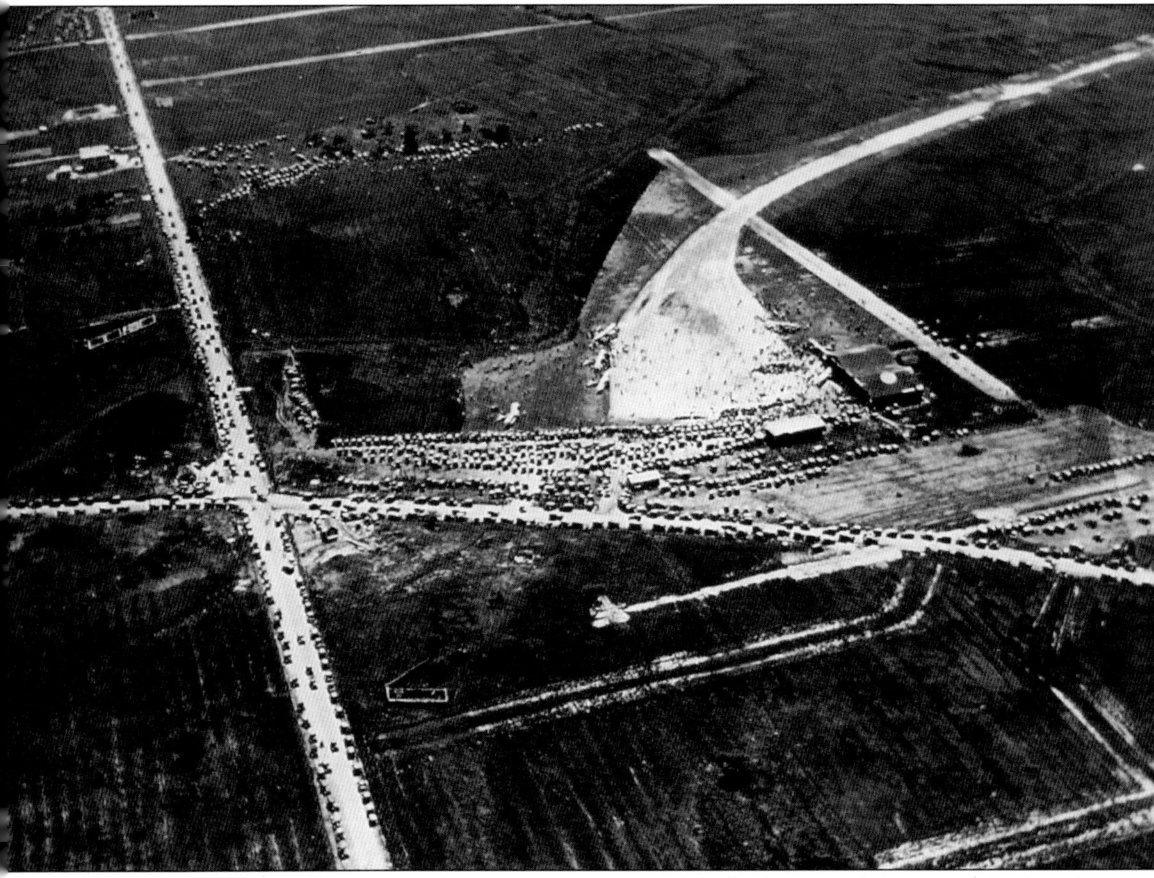

The Curtiss Aerodrome, October 19, 1924. Several hundred automobiles are parked as their occupants enjoy an air show. The view is south with Eggert Road running left to right and Town Line Road (Niagara Falls Boulevard) at left. A low-flying seaplane leaves a smoke streamer in the foreground. Present–day Curtis Parkway follows the path of the former airfield runway.

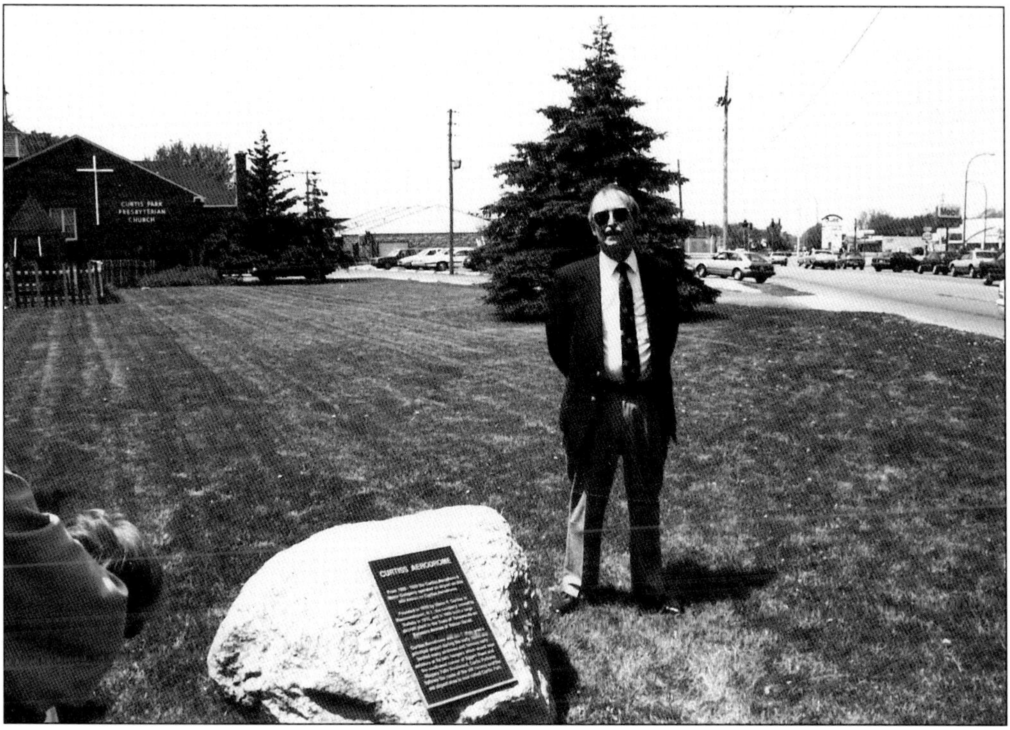

Town Historian John W. Percy at the May 1993 dedication of the historical marker for the Curtiss Aerodrome at Curtis Parkway and Eggert Road. This boulder, itself a monument to the last ice age, is a glacial erratic deposited in the town by the last ice sheet over 12,000 years ago.

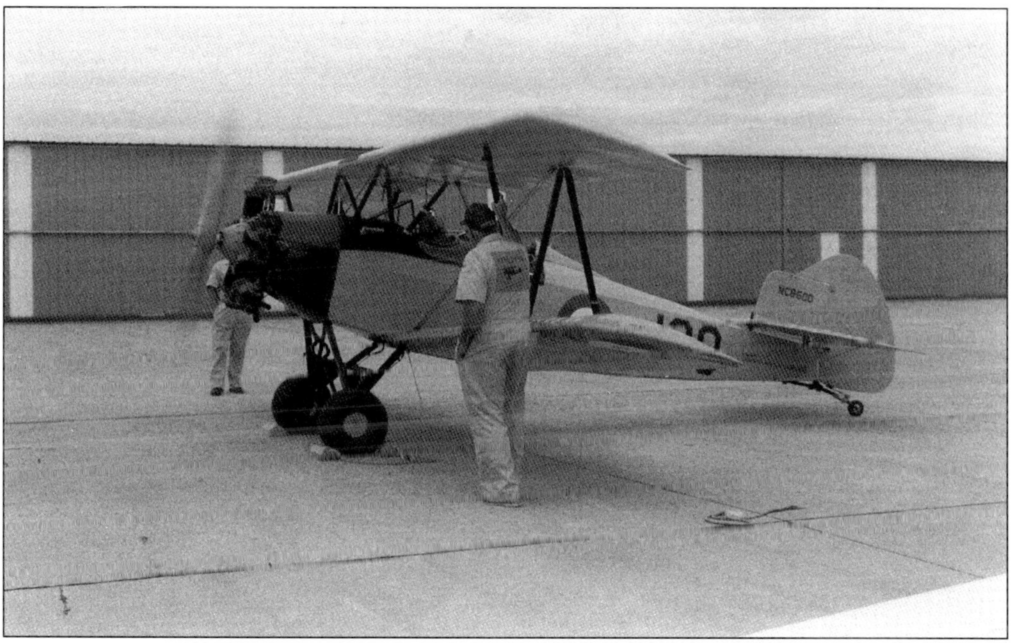

The Consolidated "Fleetster" which flew over the May 1993 dedication of the Curtiss Aerodrome monument. This was one of the last Fleetsters built at the Elmwood Avenue factory in 1929. The photograph was taken at Niagara Falls Airport where the restored plane is hangered.

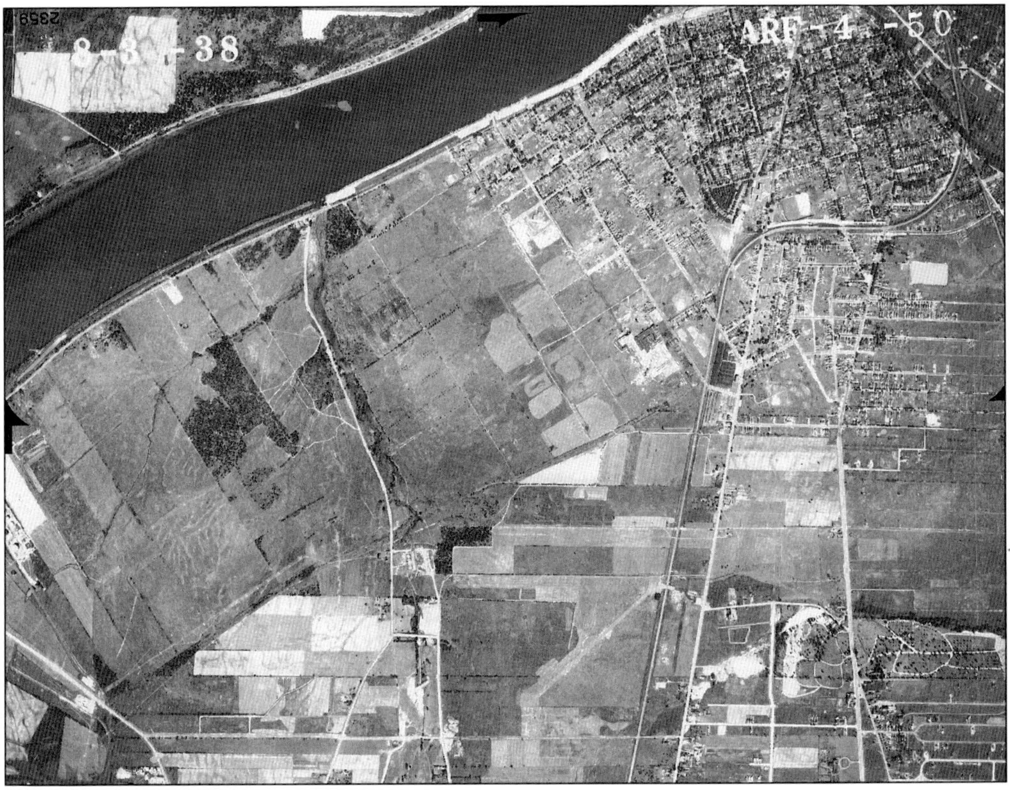

An August 3, 1938 USDA photograph of the northwest portion of town. The City of Tonawanda is at upper right, and the Niagara River at upper left. The Two Mile Creek and Road are left of center. From the right are Delaware, Elmwood, Military, and the New York Central Railroad tracks. Bell Airport's runway runs southwest from the railroad crossing.

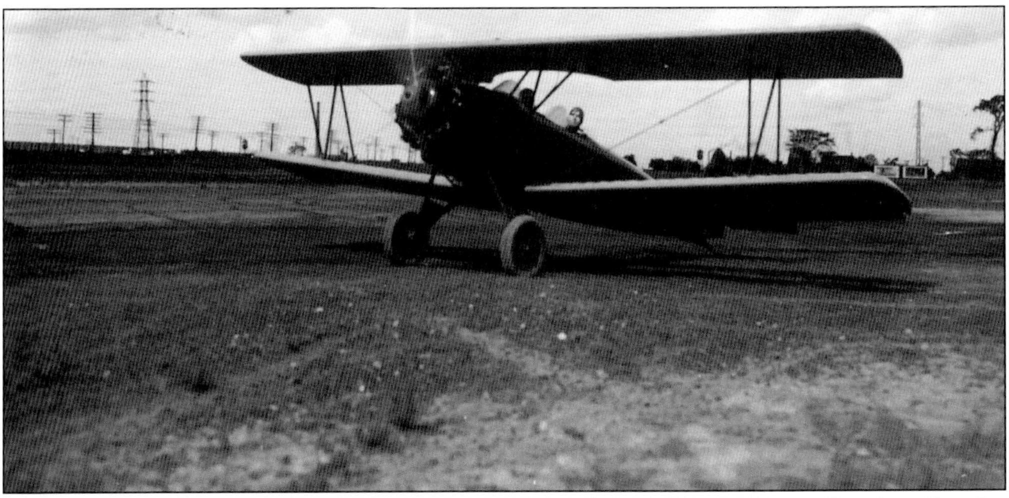

A Fleet PT-1 "Trusty" 2-place biplane at Consolidated Airfield on Military Road at Knoche Road, c. 1930. This was the standard primary trainer for the Army Air Corps into the 1930s and was also sold commercially to flight schools, businessmen, and sport pilots. It was built at Consolidated's Elmwood Avenue factory in North Buffalo and was priced at $4,985.

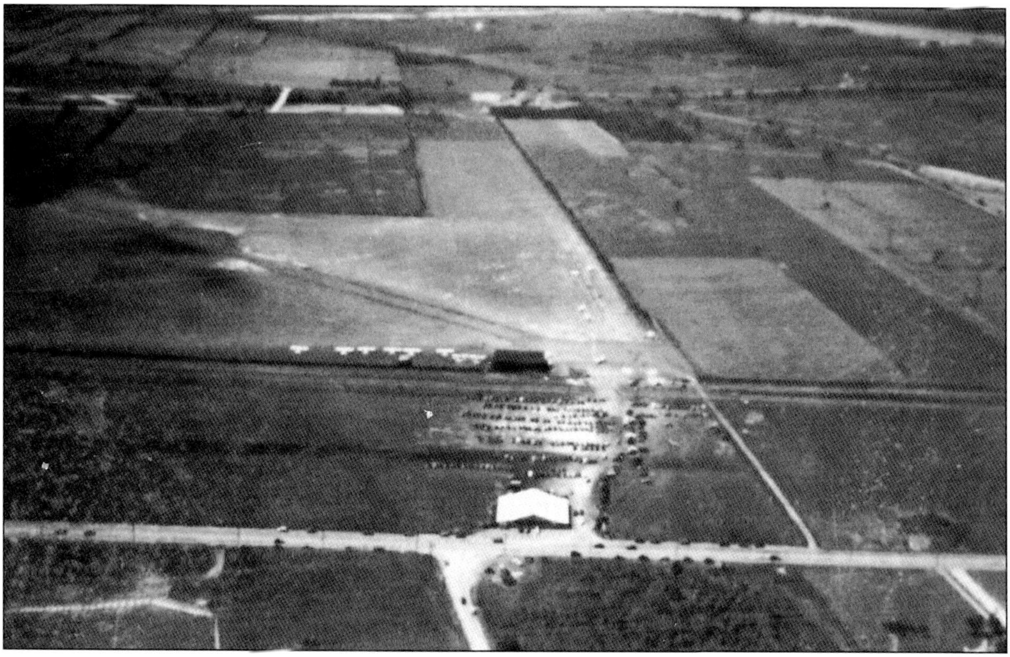

An aerial view of the western part of the town from Knoche Road (foreground) to the Niagara River (top of photo) in 1941. Bell Airport can be seen just beyond Military Road. Popular air shows were held here for many years.

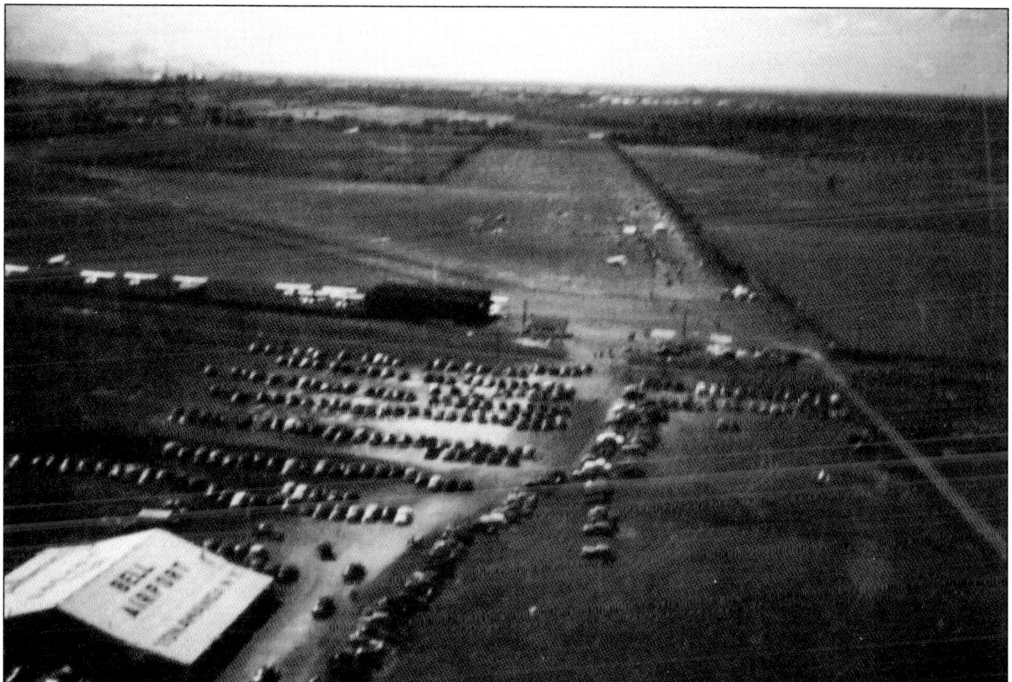

The view west over Bell Airport in 1941. The landing strip ran northeast to southwest. This airport was built just west of Military Road at the end of Knoche Road by the Consolidated Aircraft Corp. in 1929. It was a privately operated airport when it closed in 1952.

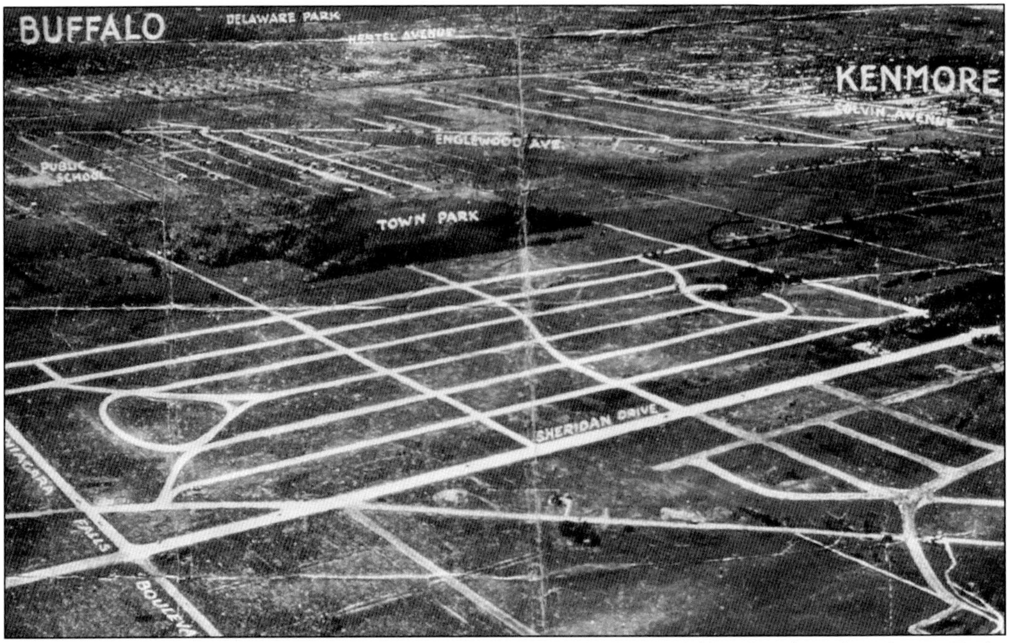

A 1930 aerial view of the former Curtiss airfield area, which would be developed as Curtis Park. Those streets are drawn in, to be constructed many years later. Sheridan Drive was opened in 1925. The town park (Lincoln Park) had yet to be developed in 1930. The public school shown is the Kenilworth area's Abraham Lincoln School.

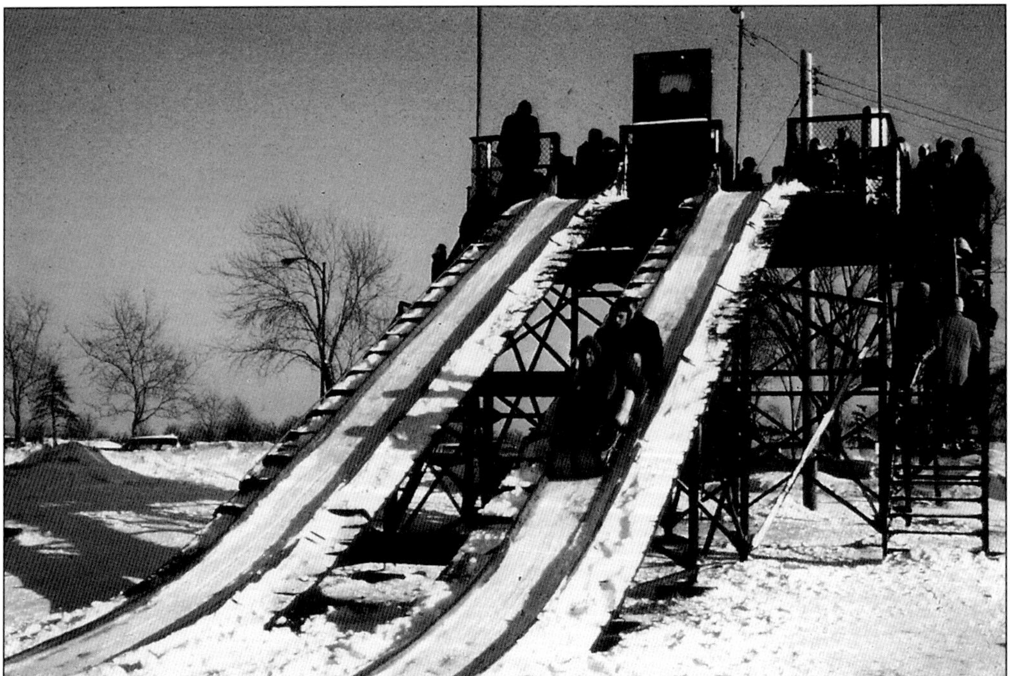

The toboggan run that stood for many years in Sheridan Park, west of the creek. The town provides a wide variety of other winter activities in the 1990s. This photograph was taken in March 1963.

Six

The Changing Landscape

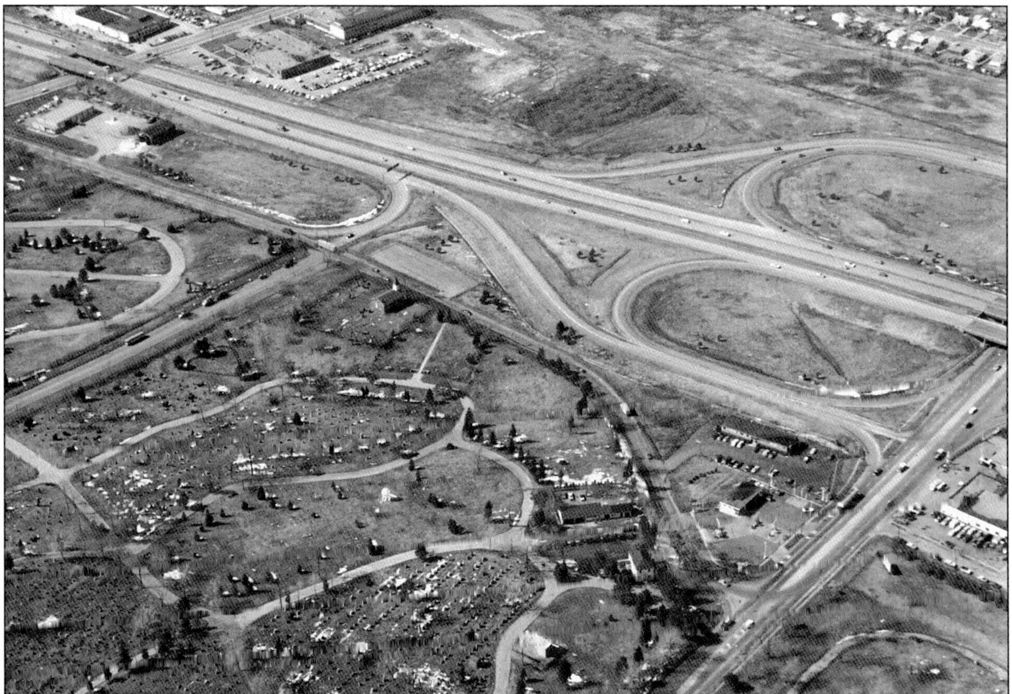

The Elmwood and Delaware Avenue exit from I-190, *c.* 1985. The Mt. Olivet Cemetery is in the left foreground. The Tonawanda-Kenmore Historical Building is in the 1849 church facing Knoche Road.

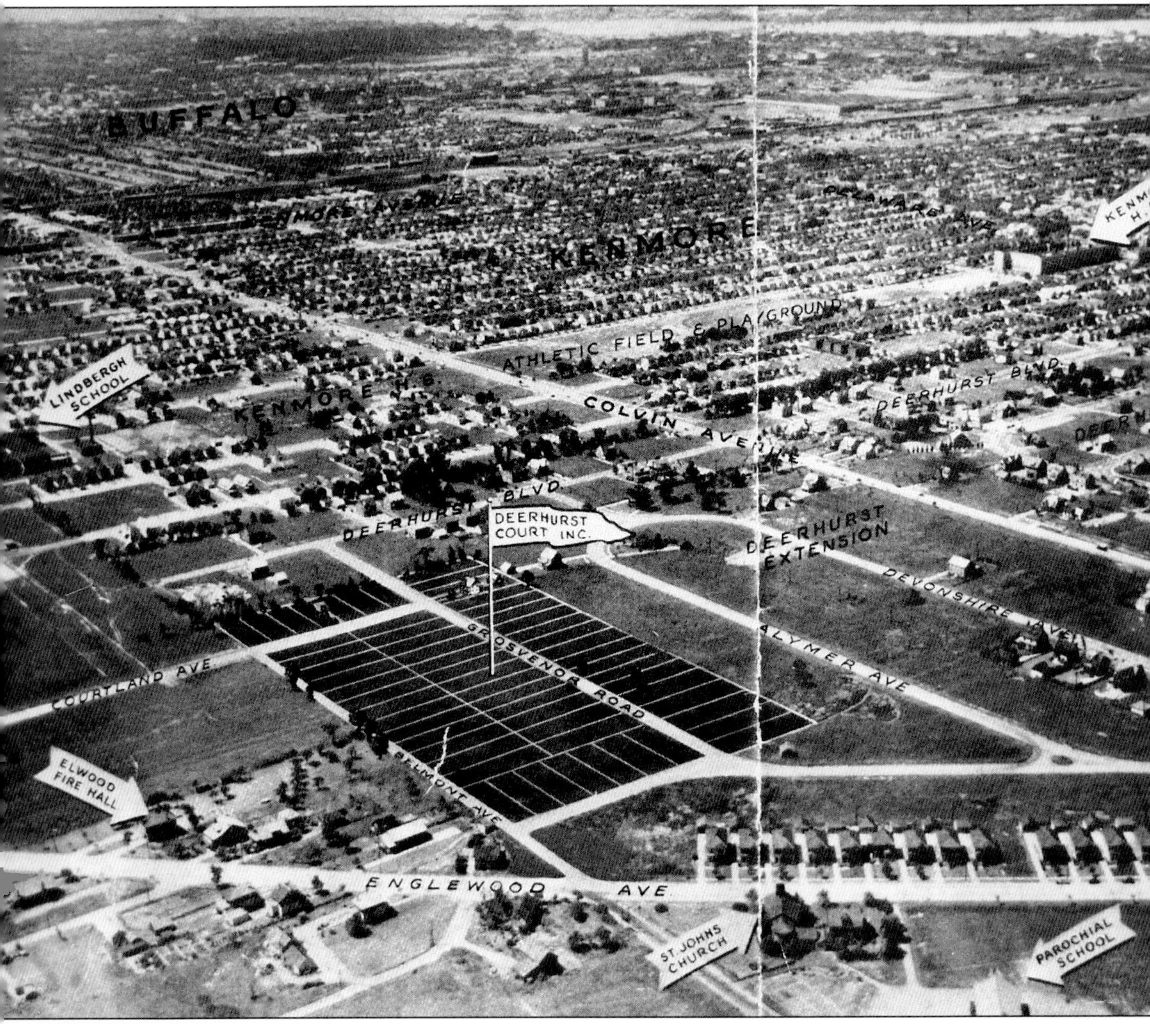

A view southwest toward Kenmore, *c.* 1937. The eastern extension of the Deerhurst Park development was just underway. Note the street name changes: Alymer became Dorset, Courtland dropped the "u," and Devonshire became a road. The original Bell Aircraft plant on Elmwood Avenue can be seen at upper right. The Niagara River is at the top of the photograph.

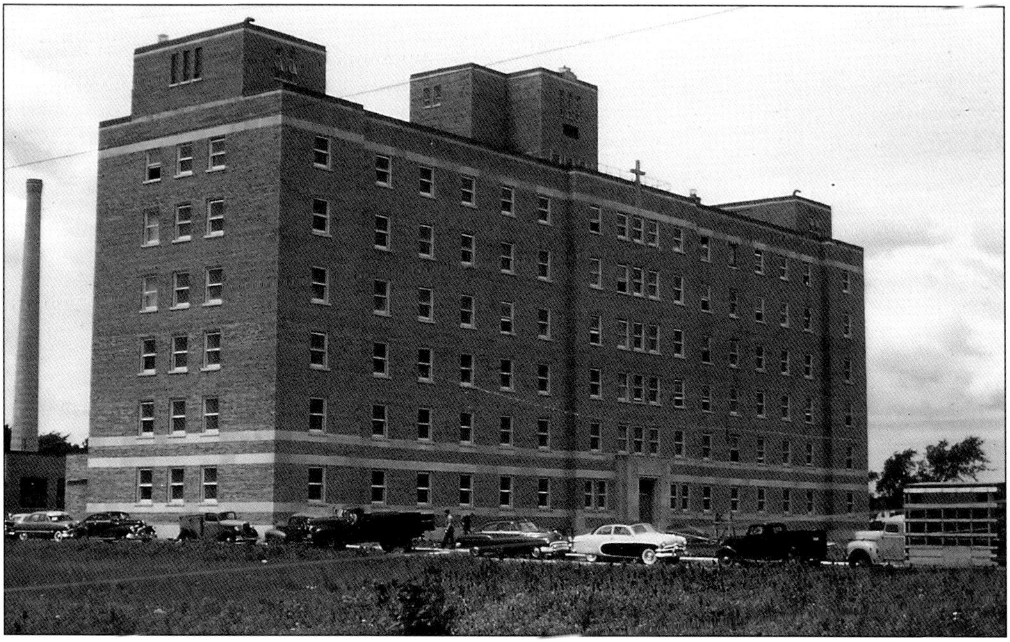

Kenmore Mercy Hospital. This original center portion facing Elmwood Avenue has been expanded many times over the years. The hospital, which opened in 1951 after five years of community fund-raising, is run by The Sisters of Mercy, who had living quarters on the top floor. The smokestack at left is part of the powerhouse.

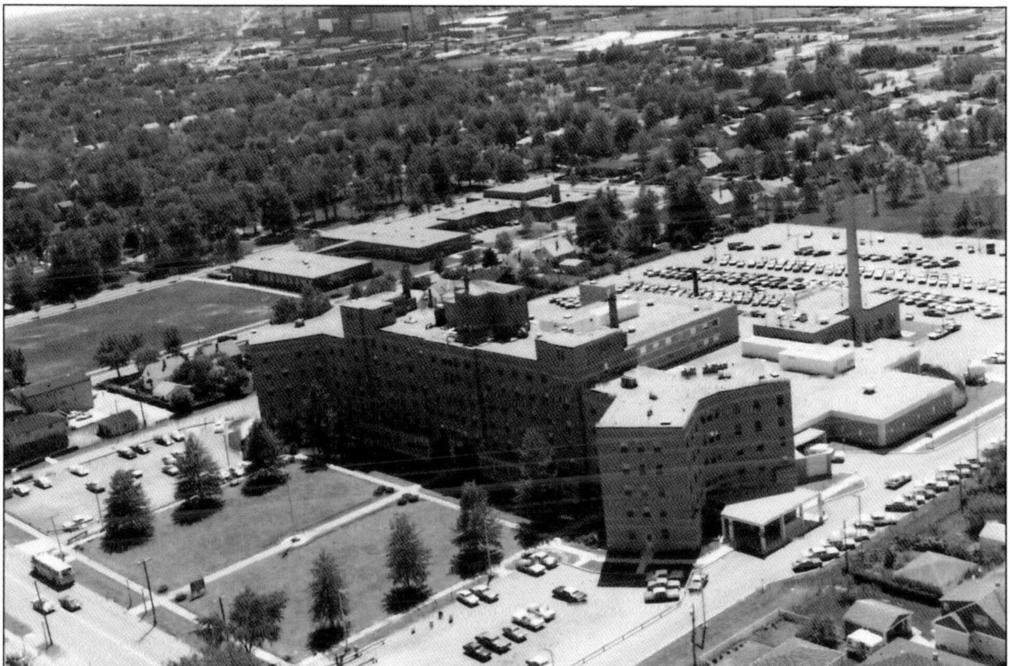

A view southwest over Kenmore Mercy Hospital, June 3, 1976. The original center portion of the building opened in 1951. The hospital is still administered by The Sisters of Mercy. (WNYHI)

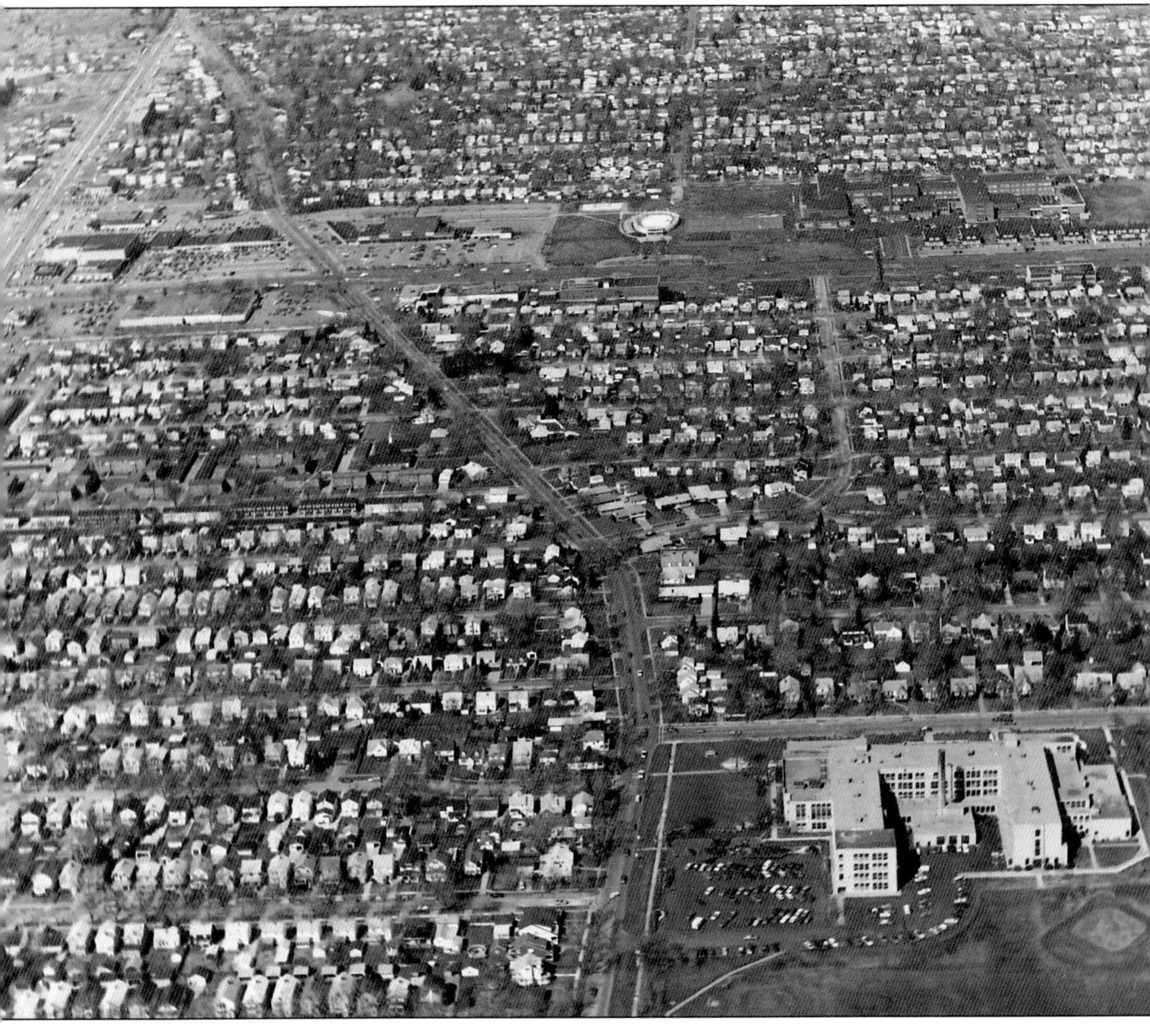

A *c.* 1985 view north along Delaware Road. Kenmore West High School, opened in 1940, is in the right foreground facing Highland Avenue. Sheridan Plaza, Delaware Pool, and the Herbert Hoover School are in the middle distance. The town's Aquatic Center replaced Delaware Pool in 1993.

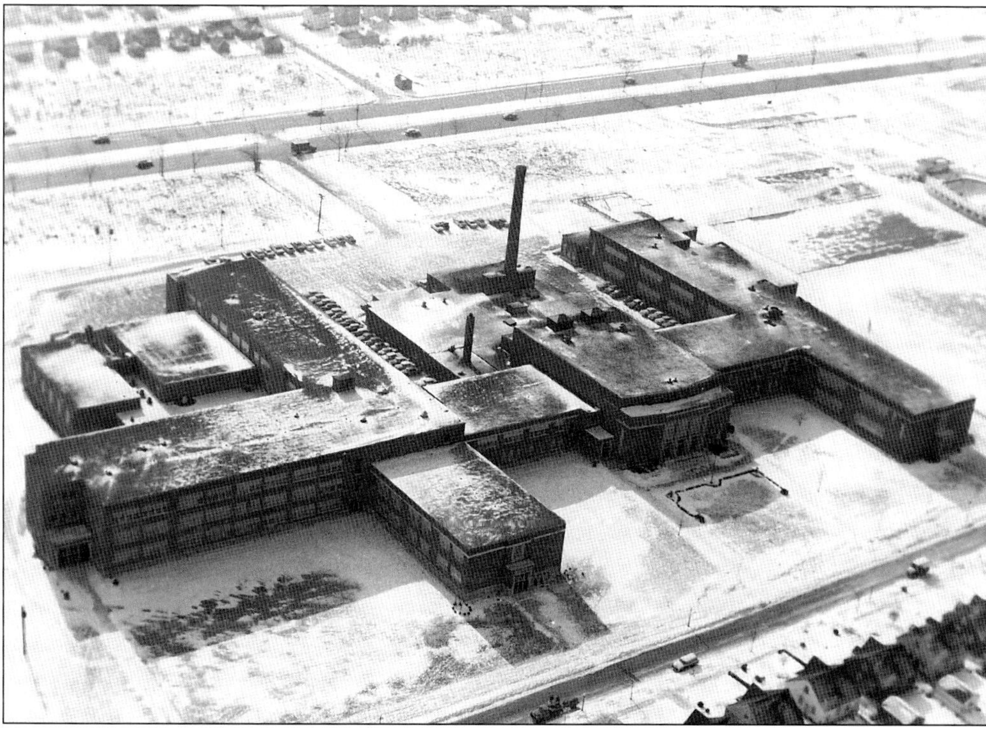

The Herbert Hoover School. This school, facing Thorncliff Road, was dedicated by former President Herbert Clark Hoover in October 1951. Pictured in this late 1950s photograph are the newly completed junior high on the left and the elementary school at right. The familiar Sheridan Drive pedestrian overpass had not yet been erected.

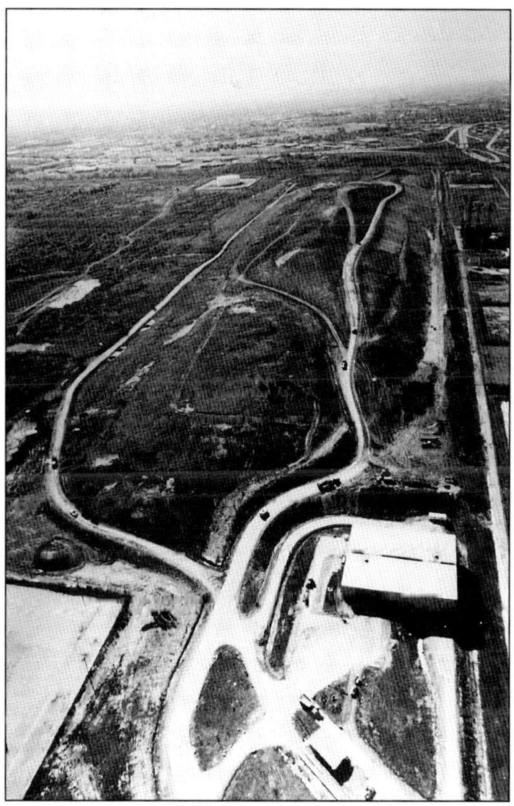

"Mt. Garbage," the Browning-Ferris dump, on May 13, 1987. The abandoned Ashland Oil Refinery is at far right; the interchange of the Niagara Thruway and the Elmer Youngmann Highway is in the distance. (WNYHI)

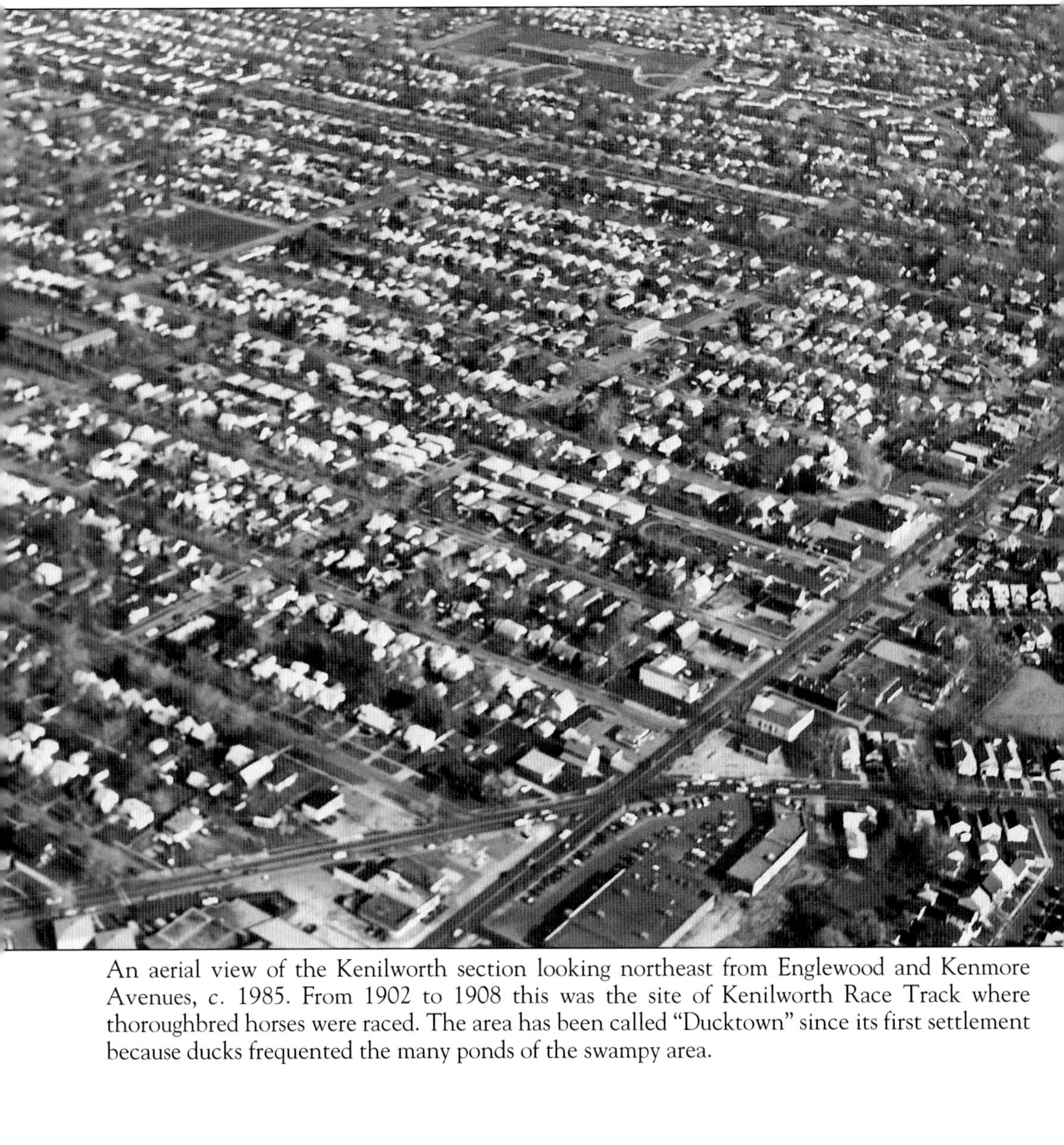

An aerial view of the Kenilworth section looking northeast from Englewood and Kenmore Avenues, c. 1985. From 1902 to 1908 this was the site of Kenilworth Race Track where thoroughbred horses were raced. The area has been called "Ducktown" since its first settlement because ducks frequented the many ponds of the swampy area.

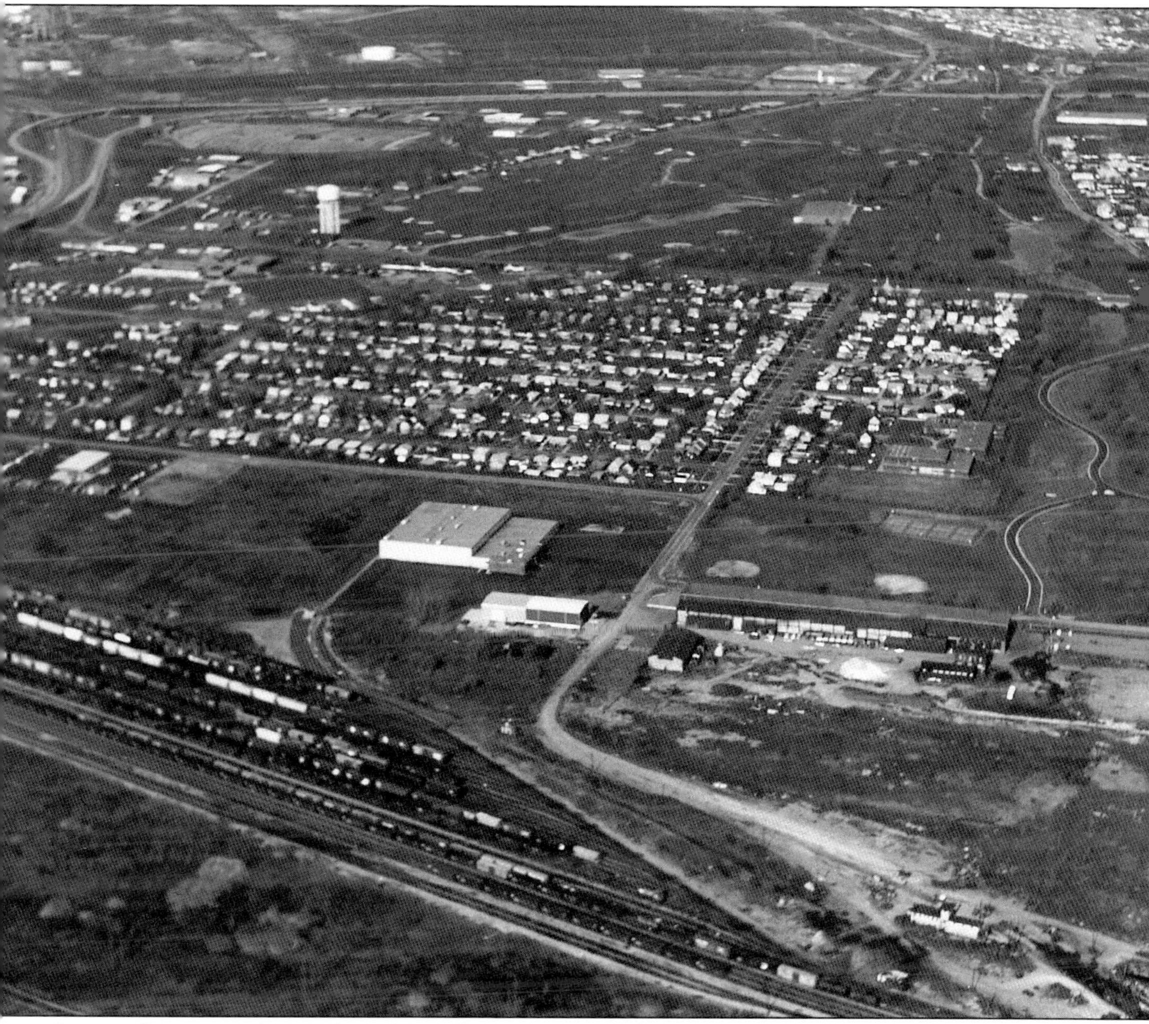

An aerial view northwest from Conrail's Kenmore Yard, *c.* 1985. The recreation and highway departments building (formerly Lake Erie Engineering) is at right along Woodward Avenue. This building was destroyed in a spectacular fire in 1995. Sheridan Park is in the upper part of this photograph. Two Mile Creek begins near the rail yard, but is piped underground until it reaches the Praxair property (at right), where it flows into the park and on to the Niagara River.

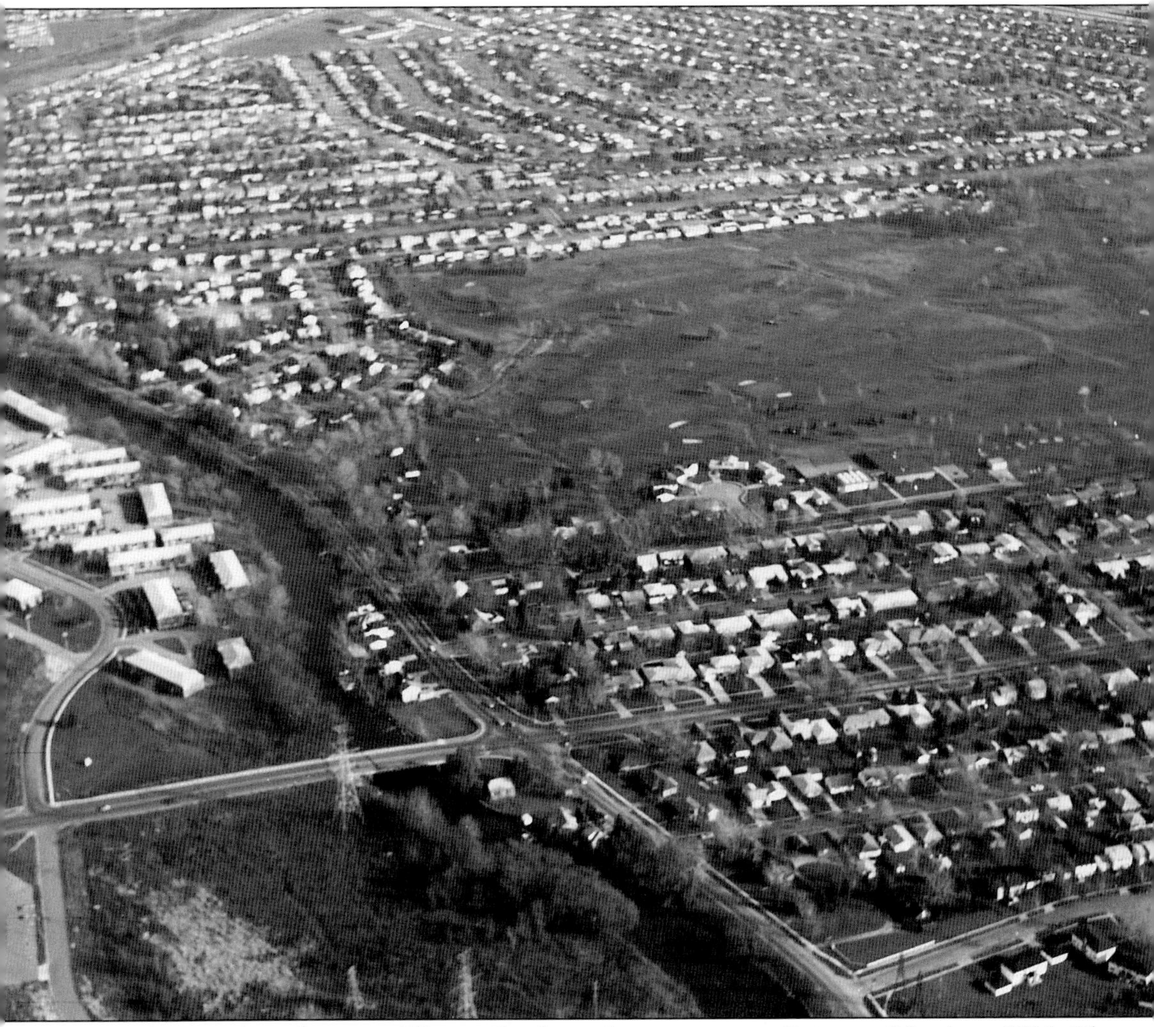

Colvin Boulevard crosses Ellicott Creek at the entrance to Raintree Island, *c.* 1985. The Brighton Golf Course is surrounded by homes built after World War II, although a few nineteenth-century houses still stand along Ellicott Creek Road.

Seven

Getting Around

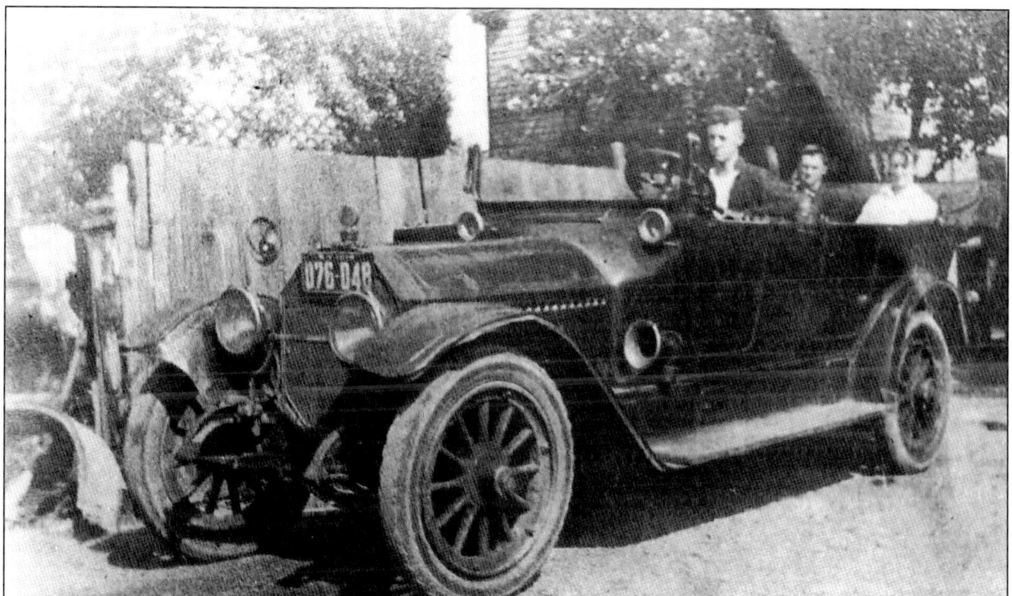

John D. Sullivan, "pilot" of a Locomobile jitney in 1914. This large automobile was one of many used to transport workers to and from River Road industries prior to 1936. One-way fare was 5¢.

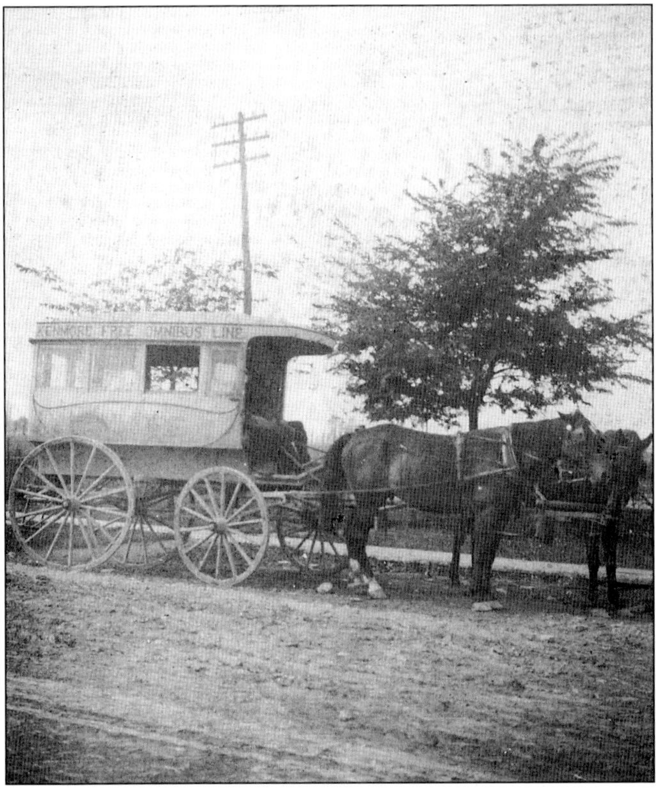

Frank Stillwell's Kenmore Free Omnibus Line, *c.* 1889. Before the trolley line opened, Frank Stillwell operated this omnibus line to transport people between the pioneer village and the New York Central belt line railroad passenger stop at Delaware Avenue.

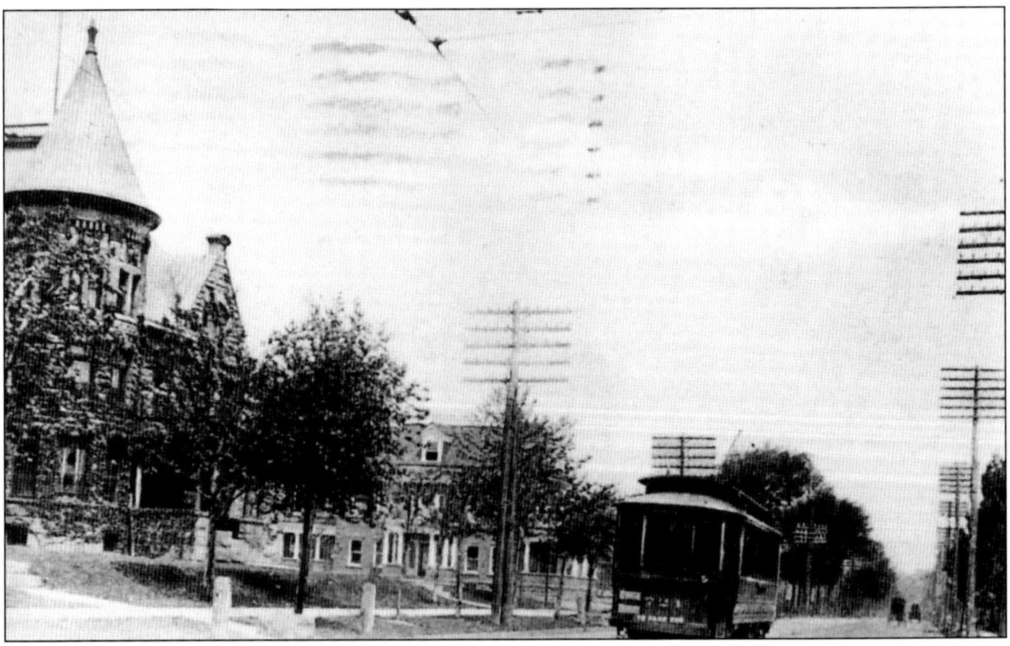

A trolley from Tonawanda slowing for the turn onto Kenmore Avenue in 1908. The George Eberhardt home is nearing completion just across West Hazeltine from his father's turreted stone home, built fifteen years earlier. Note the stone hitching posts for the Fred and LPA Eberhardt homes facing Delaware Avenue. (WNYHI)

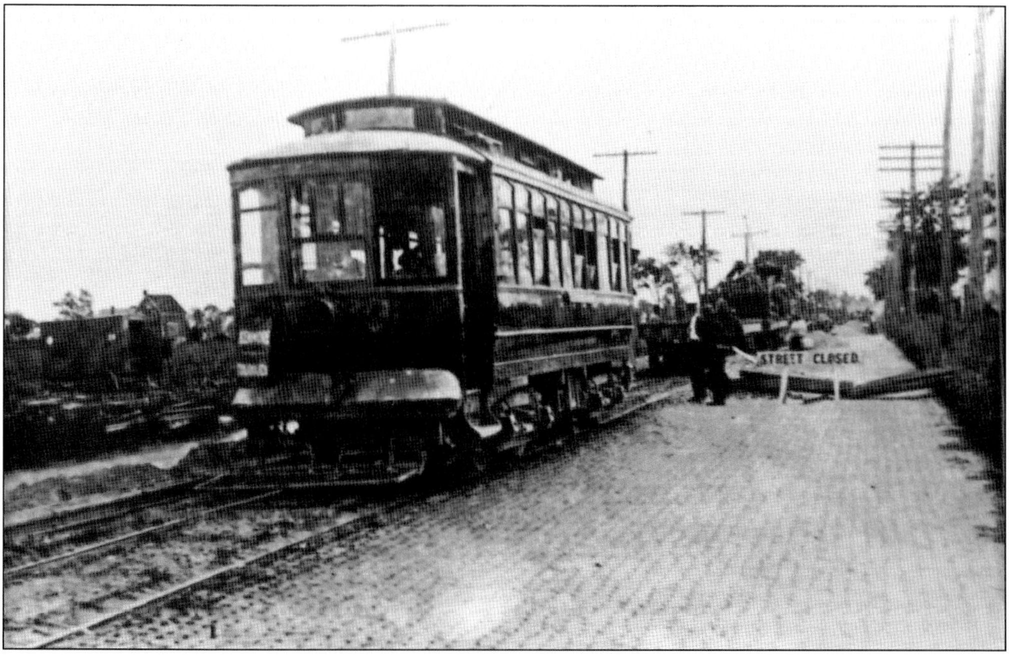

A *c.* 1913 photograph of the trolley tracks near Mount St. Mary Academy under reconstruction by the International Railway Company. The Kenmore & Tonawanda Electric Railway laid tracks along the length of Delaware Avenue in 1893.

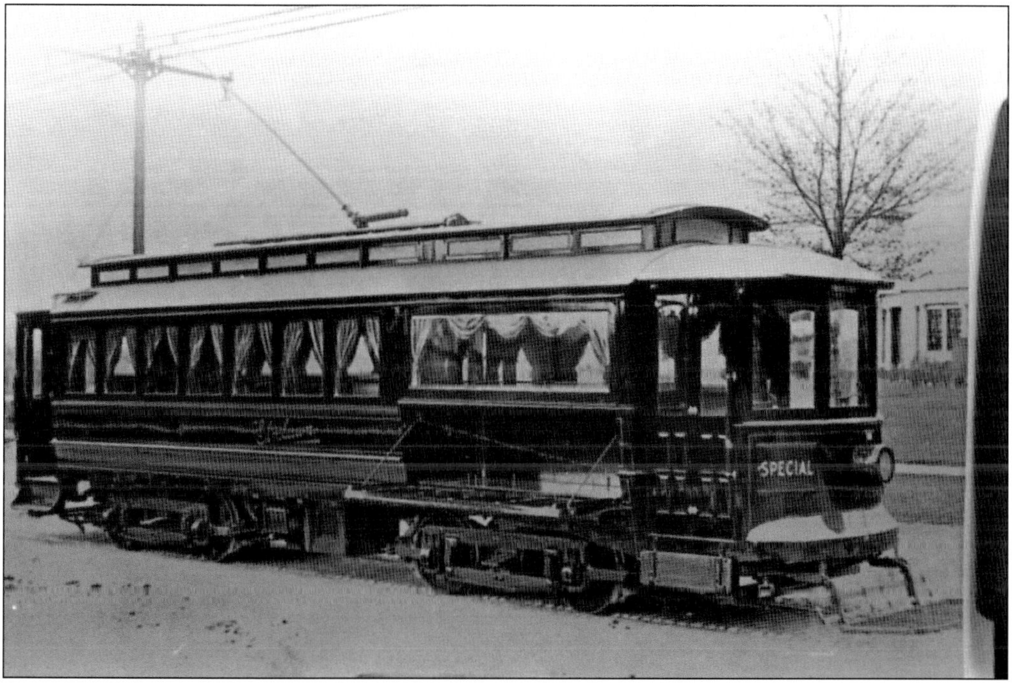

One of the two International Railway Company streetcars especially equipped for funerals. A funeral party could accompany the casket directly to Elmlawn Cemetery, where there was a spur to accommodate the trolley during the burial service. No auto procession or police escort was necessary.

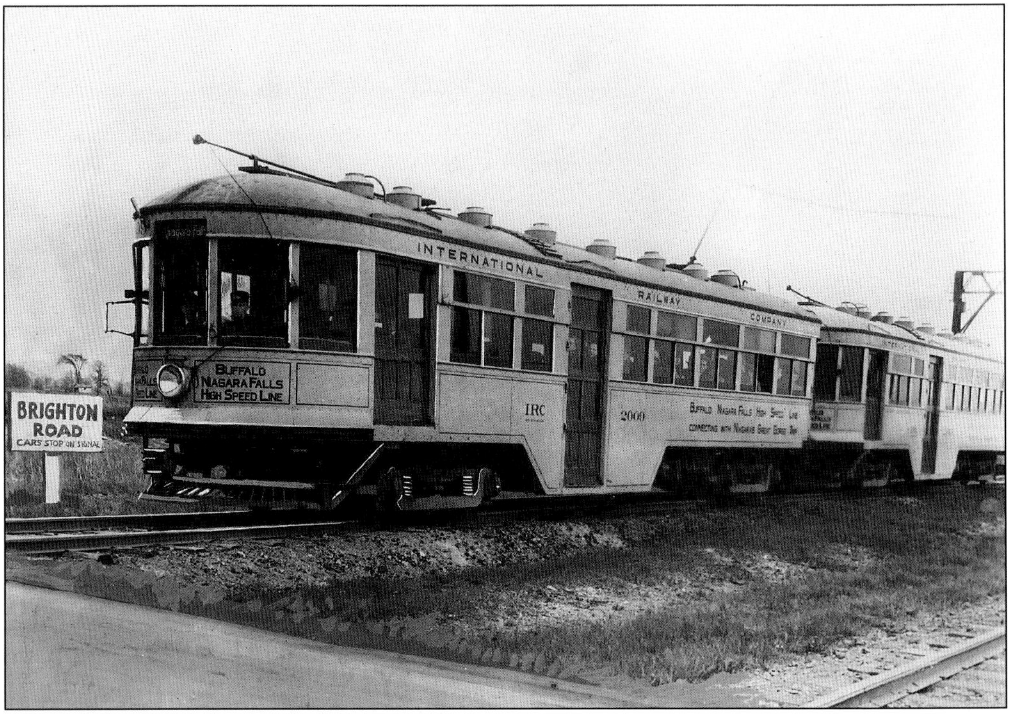

A doubleheader at the Brighton Road crossing where the tracks paralleled the Erie Railroad. The IRC ran a high-speed service to Niagara Falls from 1918 to 1937.

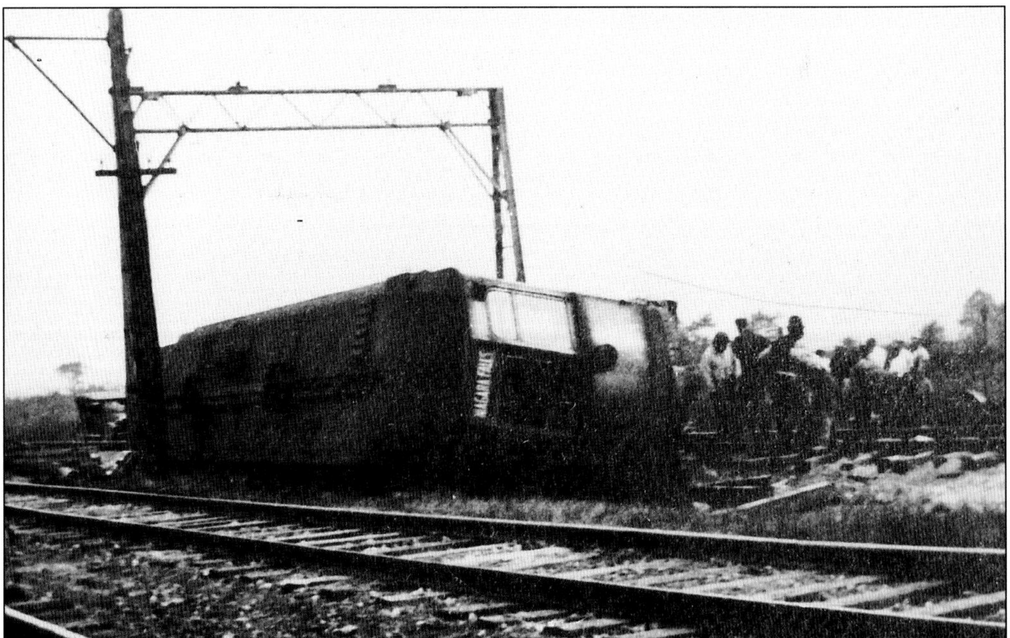

A derailed Niagara Falls high-speed trolley unit. The trolley was literally blown off the rails when the track was dynamited in August 1922 during a bitter strike by operating employees against the IRC. The late-night incident occurred just north of the Colvin-Belmont grade crossing.

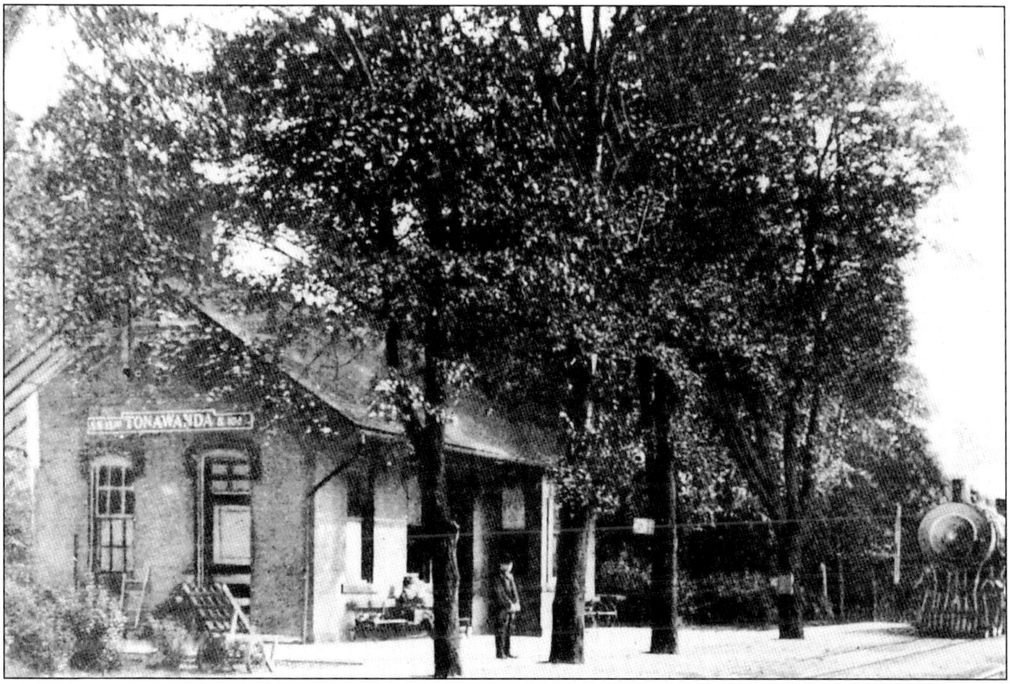

Tonawanda's railroad station on Main Street at Fletcher and Grove Streets, a regular stop on the New York Central's Niagara Falls line. Built in 1870, it was the town's second railroad station, and served until the tracks were relocated in 1922. It later became the city library and now serves as home to The Historical Society of the Tonawandas, Inc. (WNYHI)

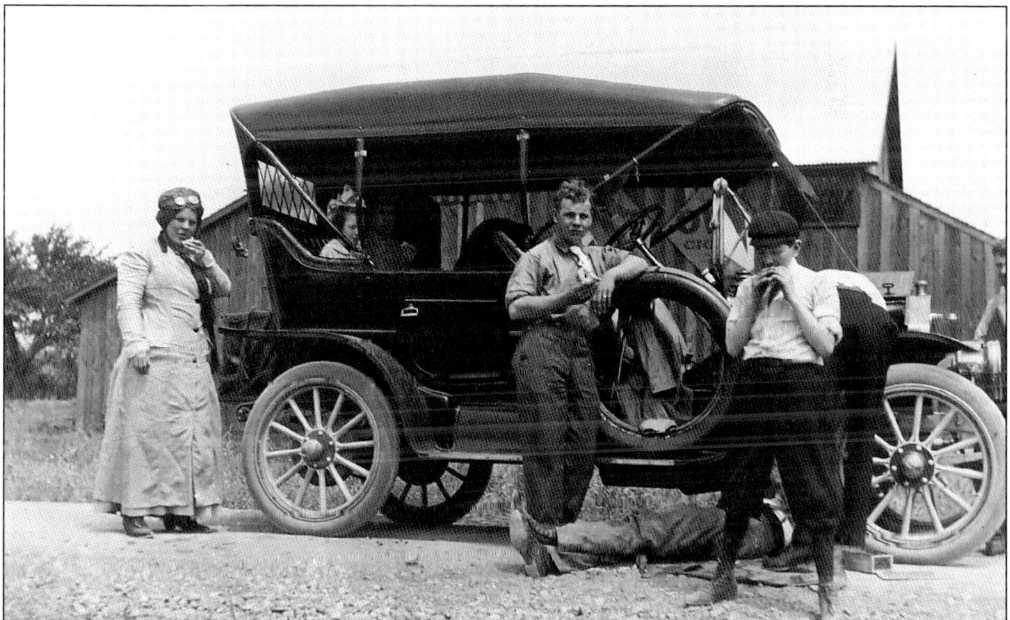

The Eberhardt family of Kenmore on an outing with their 1910 Buick. The woman with goggles is Miss Florence Eberhardt and the man leaning on the tire is Louis K. Eberhardt, both children of "L.P.A." Note the right-hand drive of this 30 horsepower, brass-trimmed auto.

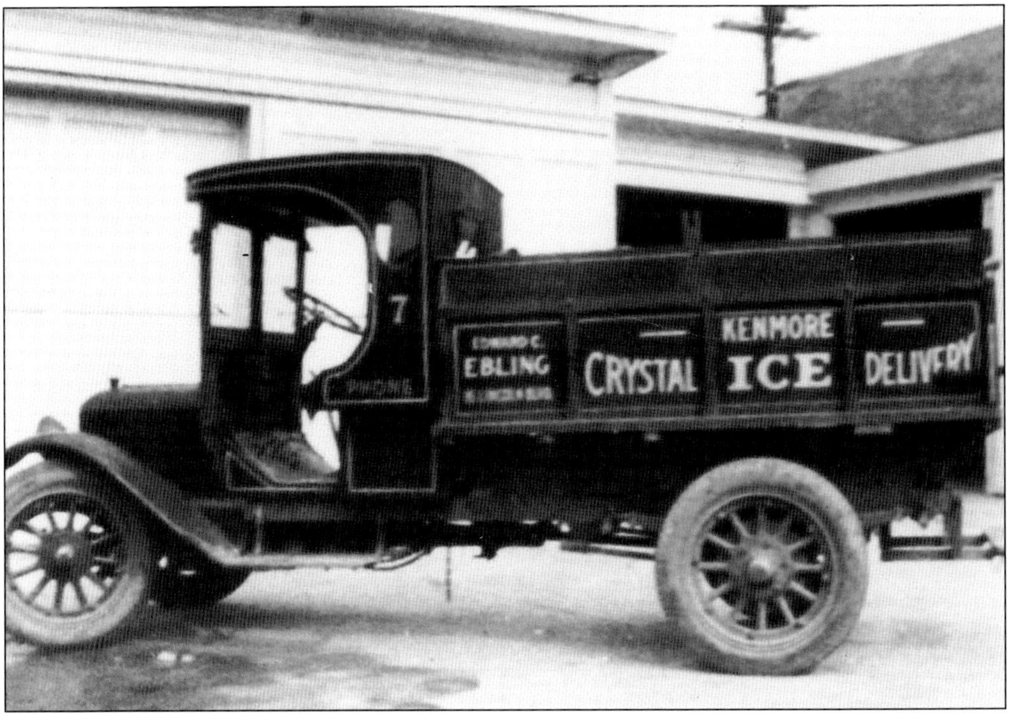

A delivery truck from Edward C. Ebling's Kenmore Coal & Ice Company, *c.* 1920. The company, located at 16 Lincoln Boulevard, also provided carting and storage service. It was one of several area companies which provided local delivery of fuel for coal furnaces and blocks of ice for refrigeration.

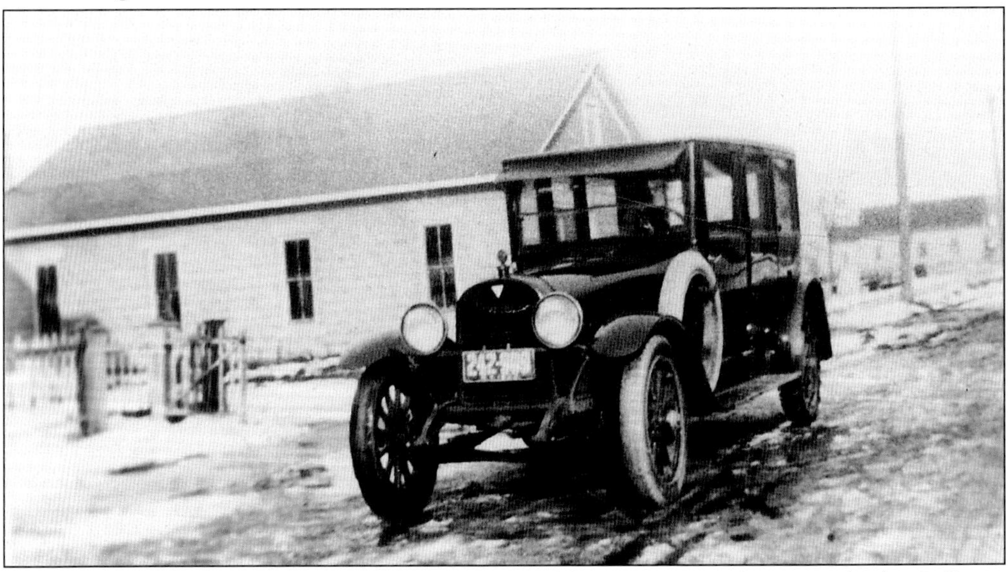

The 1923 Hudson 6-cylinder 7-passenger sedan used by George DeGlopper and John Sullivan in their jitney business along River Road. In an interview, "Sully" said that one of his cars once carried forty-eight men at once, most hanging outside the car, sitting on the hood and headlights, standing on the running boards, and lying on the roof. It is shown here parked near the American-Serbian Club on Tonawanda Street.

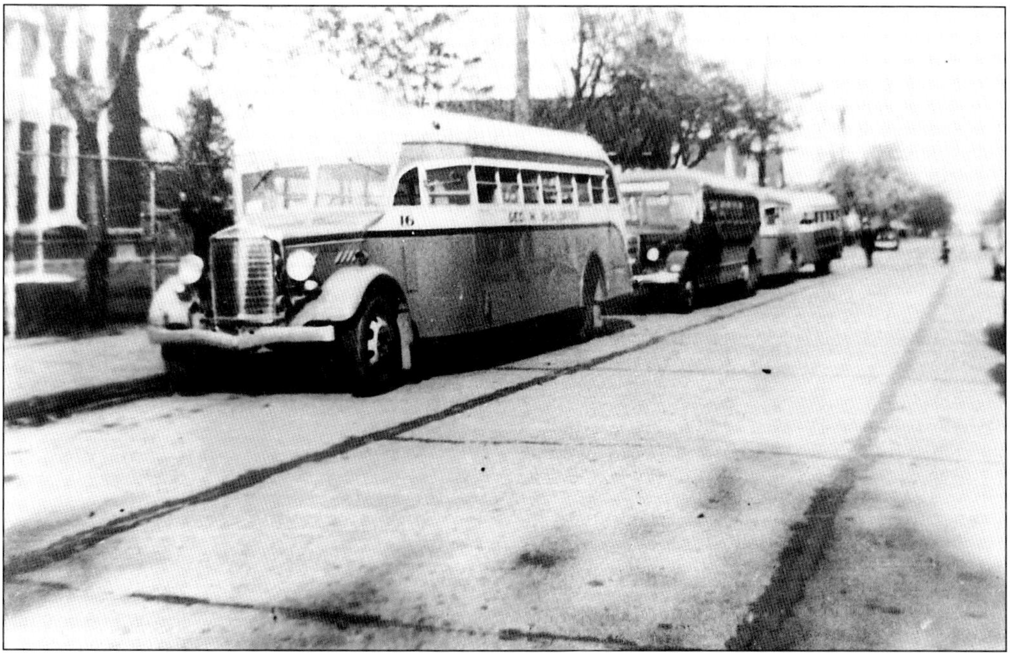

The DeGlopper bus fleet parked alongside the Harding Elementary School on Edgar Avenue, *c.* 1945. Kenmore schools also utilized Wooly Bus Lines until the district established its own transportation system.

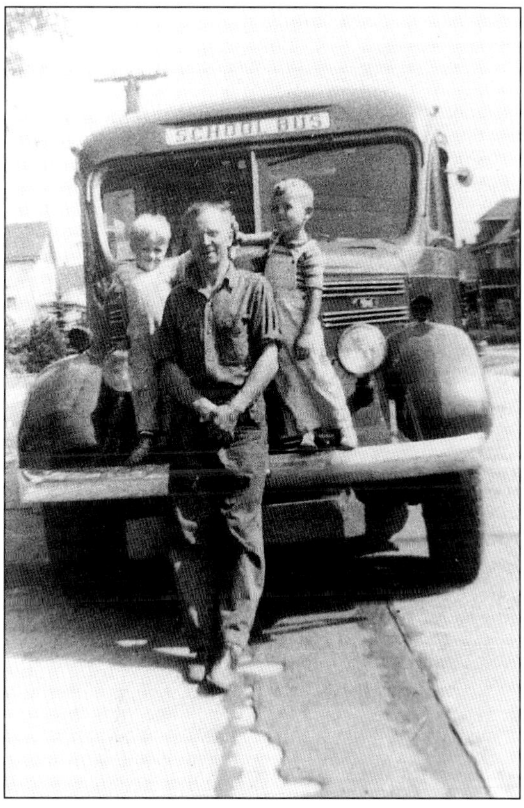

George W. DeGlopper and grandsons H. William and Donald R. DeGlopper with one of his early busses at 20 Roswell Avenue, *c.* 1945. George began the Grand Island Transit Company in 1936.

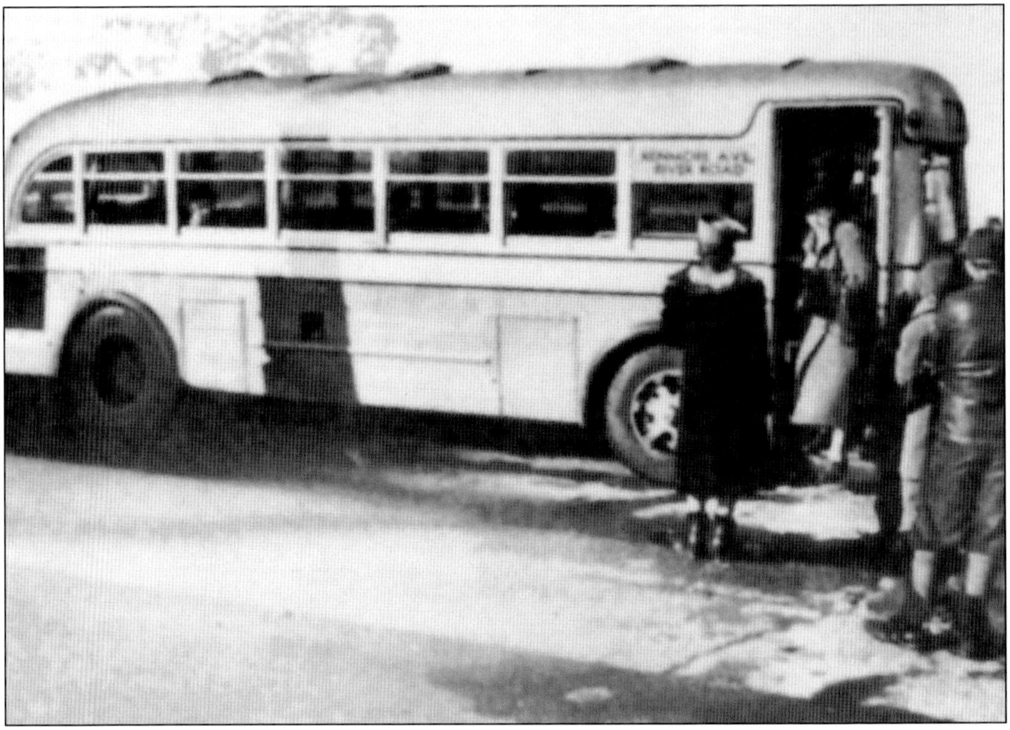

One of the "shorty" busses on the IRC Kenmore Avenue route. This route provided transportation for factory workers in the River Road area to their homes in Kenmore and North Buffalo. The fare in 1948 was 10¢ each way .

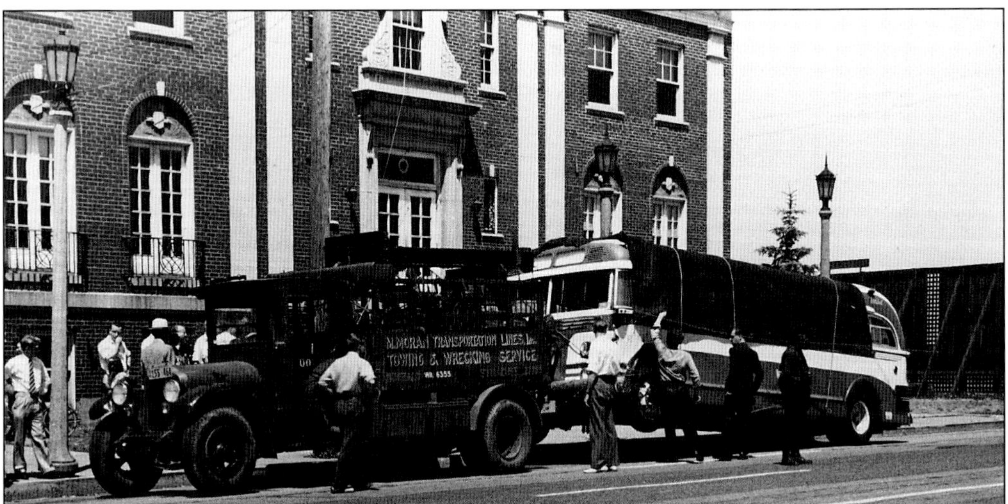

A bus being towed, *c.* 1939. Busses weren't always reliable, but they were less expensive to run then the trolley lines. Memorial Hall (1929) became the new home of the American Legion and the Veterans of Foreign Wars.

Passengers on a bus fitted with "stand-sits." In 1943, in order to accommodate more passengers during the busy wartime commutes, a few IRC busses were fitted with uncomfortable wooden benches known as "sit-stands," or worse, by their unhappy occupants. The author remembers using them on the Woodward Bus route which ran along Elmwood Avenue. (WNYHI)

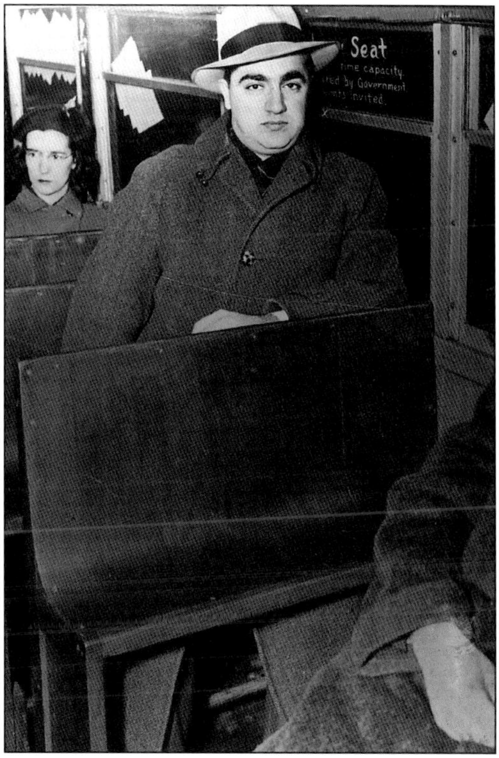

The Guenther-Dusel Hardware store and Werner's Market at Delaware Avenue and Courier, c. 1930. Delivery service was important to the relatively far-flung homes of a growing suburbia. Many families could not afford a car during the Great Depression.

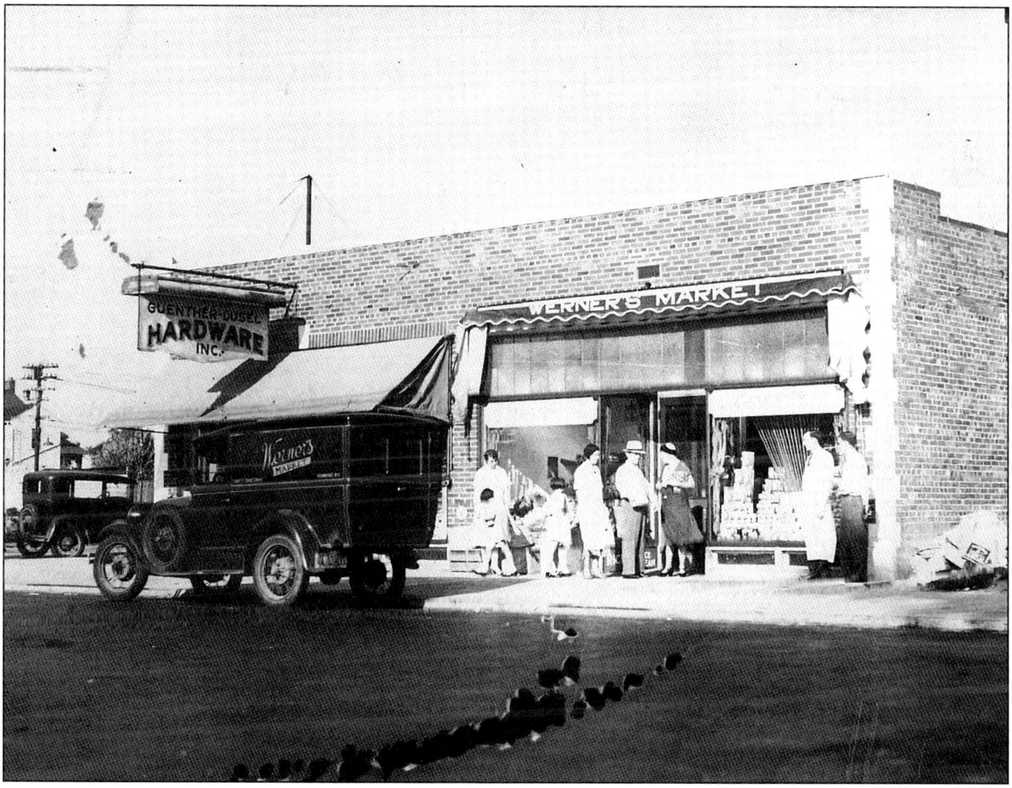

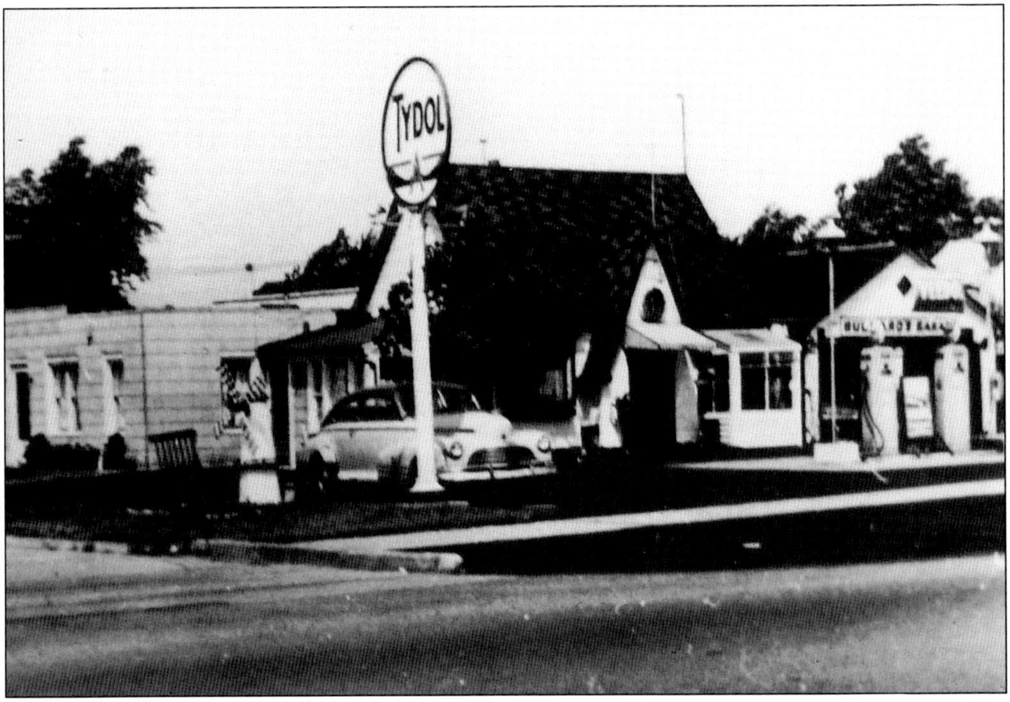

Bullard's Garage on Elmwood Avenue at Pullman Avenue, c. 1946. The building houses Marrale Motors today. Tydol gasoline stations had a national corporate architectural style. Gasoline prices hovered around 25¢ a gallon for many years after World War II.

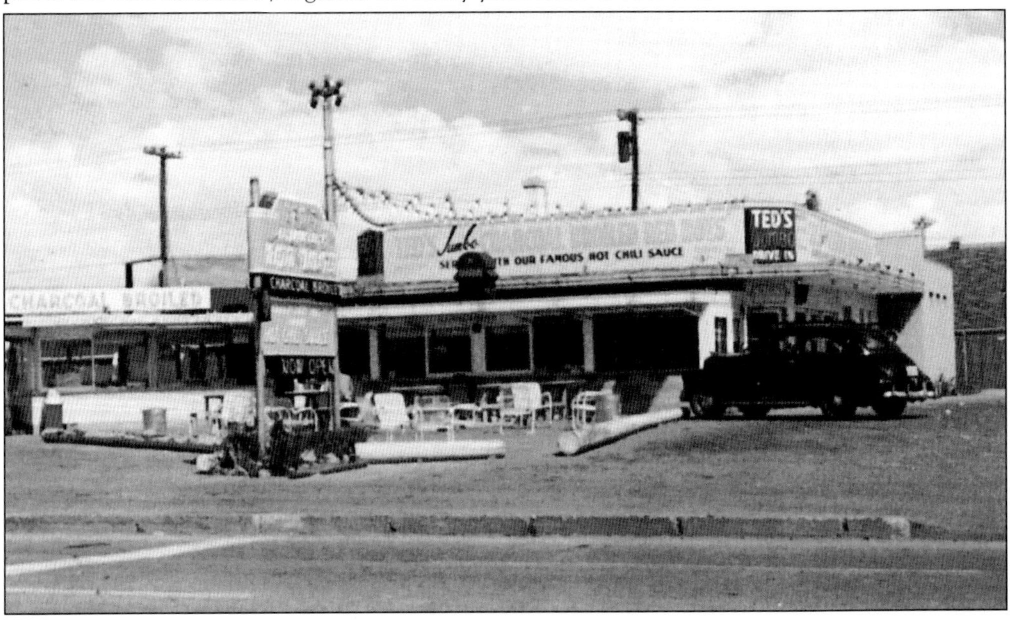

Ted's Jumbo Charcoal Broiled Red Hots, served at this site on Sheridan Drive since 1948. You could enjoy a charcoal dog with hot chili sauce and an order of fries while sitting out front watching the latest tail-finned DeSotos and Studebakers cruise by. Wash it down with a nickel Coke, then get back in your ten-year-old '46 Chevy and head west across the nearby Erie Railroad tracks toward Kenmore. (WNYHI)

Eight

Pulling Together

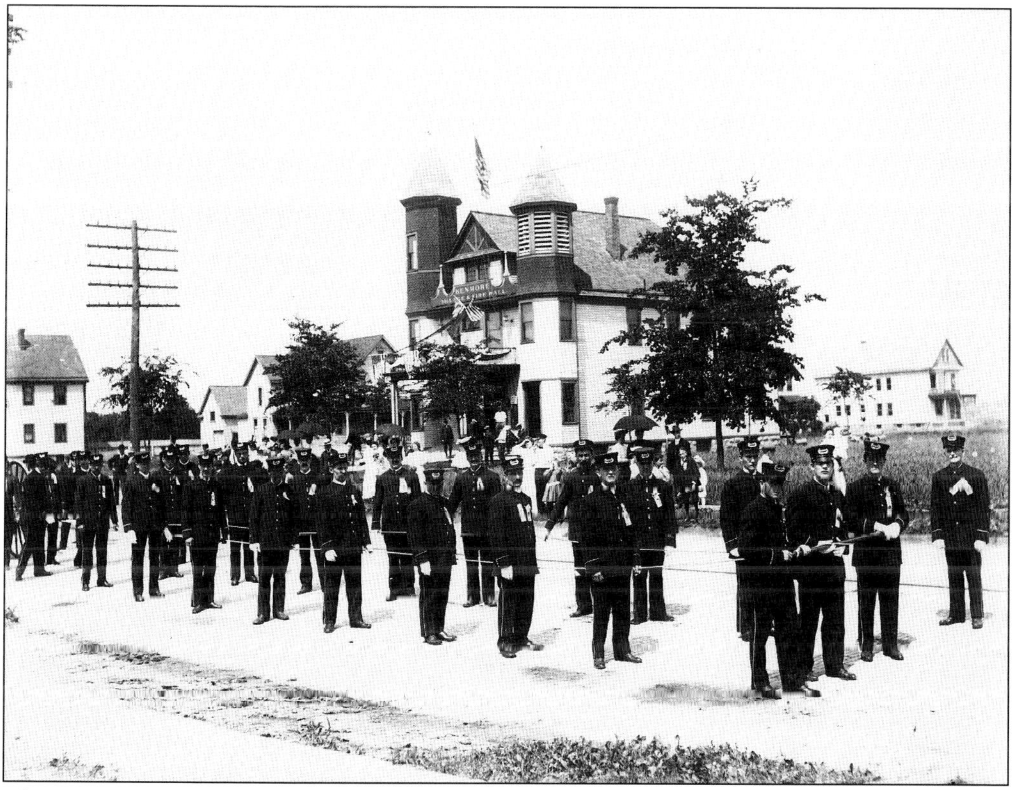

The Alert Hose Company lined up in front of Kenmore's Village and Fire Hall, 1904. The building was erected in 1903 at 2831 Delaware Avenue and served until 1929, when the present Nash Road fire hall was built. All fire equipment was hand-drawn until the first fire engine was purchased in 1919.

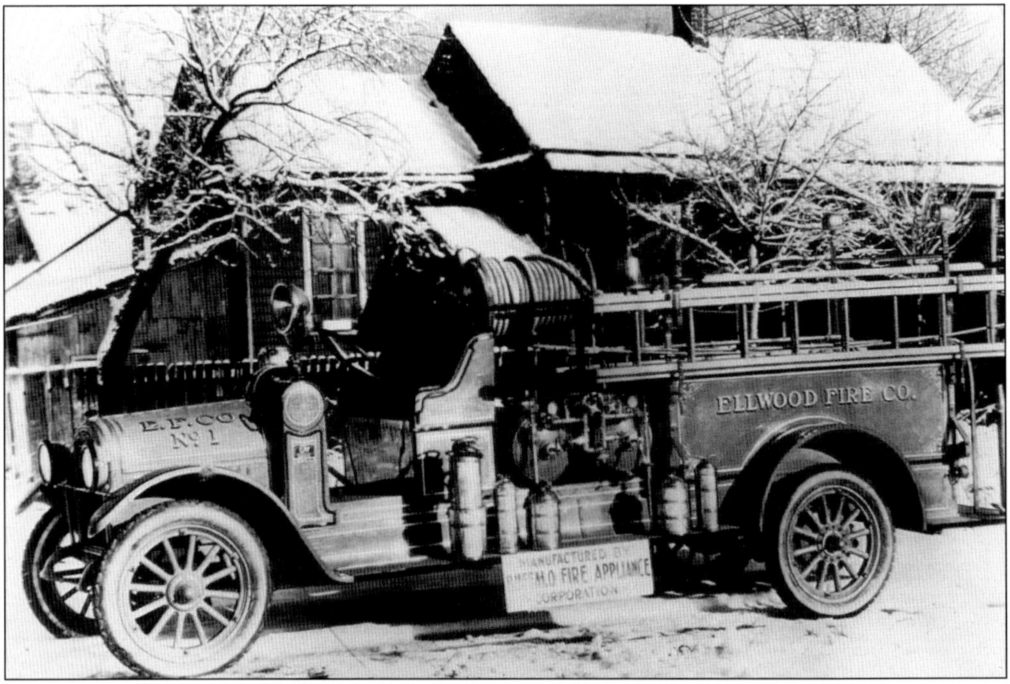

The chemical tank truck purchased by the Ellwood Volunteer Fire Company in 1924 from the Buffalo Fire Appliance Corporation for $3,250. In case of fire volunteers were summoned to the Englewood Avenue fire hall by the sound of a rim from a locomotive being hit by a sledge hammer. The rim hung on a tripod in front of the fire hall.

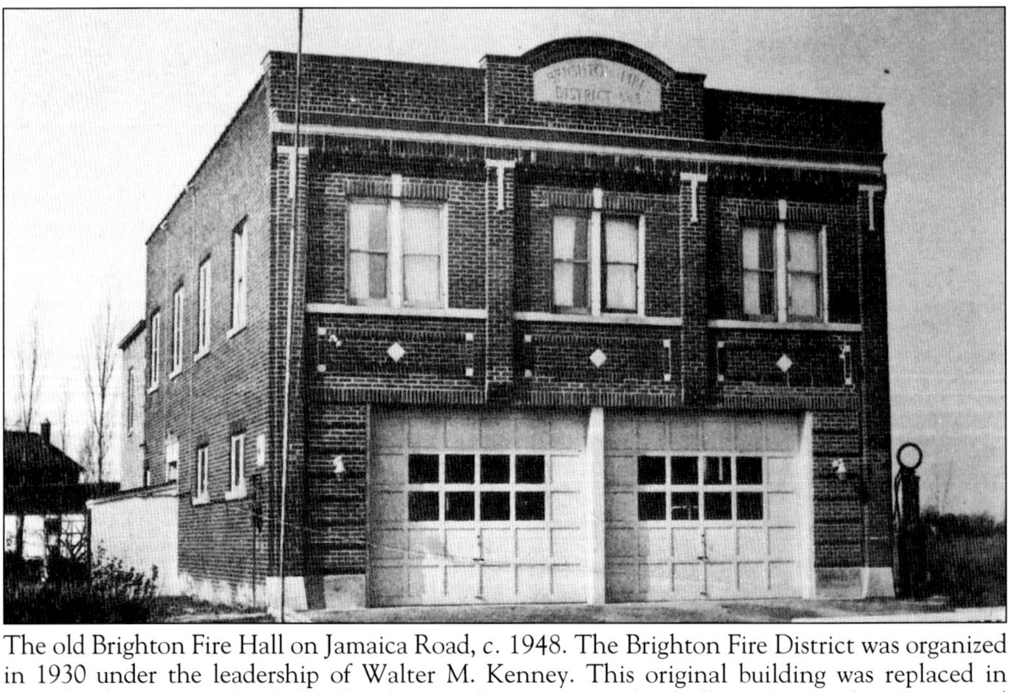

The old Brighton Fire Hall on Jamaica Road, c. 1948. The Brighton Fire District was organized in 1930 under the leadership of Walter M. Kenney. This original building was replaced in 1961 by the present fire hall. The district also maintains fire halls on McConkey Drive and Dexter Terrace.

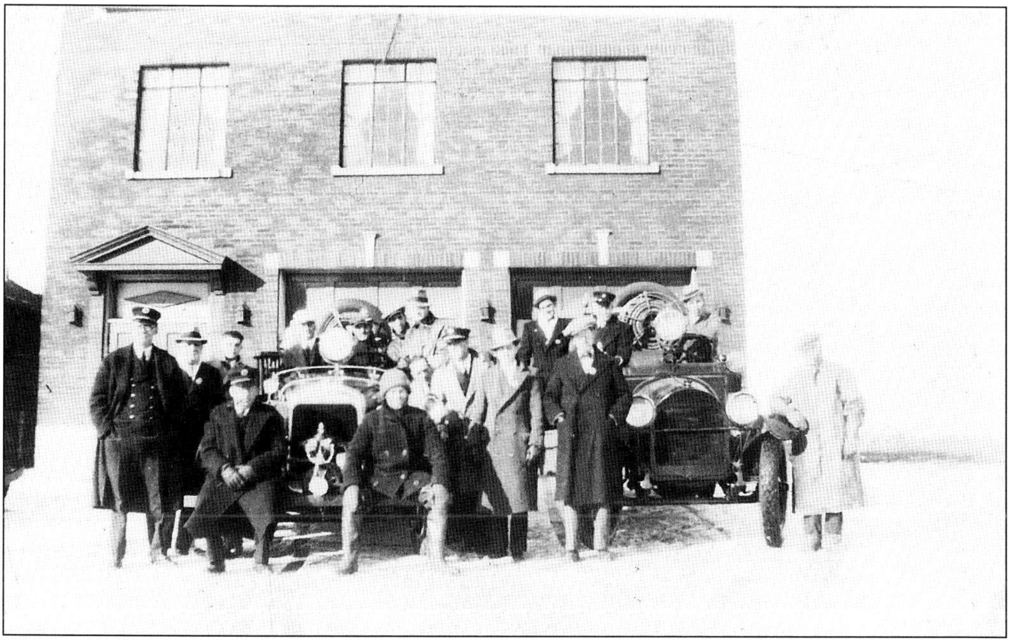

The Sheridan Park Volunteer Fire Company hall, December 30, 1934. Members of the fire company, which was organized in 1928, proudly show off their Stewart and Reo fire engines. The company began with a donated hand-pulled reel cart in 1929. (Sheridan Park VFD)

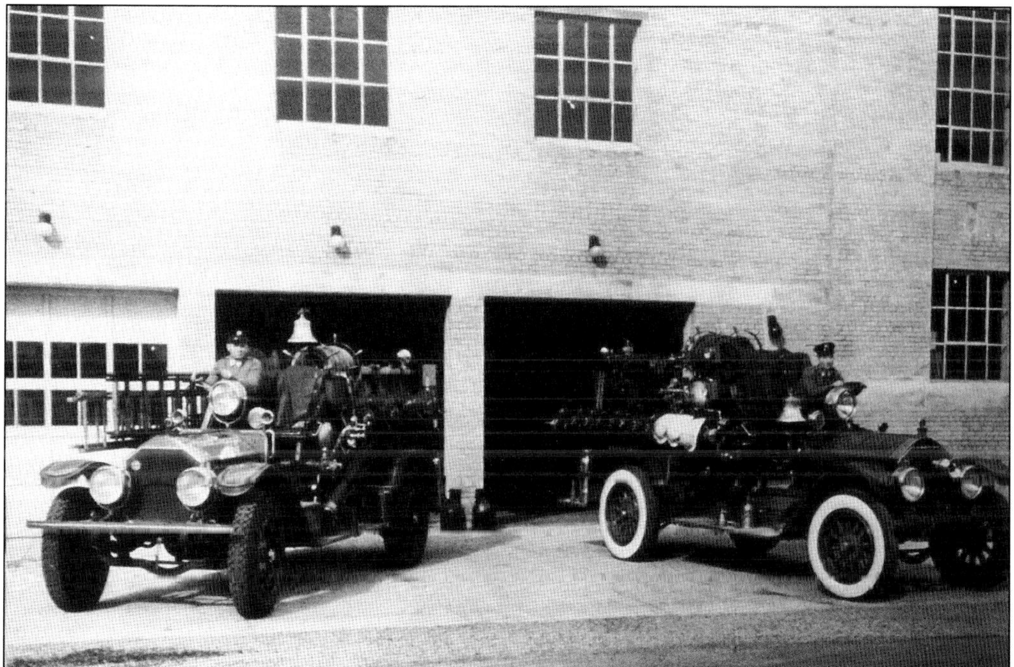

The Kenilworth Volunteer Fire Company hall on Maxwell Avenue. Two American La France pumpers are displayed outside the new building, erected in 1938 as a WPA project to replace an earlier building across the street.

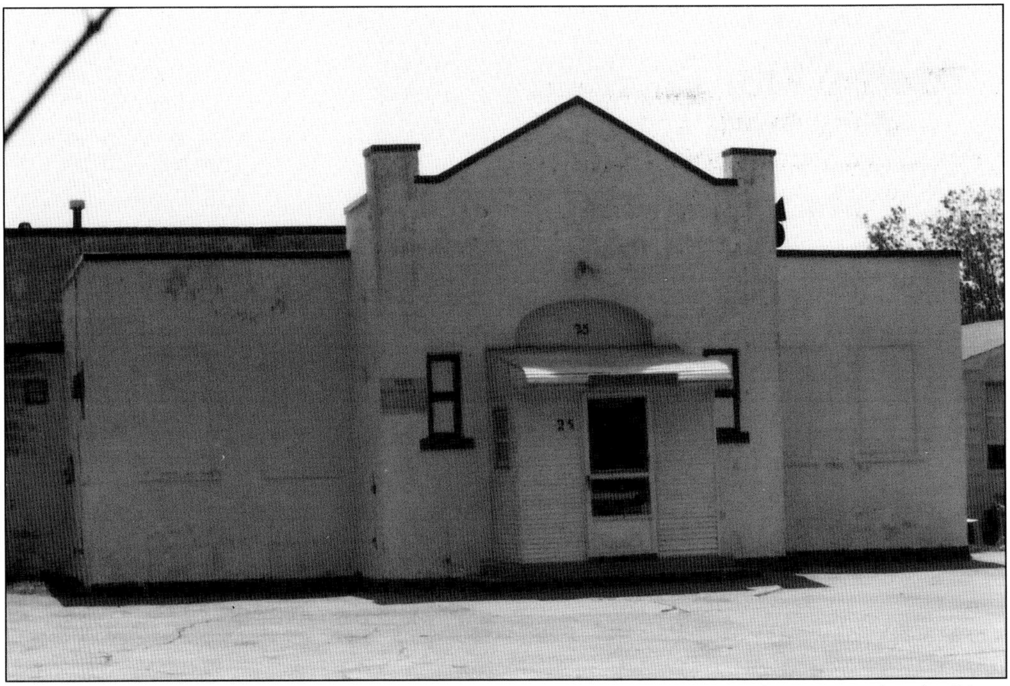

The "Town Lockup" on Roswell Avenue in the Riverside section of the town. This building was erected in 1921 as a jail for both town and village prisoners. The building also served as town court until 1930. Later it was used by the Boys Club, the Tonawanda-Kenmore Historical Society, and, after 1975, the Town Police Club.

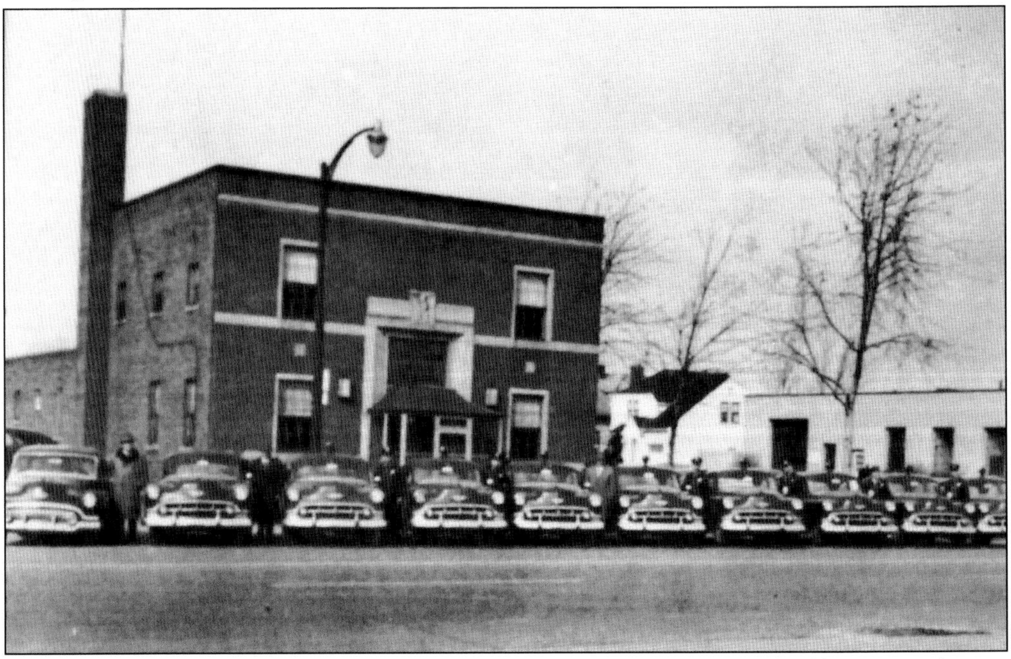

Town of Tonawanda police cars lined up in front of the headquarters building on Delaware Avenue at Westchester, 1953. Notice the "bubblegum" lights on top of the Chevrolet patrol cars. The building now houses a day-care center.

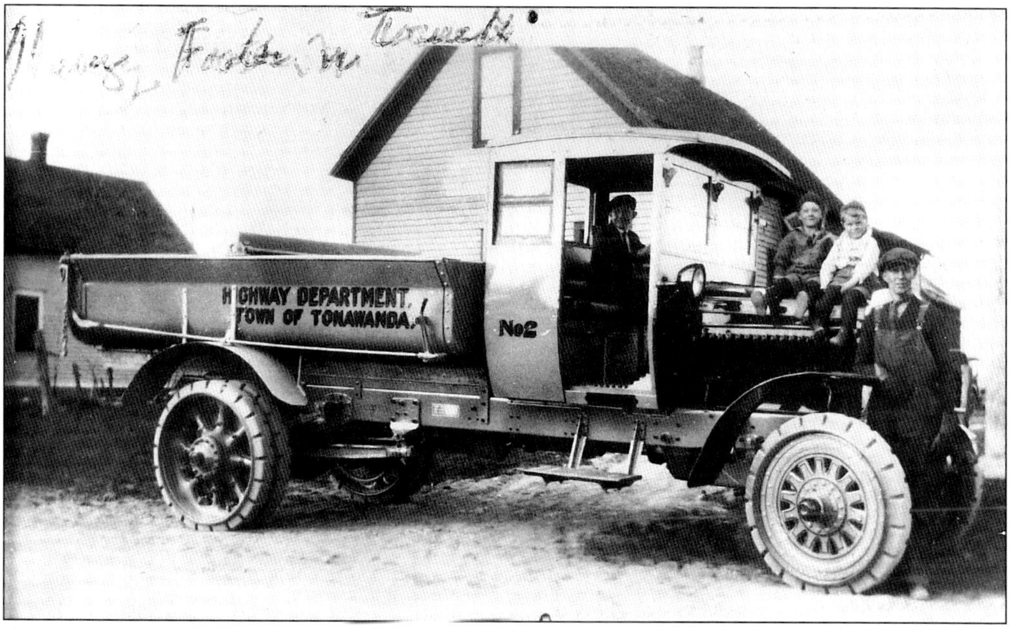

A town highway department truck on Guideboard (Eggert) Road in 1923. In the cab is Harry J. Foster, while Fred Marohn stands at the front. Carl and Robert Marohn are on the hood.

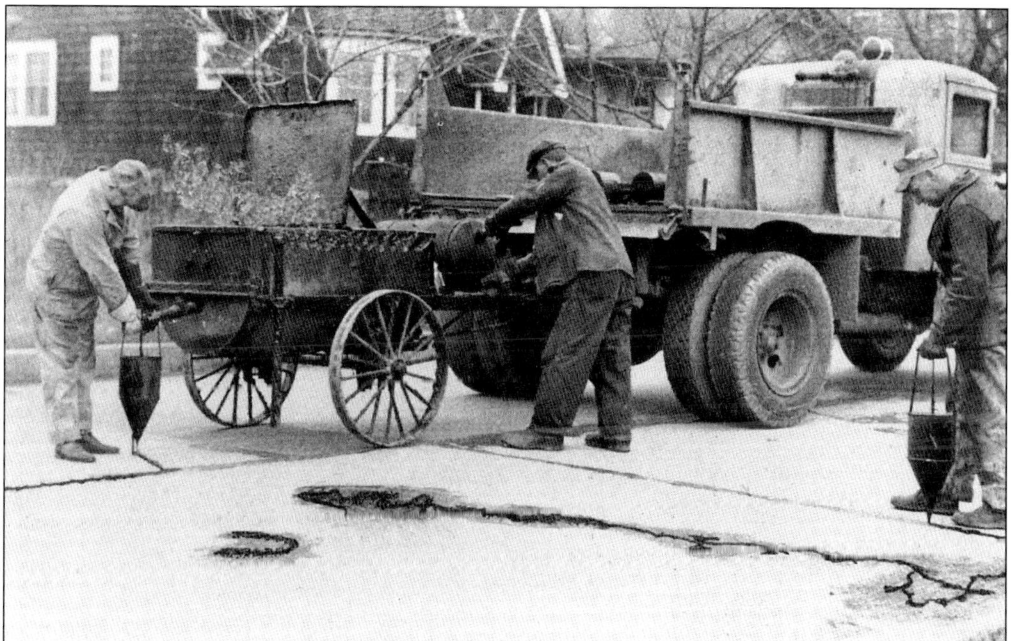

Street maintenance in the town in 1940, a constant problem in the cold season climate of freeze and thaw. Highway department personnel are using hot tar from the trailer to fill cracks in a concrete roadway.

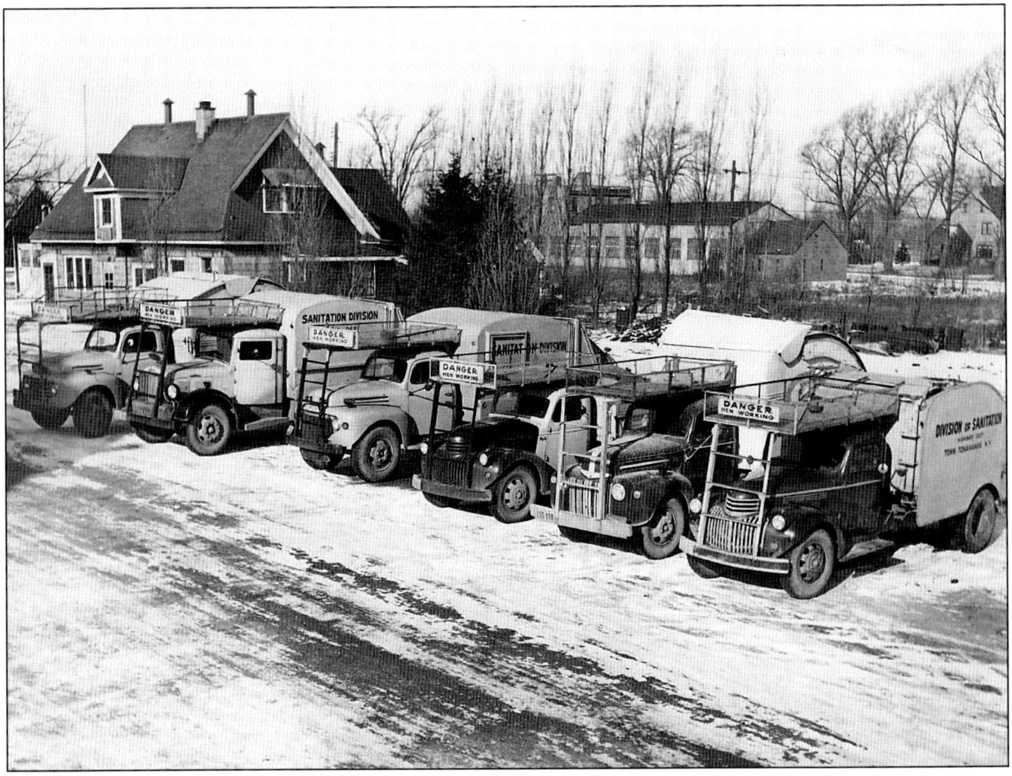

Town of Tonawanda sanitation trucks parked behind the Highway department barn on McConkey Drive in 1942. The old Schell farmhouse on Brighton Road (formerly Shell Road) can be seen at far right.

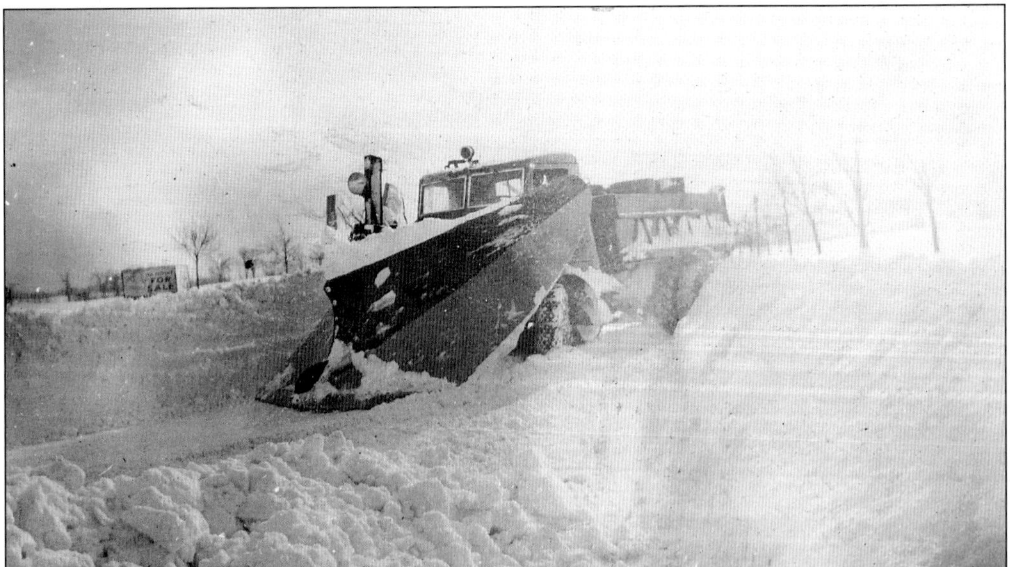

A town highway department plow at Colvin Boulevard and Eggert Road during the great snowstorm of December 8–10, 1937. Snowdrifts were so deep that many isolated homes in the town had to be supplied with food and necessities by airdrop.

Nine

GHOSTS

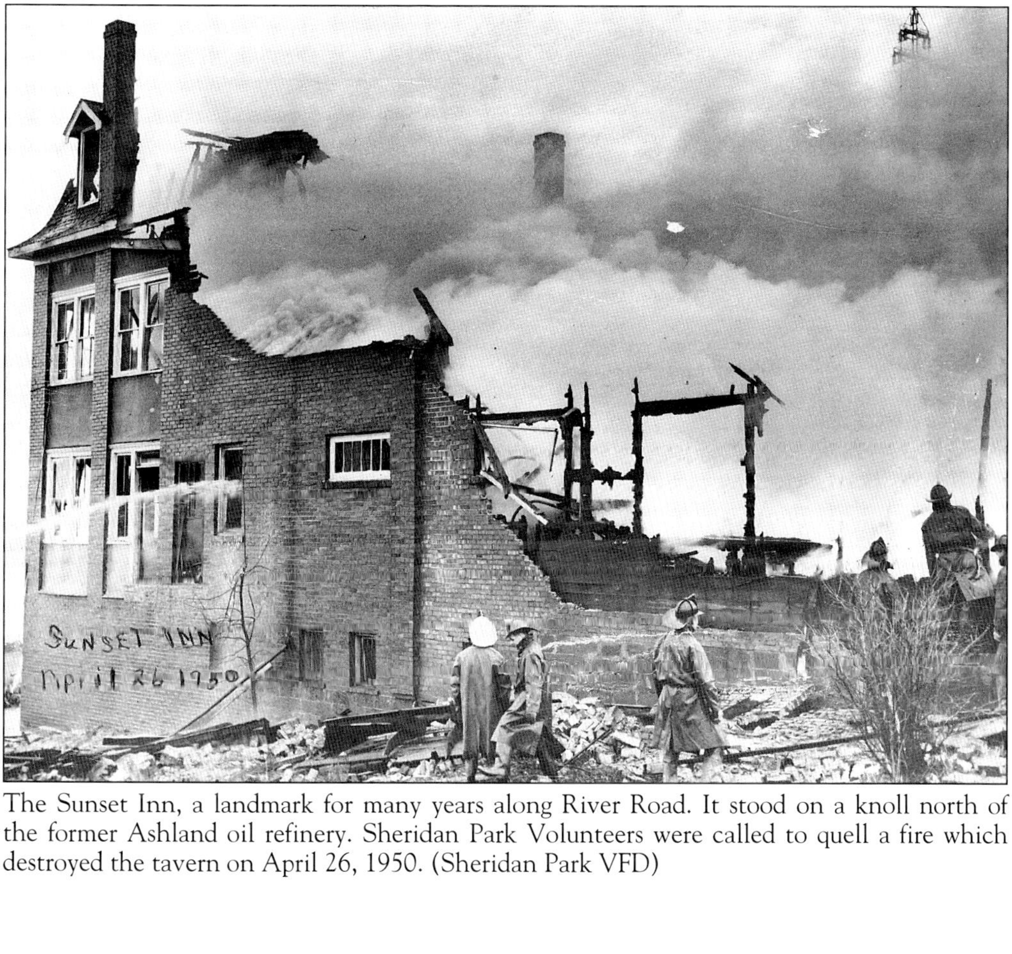

The Sunset Inn, a landmark for many years along River Road. It stood on a knoll north of the former Ashland oil refinery. Sheridan Park Volunteers were called to quell a fire which destroyed the tavern on April 26, 1950. (Sheridan Park VFD)

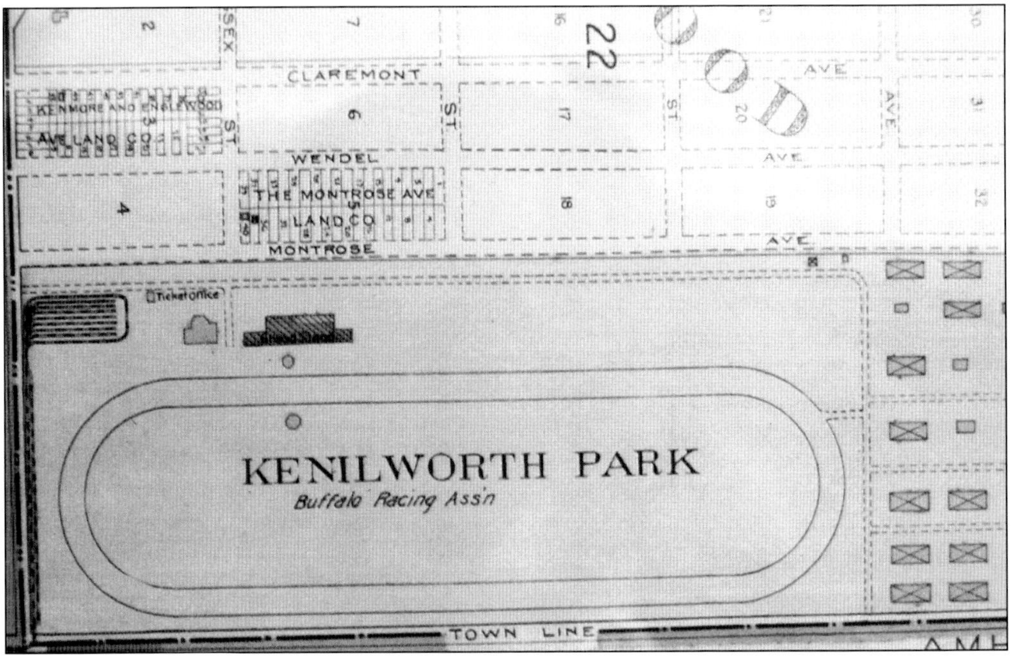

Kenilworth Park. Located in the extreme southeast corner of the town, the racetrack was in operation from 1902 to 1908. This map from a 1909 atlas shows Town Line Road (now Niagara Falls Boulevard) on the east side and an extensive trolley yard at the southwest corner of the property. The ticket office, clubhouse, and grandstand were just north of the trolley terminal. Horse barns were north of the track.

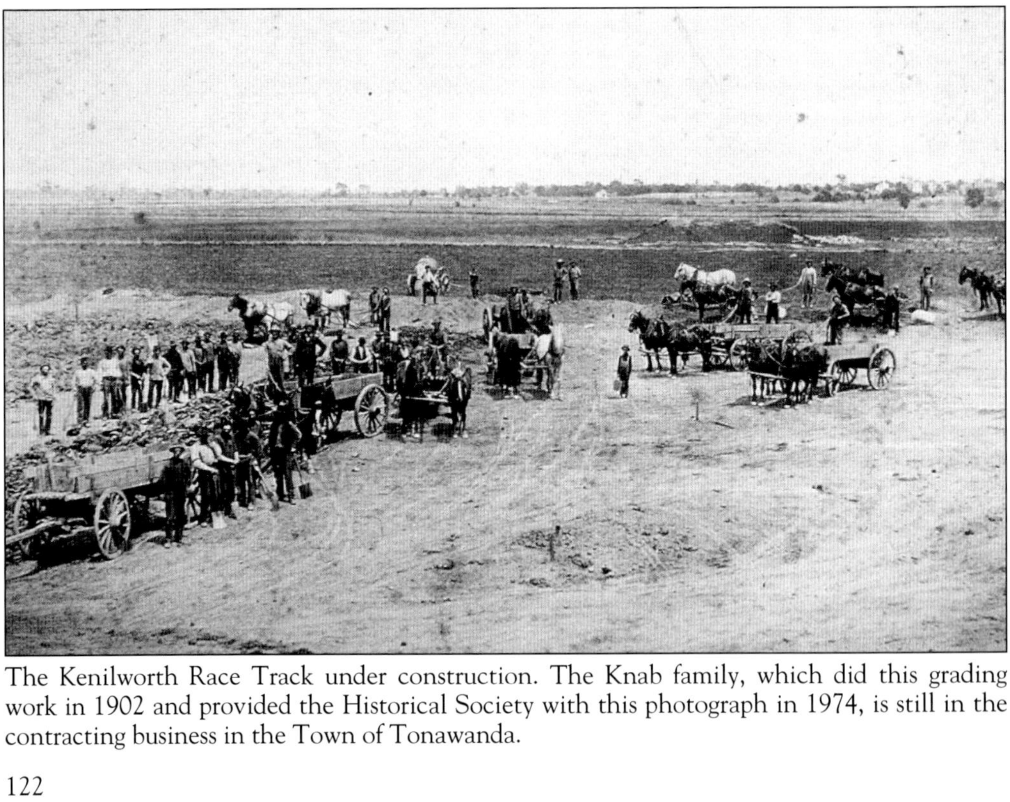

The Kenilworth Race Track under construction. The Knab family, which did this grading work in 1902 and provided the Historical Society with this photograph in 1974, is still in the contracting business in the Town of Tonawanda.

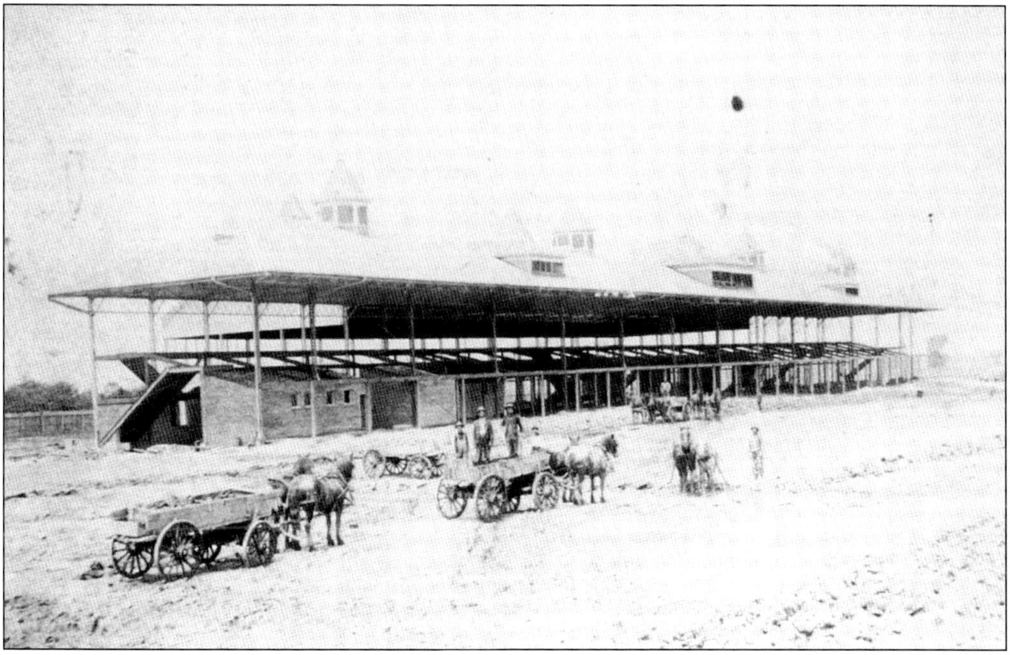

The grandstand at the Kenilworth Race Track under construction in the early summer of 1902. An unseasonably wet spring and delayed delivery of materials prevented construction from getting underway until March 19. The stand was built to hold 4,000 spectators. (B&ECHS)

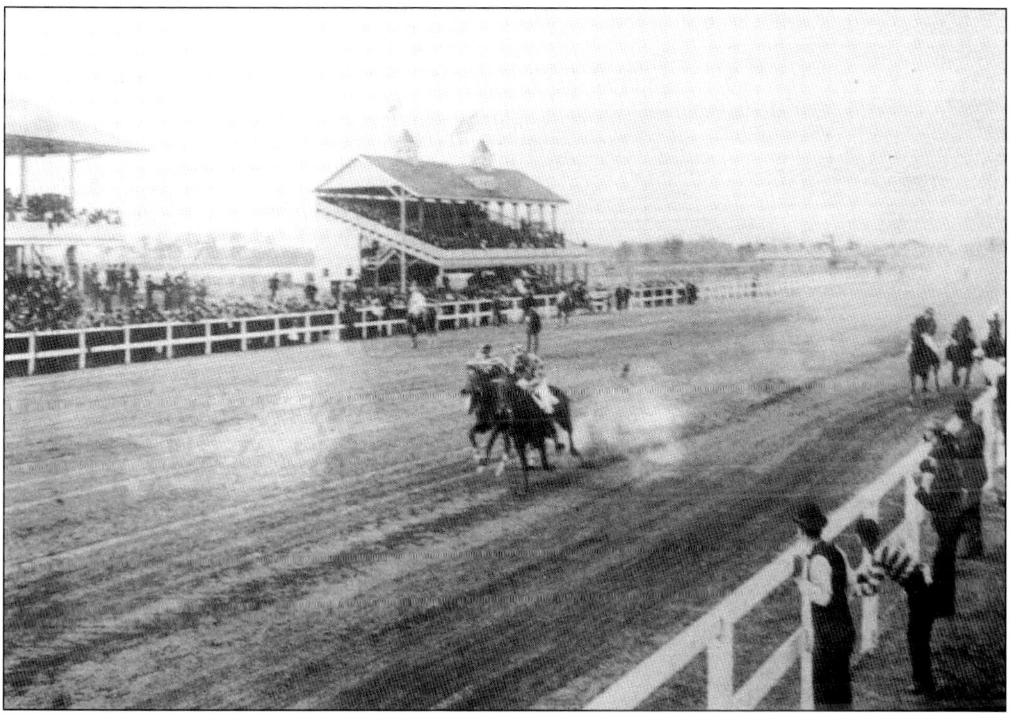

Opening day. Nearly 10,000 people attended the opening of the track on August 30, 1902. The derby wasn't much of a contest though because the favored Sombrero led from start to finish around the one-mile track. (B&ECHS)

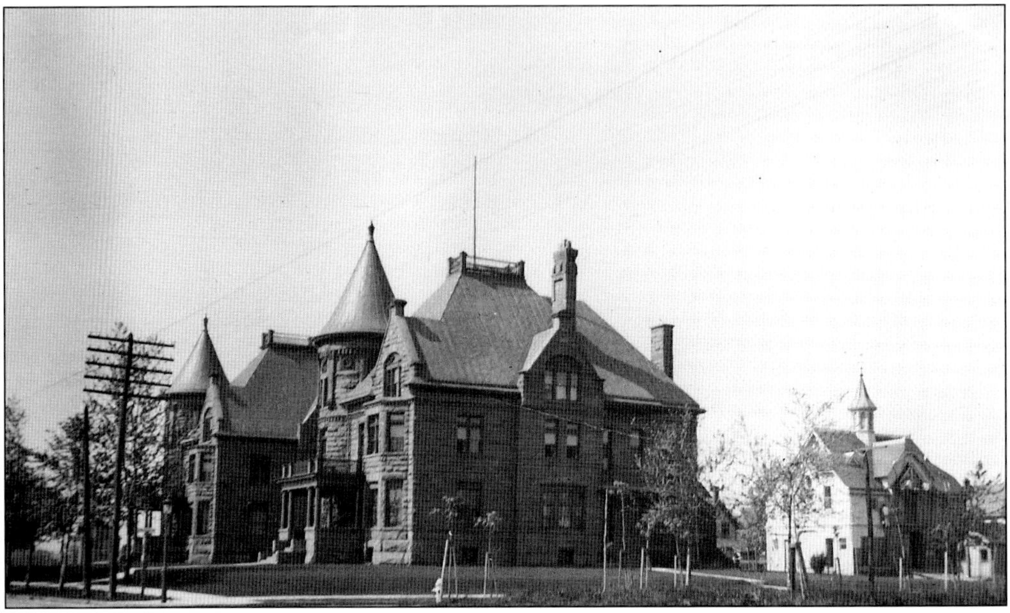

A turn-of-the-century view southwest at the L.P.A. and Fred Eberhardt mansions. The far building still stands as the Jack Hunt Coin Mansion. Behind L.P.A.'s home is his carriage house, which originally stood across Delaware Avenue. It was moved after L.P.A.'s first home burned in 1894.

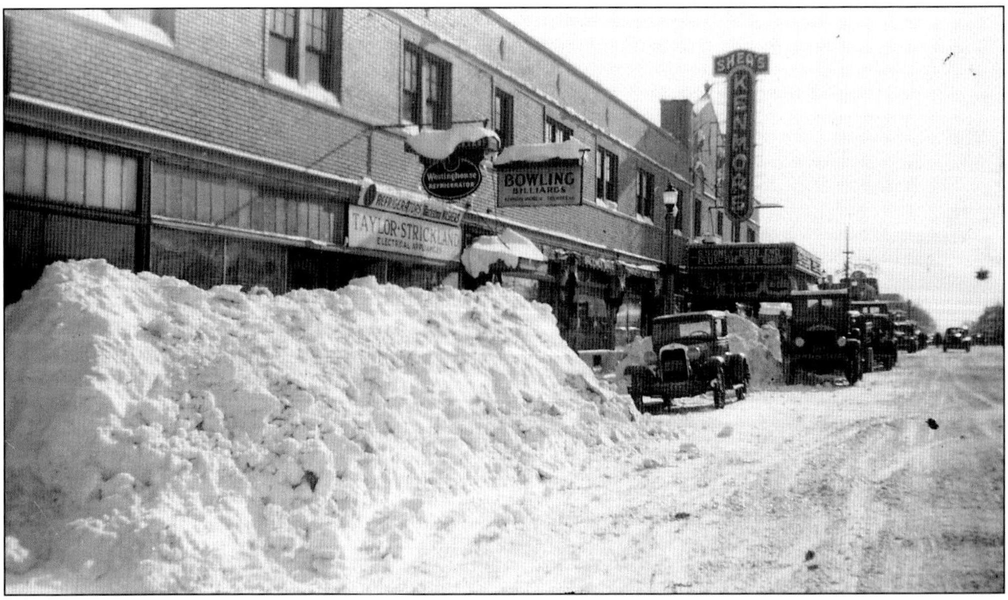

The Kenmore Theater block on March 27, 1936, ten days after the infamous St. Patrick's Day snowstorm. This storm hit the area by surprise just as the hint of spring was in the air.

Dismantling the internationally famous elephant ivory sign atop the closed Wood & Brooks Company, c. 1982. The factory had manufactured piano keys at Kenmore Avenue and Ontario Street since the early twentieth century.

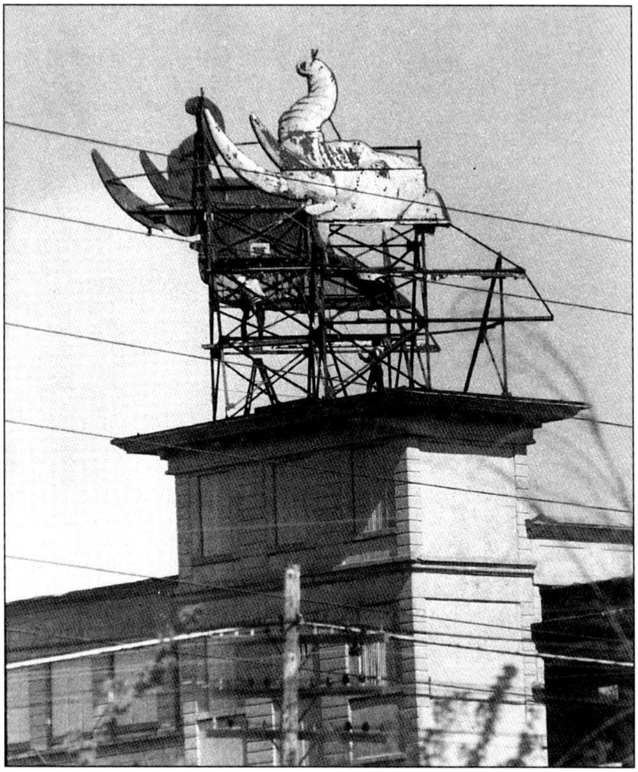

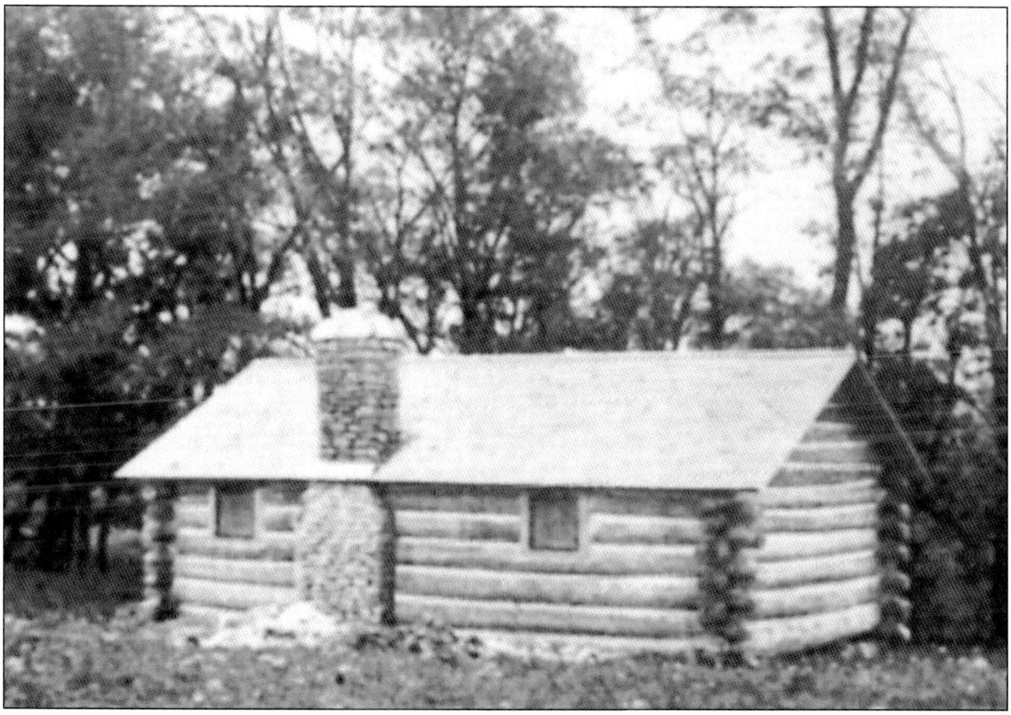

The Boy Scout cabin built in 1926 in the area that became Sheridan Park. A Girl Scout cabin was built later. These cabins were used by local scout troops for campouts.

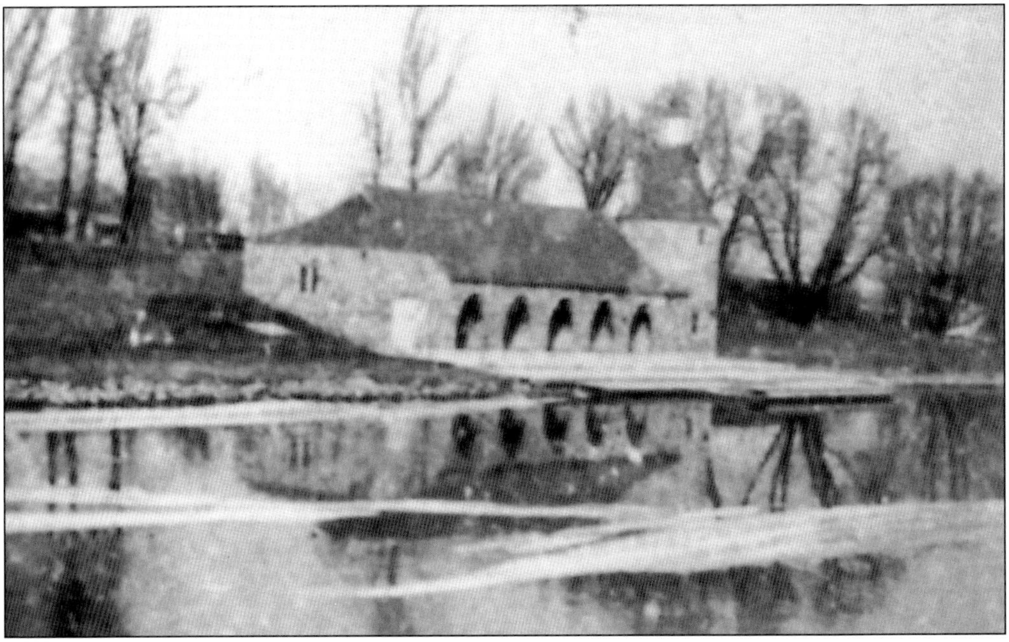

The stone rental boathouse on the island in Ellicott Creek Park, *c.* 1948. Built during the Great Depression, the boathouse lost its roof and interior when it burned many years ago.

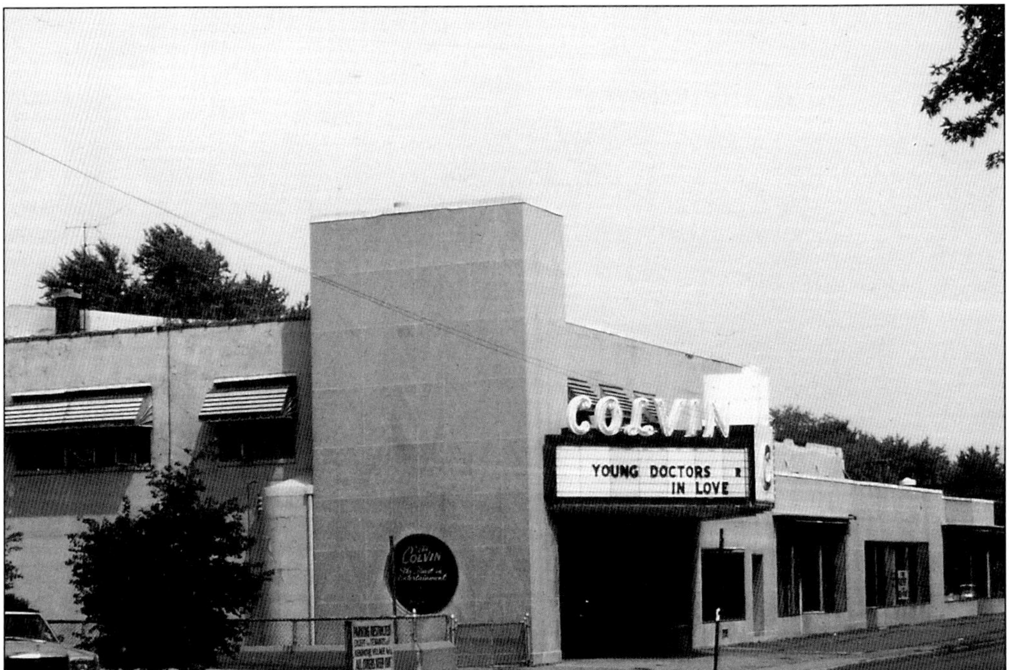

Basil's Colvin Theater on Kenmore Avenue east of Charleston Avenue. The art-deco theater opened Sunday, April 9, 1944, after a three-year delay due to shortages of construction materials during World War II. It was torn down in 1982 to make way for a high-rise apartment building.

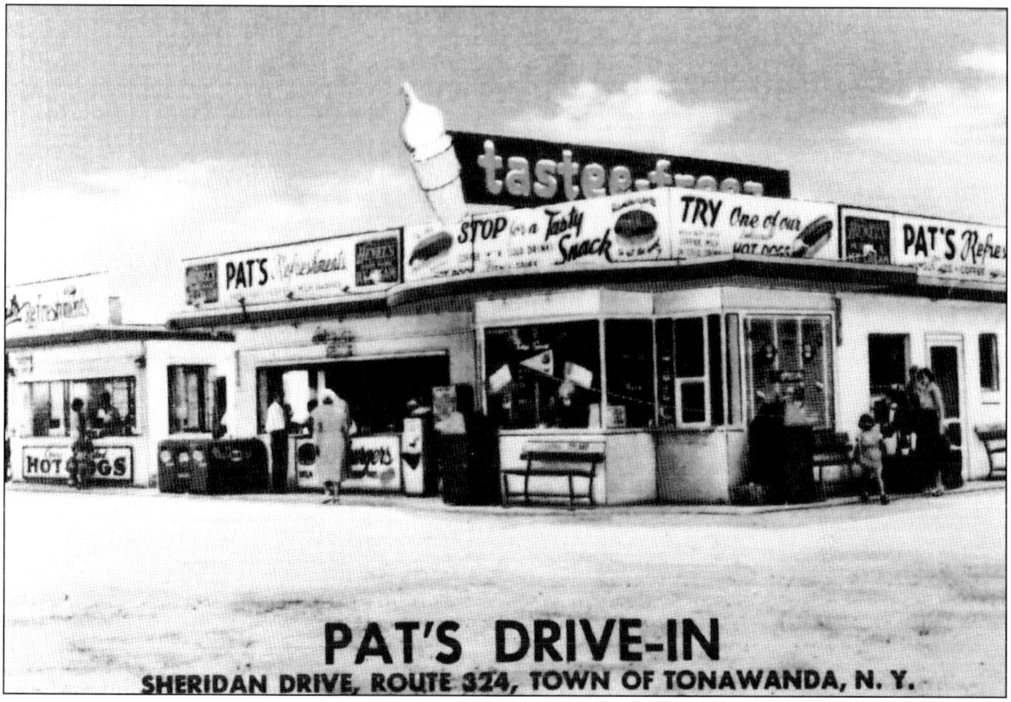

Pat's Drive-In, for many years a popular gathering place on Sheridan Drive at Parker Boulevard. Pat's served the last of its special hot dogs in September 1983, with a nostalgia party which included 1950s prices and a classic automobile show. This is a *c.* 1950 postcard. Walgreen's occupies the site now. (WNYHI)

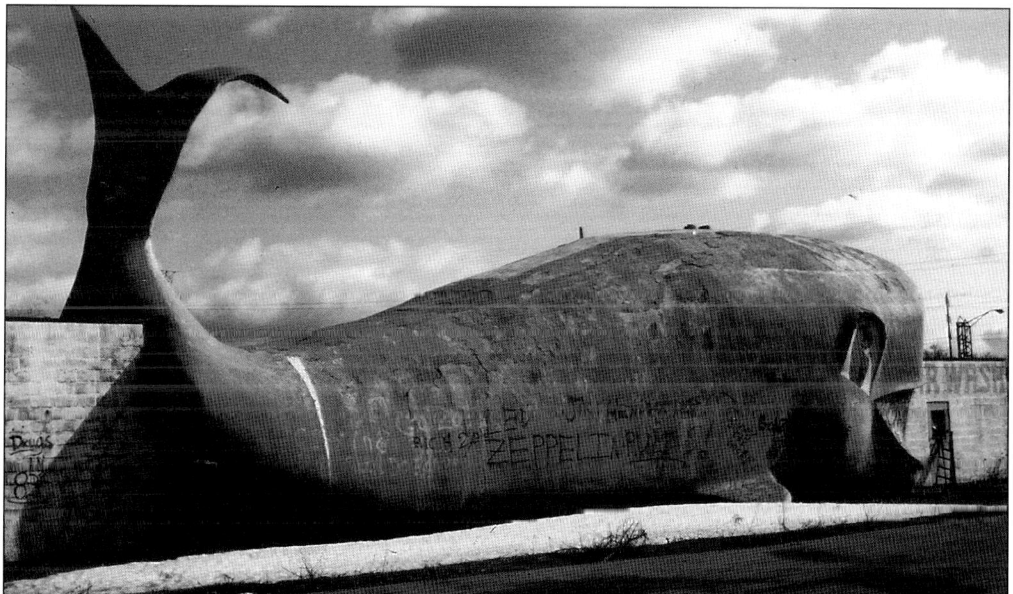

Remember "The Blue Whale?" It was a car wash on Young Street at the Tonawanda city line during the 1970s and '80s. Dirty cars drove in the tail and clean cars drove out the whale's mouth (when it worked). Its later years saw it as a target for graffiti "artists." Today, a Wendy's restaurant stands on the site.

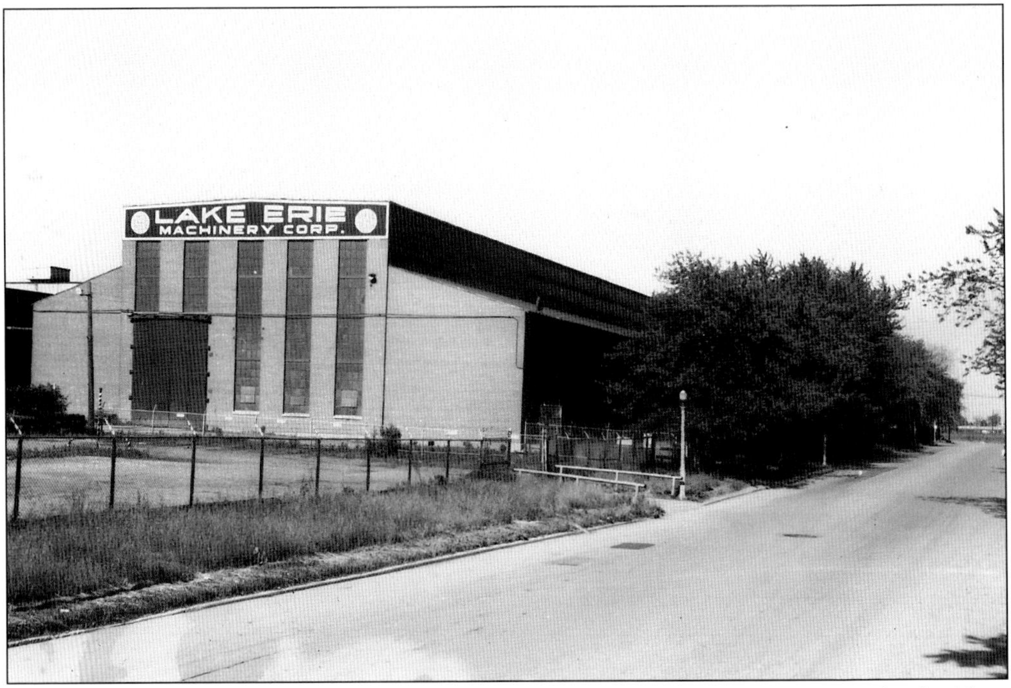

The Lake Erie Engineering Corporation on Woodward Avenue, June 8, 1962. This building became the town highway and recreation departments building in 1973. It was destroyed by fire in July 1995. (WNYHI)

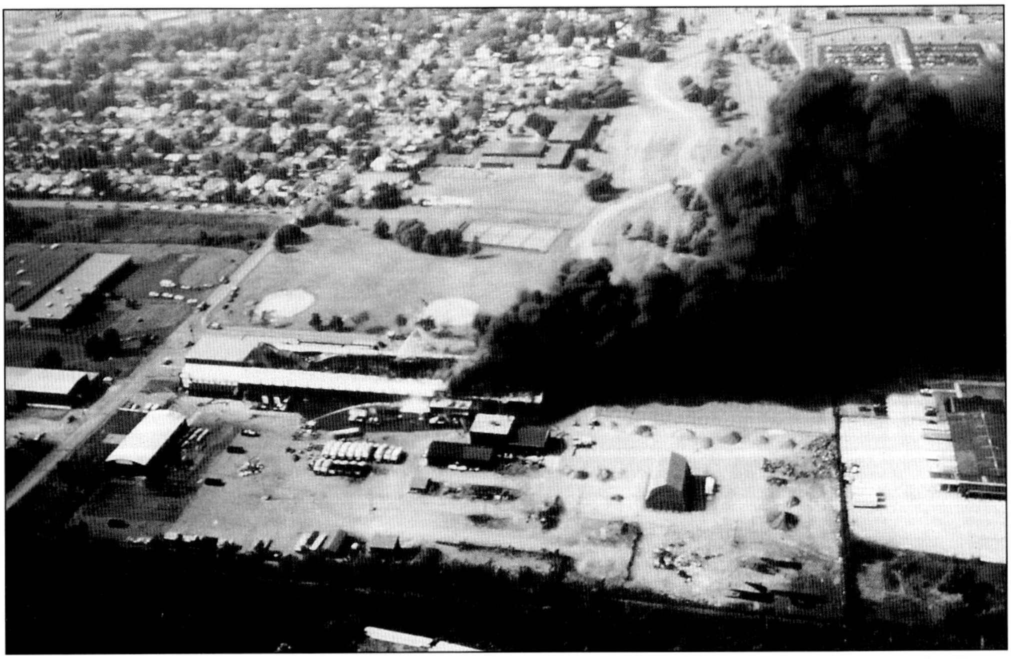

The spectacular fire that destroyed the Town's highway and recreational departments' facilities in July 1995. The former Lake Erie Engineering Corporation building on Woodward Avenue was a total loss. Riverview Avenue is at left; the Praxair Corporation is obscured by the heavy smoke.